# A SOCIAL INCLUSION ROADM

This independent study was commissioned by the Belgian Ministry of Social Integration in the context of the 2010 Belgian Presidency of the Council of the European Union (EU) during the second semester of 2010. It does not necessarily represent the views of the Government of Belgium. The three authors have written in a strictly personal capacity, not as the representative of any Government or official body.

Hugh Frazer, National University of Ireland, Maynooth, Ireland
Eric Marlier, CEPS/INSTEAD Research Institute, Luxembourg
Ides Nicaise, HIVA and Department of Education Sciences, K.U. Leuven, Belgium

Hugh Frazer
Eric Marlier
Ides Nicaise

# A Social Inclusion Roadmap for Europe 2020

Antwerpen-Apeldoorn

Hugh Frazer, Eric Marlier & Ides Nicaise
A Social Inclusion Roadmap for Europe 2020
Antwerp / Apeldoorn
Garant
2010

212 p. – 24 cm
D/2010/5779/78
ISBN 978-90-441-2667-9
NUR 740/747

Cover Design: Filip De Baudringhien

Garant
Somersstraat 13-15, 2018 Antwerp (Belgium)
Koninginnelaan 96, 7315 EB Apeldoorn (The Netherlands)
Garant/Coronet Books, 311 Bainbridge Street Philadelphia PA 19147 (USA)
Garant/Central Books, 99 Wallis Road, London E9 5LN (England)
Garant/University Book House, 130 Planning Street – Box 16983, Al Ain (United Arabic Emirates)
www.garant-uitgevers.be   info@garant.be
www.garant-uitgevers.nl   info@garant-uitgevers.nl

# Contents

# Foreword by Mr. Philippe Courard, Belgian Secretary of State for Social Integration and Combating Poverty

Our common involvement in the European Year for combating Poverty and Social Exclusion is a challenge and an opportunity. While 2010 is a major milestone in the European Strategy which was launched in Lisbon in 2000, it also closes the first decade of the "Open Method of Coordination" (OMC) in the field of social inclusion.

Unfortunately, this decade cannot be considered a success in the fight against poverty and social exclusion. As far as statistics are able to show, it seems that poverty has not declined – not even before the financial crisis of 2008. The promise of "more social cohesion" included in the Lisbon agenda thus has not been fulfilled. Eighty million EU citizens are currently at risk of poverty, which is equivalent to the population of the largest EU Member State.

This does not mean that the past decade of cooperation in the field of social inclusion was a complete failure. The fact that the OMC has been pursued and strengthened, the wide support that it has received, the approval of the new EU Lisbon Treaty which mentions the fight against social exclusion as a key objective and contains a chapter on fundamental social rights – all these elements are hope-giving. Today, only a minority of EU citizens would question that poverty and social exclusion must be tackled at all policy levels, that is EU, national, regional as well as local levels. A common language has been developed. Room has been shaped for an increasingly critical and informed debate about the roots of exclusion in our economic, social, educational and cultural systems.

The EU Belgian Presidency in the second half of 2010 is putting social inclusion very high on the EU policy agenda. During our Presidency we want to ensure that appropriate arrangements are put in place to ensure more effective EU coordination and cooperation in the social field. This is vital if we are to achieve the ambitious social inclusion objectives of the Europe 2020 agenda. Within this overall context, we then want to move ahead, as far as possible, in relation to three key issues.

First, a concrete agenda must be set for the implementation of the European Commission Recommendation on Active Inclusion. All three pillars (adequate minimum income, inclusive labour markets and access to quality services) must be developed, step by step, with the same horizon as the Europe 2020 agenda. The need to address the lack of clarity that currently exists as to what constitutes an "adequate" minimum income to live life with dignity is particularly important. For this, as argued by the authors of this book, the European Commission and Member States should initiate a process to agree on common criteria which would assist Member States in ensuring that their MISs meet the requirements of the 1992 EU Council Recommendation on common criteria concerning sufficient resources and social assistance in social protection systems and of the 2008 Commission Recommendation on the active inclusion of people excluded from the labour market. Once these criteria are agreed, the possibility of incorporating them into an EU Framework Directive on the adequacy of minimum income schemes should be explored.

Secondly, child poverty and social exclusion must be eradicated. The subsidiarity principle can be no excuse for the EU to refrain from action. All political leaders, administrators and professionals must keep in mind that children born in poverty face a substantial risk of getting stuck in poverty throughout their youth and into adulthood. This is not acceptable. Allowing child poverty to persist is also irrational, because the long-term burden on the European economy may far exceed the cost of immediate strategic action. We want to step up the policy debate – while giving a voice to the children themselves – and facilitate the preparation of a European Commission Recommendation on the basis of which common policies to better tackle child poverty and social exclusion can be built.

Thirdly, hundreds of thousands of people throughout the EU are still deemed to sleep rough or beg for shelter across Europe – and many of them probably belong to the poorest among the poor. The EU should be concerned, particularly because part of the homeless population errs across national borders within the EU, looking for a place where they can build a more decent living. Lack of consensus on common policies, beginning with a common definition and conceptual framework, appears to constitute an obstacle for a breakthrough in EU policy towards the homeless. The Belgian Presidency has therefore decided to endorse the proposal of the European Federation of National Organisations Working with the Homeless (FEANTSA) and to host a Consensus Conference in December 2010 where all stakeholders, supported by a preparatory committee and a jury of outstanding EU citizens, will contribute to defining such a common framework.

The three priorities set out above are just stepping stones towards a more inclusive Europe. We are aware of the limitations of these actions (bearing in mind the weak competencies of EU institutions in this field). This means that our objectives must be both ambitious and feasible within the short run. At the same time, in order to strengthen the legitimacy of EU action in the field of social protection and social inclusion, horizontal objectives need to be pursued such as the active participation of stakeholders (including people experiencing poverty and social exclusion), and the systematic inclusion of poverty proofing within the policy impact assessment procedures, in all policy debates.

In order to prepare the ground for this agenda, the Belgian Presidency appointed three European experts to write this book. Their remit was to take stock of the progress made during the past ten years, in relation to European social inclusion policy in general as well in as each of the three priority areas mentioned above – child poverty and social exclusion, active inclusion and homelessness and housing exclusion. They were also asked to carry out an independent assessment of policies in these areas, both at EU and Belgian levels – with Belgium just standing as a concrete example, with its strengths and weaknesses, but of course without any claim of Belgium having to teach lessons to other Member States. Finally, they were asked to formulate concrete recommendations for further action at EU, national and sub-national levels. We hope that their ideas will stimulate an open, critical debate that can result in useful conclusions for action.

*Philippe Courard*

# Preface

2010, the European Year for Combating Poverty and Social Exclusion, is both an opportunity for evaluation and for the preparation of the objectives for the next decade in the context of the Europe 2020 strategy. Is there reason to celebrate? Sadly not. In spite of the several positive developments encouraged by the Social OMC, this process has failed in one of its main goals. Indeed, there has been little progress made towards achieving the overall objective set in Lisbon ten years ago of making a decisive impact on the eradication of poverty and social exclusion by 2010, though some would argue that this was not something that such a process could achieve. The harsh reality is that the at-risk-of poverty rate for the 15 countries that were members of the EU in 2000 has remained stable: the EU-15 weighted average was 15% in 2000 and in 2008, the most recent data available, it is 16% (for the 12 newer Member States, the average poverty risk rate in 2008 is 17%; the 2008 EU-27 average is 17%).[1] In relation to "material deprivation", the situation is however a bit more encouraging at least in the newer Member States. Indeed, if the EU-15 average has remained stable between 2005 and 2008 (12-13%), it has dropped in the 10 newer EU countries for which data are available though it still remains 2.5 times as high as in the older Member States (2005: 43%, and 2008: 29%).[2]

On 17 June 2010, all 27 EU Heads of State and Government adopted the "headline target" for the EU as a whole of "promoting social inclusion, in particular through the reduction of poverty, by aiming to lift at least 20 million people out of the risk of poverty and exclusion" (conclusions of the March 2010 European Council). This renewed political commitment and focus on issues of poverty and social exclusion at EU level creates a real opportunity. A key challenge during the Belgian Presidency of the EU (second semester of 2010) will be to build on the progress made during the Spanish Presidency (first semester of 2010) and to put in place new governance arrangements that will trans-

---

1  According to the EU definition, people "at risk of poverty" are people living in a household whose total equivalised income is below 60% of the median national equivalised household income. All the figures presented in this paragraph are from the *Community Statistics on Income and Living Conditions EU-SILC)* data source.

2  As indicated in Chapter 1 (Section 1.3.1), this EU indicator significantly improves the multi-dimensional coverage of the EU portfolio for social inclusion. It focuses on the proportion of people living in households who cannot afford at least 3 items out of a list of 9. Figures for the newer Member States do not include Bulgaria and Romania as data for these countries are not available for all 4 years considered here. In 2008, the national rate of material deprivation (EU definition) is 51% for Bulgaria and 50% for Romania.

late this political commitment into effective action. The issues raised in this book are very relevant to this task. In particular, it is the authors' hope that their concrete recommendations for an EU roadmap for developing EU and (sub-)national policies to better tackle poverty and social exclusion will be of assistance. Overall, their aspiration is that this book will contribute to meeting the challenge of building a truly inclusive and social Europe.

This volume consists of four main chapters. Chapter 1 sets the overall EU context for the study by summarising briefly the main elements of and the key lessons from the social inclusion strand of the Social Open Method of Coordination (OMC) between 2000 and 2010. It also makes various suggestions as to how the Social OMC (in particular its social inclusion strand) could be strengthened in the post-2010 period and more specifically in the context of the so-called "Europe 2020 agenda". Chapters 2, 3 and 4 are then thematic chapters, with Chapter 2 focusing on child poverty and social exclusion, Chapter 3 on active inclusion, and Chapter 4 on homelessness and housing exclusion. The three thematic chapters draw on the rich material that has been developed on each of these issues in 10 years of the Social OMC. Each thematic chapter starts by examining the situation at EU level and is then followed by an in-depth analysis of the specific situation in Belgium; it closes with a section presenting the main conclusions at EU level and proposing concrete recommendations for strengthening EU action in those fields. Chapter 5 explores ways of making social inclusion a corner stone of EU and Member States' policies. Finally, Chapter 6 draws together the overall conclusions.

The authors would like to thank Bill Edgar for his important contribution to the EU section of Chapter 4, Sebastiano Cincinnato for his assistance in preparing the Belgian sections of Chapters 2-4, and Kate Holman for assistance with editing. The authors' thanks also go to Magda De Meyer and Julien Van Geertsom from the Belgian Presidency for helpful comments on earlier versions. They should not, however, be held responsible in any way for the contents of the volume.

# 1 Setting the Overall EU Context

## 1.1 Introduction

2010 is a critical year for the future of social inclusion issues at European Union (EU) level. The Lisbon process, which started in 2000 and which set the context for work on tackling poverty and social exclusion for the last decade, comes to an end. Thus new political directions and new arrangements to implement them will have to be agreed during the course of this year. The place that social inclusion issues will have in these new arrangements will significantly determine what is possible to achieve in the coming decade. 2010 is also the European Year for Combating Poverty and Social Exclusion. This provides an important opportunity to raise public and political awareness of these issues and thus to increase pressure to develop stronger political and institutional arrangements for the future.

The Belgian Presidency of the EU during the second half of 2010 can play a key role in the incubation of the new arrangements for promoting social inclusion in the post 2010 period. It has commissioned this volume to assist in that process. The purpose of the volume is thus to reflect on the experience of tackling poverty and social exclusion over the last decade through the Social Open Method of Coordination (OMC) and in particular its social inclusion strand (i.e., the OMC on poverty and social exclusion). It is also to make concrete recommendations on how efforts in this area could usefully be strengthened in the future at the national and/or EU levels. In doing so, we (the authors) focus particularly on three issues: Child poverty and social exclusion (Chapter 2); Active inclusion (Chapter 3); and Homelessness and housing exclusion (Chapter 4). As asked for by the Belgian Presidency, we have given the most in depth attention to the issue of child poverty and social exclusion.

This introductory chapter sets the context for the rest of the volume by summarising briefly the main elements of and some lessons from the social inclusion strand of the Social OMC between 2000 and 2010. It then goes on to make some suggestions as to how future EU coordination in the social field (in particular its social inclusion strand) could be strengthened in the post-2010 period and more specifically in the context of the so-called "Europe 2020 agenda" (European Commission, 2010b).

This volume draws on an extensive range of sources most of which have been generated by the process.[3] These include the formal aspects of the process such as the National

3  Much of the material generated by the social inclusion process should be available on the web-site of the Directorate-General "Employment, Social Affairs and Equal Opportunities" (DG EMPL) of the European Commission at: http://ec.europa.eu/social/main.jsp?catId=750&langId=en.

Action Plans on poverty and social exclusion (NAPs/inclusion) and the joint analysis of these Plans by the European Commission and EU Member States summarised in the "Joint Reports on Social Protection and Social Inclusion". They also include the many reports emerging as a result of the wide range of work funded by the European Commission in support of the process.[4]

## 1.2 The social inclusion strand of the current Social OMC: 2000-2010

### 1.2.1   What it is and what have been its main elements

*Main elements*
Since 2000, EU Member States and the European Commission have been cooperating in the field of social policy on the basis of the so-called *Open Method of Coordination (OMC)*. This has provided the context in which efforts to tackle poverty and social exclusion in the EU have been implemented. The OMC has developed significantly over the last decade and now covers EU cooperation in three main policy areas or "strands": social inclusion (formally launched at the March 2000 Lisbon European Council as the OMC on poverty and social exclusion[5]), pensions (launched in 2001) and health care and long-term care (2004). It also includes information exchanges in the field of *making work pay*. Since 2006, the three social "processes" that were progressively implemented under the OMC (one process for each main strand) have been *streamlined* into one integrated "Social OMC" built around 12 commonly agreed EU objectives (three for each main strand as well as three "overarching" objectives which address horizontal issues that cut

---

4     In this regard, we would like to acknowledge the contribution of the members of the European Commission funded EU Network of Independent Experts on Social Inclusion as their published reports have been an important source of material when drafting this volume. For information on this Network, see:
http://www.peer-review-social-inclusion.eu/network-of-independent-experts.

5     The European Council, which brings together the EU Heads of State and Government and the President of the European Commission, defines the general political direction and priorities of the EU. The decisions taken at the European Council meetings (or "Summits") are summarised in "Presidency Conclusions" available from the website of the EU Council of Ministers:
http://www.consilium.europa.eu/showPage.aspx?id=1&lang=en.
All Presidency websites can also be found at this address. Since the March 2000 Lisbon Summit, the European Council holds every spring a meeting that is more particularly devoted to economic and social questions – the "Spring European Council". With the entry into force of the Treaty of Lisbon on 1 December 2009, it has become an official institution and has a President.

across them[6]).

The Social OMC is coordinated by the Social Protection Committee (SPC). The SPC consists of officials from mainly Employment and Social Affairs Ministries in each Member State as well as representatives of the European Commission. It reports to the EU "Employment, Social Policy, Health and Consumer Affairs" (EPSCO) Council of Ministers.

The Social OMC has essentially been a "soft" process as it is a voluntary and agreed cooperation based on shared concerns. Responsibility for developing and implementing policies remains with countries. There are no externally imposed framework and goals imposed on Member States and there are no sanctions that can be applied to countries that do not make progress on the commonly agreed objectives. Much of the emphasis is on information exchange and mutual learning. However, to some extent *peer pressure* is present as a result of the regular monitoring and reporting and, more recently, some international benchmarking.

In this volume, our focus is on the social inclusion strand even if the development of work in this area (and especially in the four issues highlighted above) cannot be considered in isolation from the wider context of the EU Social OMC.

The *Social Inclusion Process*, which the EU has developed between 2000 and 2010, has consisted of five main elements:
- a set of common EU objectives for combating poverty and social exclusion;
- two- to three-yearly *NAPs/inclusion*, which are the means by which Member States translate the common objectives into national policies and which are drawn up on the basis of a common framework;[7]
- an agreed set of commonly agreed indicators to enhance the analysis of poverty and social exclusion and to measure progress towards achieving the common objectives, which is the responsibility of the EU Social Protection Committee

---

6    The 12 EU objectives for the streamlined Social OMC were adopted by the EU in March 2006: see http://ec.europa.eu/social/main.jsp?catId=755&langId=en.
     The "overarching objectives" of the Social OMC provide linkage across the three social policy strands as well as between the EU social, economic and employment strategies. For instance, the third overarching objective is "to promote good governance, transparency and the involvement of stakeholders in the design, implementation and monitoring of policy".

7    Since the 2006 streamlining of the Social OMC, NAPs/inclusion are now one specific chapter of the streamlined "National Strategy Reports on Social Protection and Social Inclusion" (NSRSPSIs). Prior to 2006 they were known as National Action Plans against poverty and social exclusion.

(SPC) and its Indicators Sub-Group;[8]

- a process of regular monitoring and reporting on progress, which has resulted in regular reports on social inclusion in the EU: the *Joint Reports on Social Protection and Social Inclusion;*[9]
- a Community action programme to underpin and reinforce the process and particularly to encourage mutual learning and dialogue between Member States and to stimulate innovation and the sharing of good practice.[10]

### *Focus on key policy themes*

With the evolution of the Social OMC a consensus has progressively developed as to what are the key policy priorities for tackling poverty and social exclusion across the Union. Seven in particular stand out:

- increasing labour market participation, with a particular emphasis on expanding active labour market policies and ensuring a better linkage between social protection, lifelong learning and labour market reforms;
- modernising social protection systems so that they are sustainable, ensure adequate incomes and provide incentives to take up work;
- improving access to quality services, particularly to healthcare and long term care services, social services and transport;

---

8   The commonly agreed indicators for the Social OMC are organised according to the structure of the common objectives for the Social OMC: one set of indicators and "context information" appropriate to the overarching objectives agreed for the Social OMC as a whole and one appropriate to each of the three social strands covered by the Social OMC (i.e., social inclusion, pensions and healthcare and long-term care). The most recent list of indicators was adopted in the second half of 2009 and provides for each indicator the agreed definition and socio-demographics breakdowns (European Commission, 2009a). For more information on the EU social indicators (their construction and their use in the policy process), see for instance Atkinson *et al* (2002) and Marlier *et al* (2007).

9   See: http://ec.europa.eu/social/main.jsp?catId=757&langId=en.

10  The first Community Action Programme (*Programme of Community action to encourage cooperation between Member States to combat social exclusion*) covered the period 2002-2006. It was followed by the *Community Programme for Employment and Social Solidarity* (PROGRESS; 2007-2013). These programmes have promoted *inter alia*: research, policy analysis (e.g. the EU Network of Independent Experts on Social Inclusion) and the collection of data (e.g. Member States have received significant funding from these Programmes to launch the *Community Statistics on Income and Living Conditions instrument* (EU-SILC) instrument, which is a major EU reference data source for indicators and statistics used in the context of the Social OMC); the exchange of good practice (through transnational exchange projects, peer reviews and studies), the networking across Europe of NGOs and regional and local authorities active in combating the risks of poverty and social exclusion; and the funding of European conferences on poverty and social exclusion.

- tackling disadvantages in education and training, including reducing early school leaving and promoting lifelong learning;
- eliminating child poverty and social exclusion, with a special emphasis on early intervention and enhancing income support for families at risk;
- ensuring decent accommodation and tackling homelessness;
- overcoming discrimination and increasing the integration of people with disabilities as well as immigrants and ethnic minorities, particularly the Roma[11].

Member States also widely recognise that in pursuing these priorities it is important to give particular attention to those in urban and rural communities facing multiple disadvantages and to mainstreaming the issue of gender throughout these priorities with a view to promoting gender equality.

From about 2006, work in the Social Inclusion Process was focussed increasingly around these themes. Priorities 1-3 have come together under the umbrella of Active Inclusion leading to the Commission Recommendation on Active Inclusion (2008)[12], priorities 5 and 6 have led to thematic years devoted to child poverty (2007) and homelessness and housing exclusion (2009).

*Focus on better governance*
Another feature of the Social OMC in general and its social inclusion strand in particular has been the focus on promoting better governance. (For a more detailed discussion of this, see Frazer, 2007.) Eight key themes stand out in this regard:
- the need to mobilise and involve all actors – government agencies, social partners, non governmental organisations and the research community – in the design, implementation and monitoring of policies and programmes;
- the importance of including people directly experiencing poverty and social exclusion in the process;
- the importance of developing comprehensive, multidimensional and strategic responses to poverty and social exclusion which are evidence-based and which are aimed at achieving clearly defined and quantified objectives adopted as a result of a rigorous diagnosis of the causes of poverty and social exclusion;
- the need to mainstream the social inclusion objectives into national policy making so as to ensure that all relevant policy areas and budgetary decision-making processes take into account the need to promote greater social inclusion;
- the importance of ensuring effective coordination of different departments and policy areas so that their efforts are mutually reinforcing;
- the need to ensure effective links between national and sub-national levels of

---

11   A more detailed description of these policy challenges can be found in Council, 2005.
12   http://eur-lex.europa.eu/LexUriServ/LexUriServ.do?uri=OJ:L:2008:307:0011:0014:EN:PDF.

government as it is at the local level that most social inclusion policies are actually delivered;

- the importance of delivering policies on the ground in a coordinated and integrated manner involving partnerships between the different agencies and involving all actors including those experiencing poverty and social exclusion;
- the importance of establishing clear procedures for the monitoring of and reporting on the implementation of strategies and for the assessment of the impact of policies.

### 1.2.2    Main strengths and weaknesses to date

In looking to the future of the Social OMC and its social inclusion strand post-2010, it is important to identify what its strengths have been to date that can be built on and what its weaknesses have been that need to be addressed in developing future arrangements. Drawing on our own experience of the Social OMC and the work of various commentators (see, for instance, Frazer and Marlier (2008) and Zeitlin (2007)), we believe that the following are some of the key strengths and weaknesses.

#### Strengths
The Social OMC, while it has had less impact than many would have hoped, has made a useful contribution to efforts to tackle poverty and social exclusion in a number of different ways. Ten in particular stand out:

- the Social OMC has helped to keep poverty and social exclusion on the EU agenda (if not always as strongly as many would wish) and has created a space in which it has been possible to argue for enhanced efforts at EU and national (and sub-national) levels to prevent and tackle poverty and social exclusion;
- it has provided an opportunity to highlight at EU level the importance of ensuring that economic, employment and social policies are made mutually reinforcing and also an opportunity to insist that economic and employment objectives should take more into account social inclusion outcomes;
- it has contributed to Member States developing a common understanding of concepts (e.g. multidimensionality, mainstreaming, evidence-based strategies and quantified objectives, partnership between actors, participation, policy impact assessments) and to them identifying and agreeing on key policy priorities;
- it has generated a considerable body of very useful learning about how best to tackle and prevent poverty and social exclusion;
- it has achieved progress in improving data, defining commonly agreed indicators and developing a stronger analytical framework so as to better understand and assess the phenomena at stake as well as better monitor and report on

progress[13];

- it has led to improvements in governance of social inclusion issues in several Member States;
- in those Member States who have chosen to make full use of the Social OMC, it has proved to be a very helpful tool in strengthening their national and sub-national efforts to promote social inclusion;
- it has ensured that the need for a response to the social impact of the financial and economic crisis has been articulated in EU debates;[14]
- it has mobilised a wide range of actors and fostered EU wide networks of people involved in the struggle against poverty and social exclusion[15] and it has given a voice to those experiencing poverty and social exclusion[16];
- it has led to 2010 being designated the European Year for Combating Poverty and Social Exclusion.

*Weaknesses*
A major failing of the Social OMC is clearly that it has resulted in little progress being made towards achieving the overall objective set in Lisbon of making a decisive impact on the eradication of poverty and social exclusion by 2010, though some would argue that this was not something that such a process could achieve. Eleven explanations are often put forward by commentators for the relatively limited impact of the Social OMC:

- it has had low political status and there has been a lack of political leadership at EU level, particularly vis-à-vis the other strands of the Lisbon agenda (growth and jobs);
- *feeding in* and *feeding out*, i.e. the expectations that the Social OMC agenda should parallel and interact closely with the Growth and Jobs agenda ("feeding in" to growth and employment objectives while growth and employment programmes should "feed out" to advance social cohesion/inclusion goals, have

---

13  Overall, experience with the Social OMC has enabled the identification of key elements necessary for effective systems for monitoring performance on poverty and social exclusion. We come back briefly on these in Chapter 2, Section 2.3.9. See also present Chapter (Section 1.3) for a short discussion on how the Commission and Member States could usefully make a more rigorous, intensive and visible use of the commonly agreed indicators for the Social OMC.

14  In this regard, it is encouraging that the 2010 *Joint Report on Social Protection and Social Inclusion* clearly recognises that "the crisis has emphasised the added value of policy coordination through the Open Method of Coordination on Social Protection and Social Inclusion (Social OMC) and provided further incentive to reinforce and exploit its potential fully" (Council, 2010).

15  For a list of the Networks supported as part of the process and for the links to the different Networks' web-sites, see aforementioned European Commission's web-site.

16  See for instance European Anti-Poverty Network (2009b). For the reports summarising the main outcomes of the annual EU Meetings of People Experiencing Poverty, see:
http://www.eapn.eu/content/view/600/14/lang,en/.

been disappointingly weak – they have existed more in theory than in practice and, more broadly, linkages with other EU policy areas (e.g. competition, agriculture, health, education, justice, migration) have been very limited;

- the Social OMC has been too "soft" as there are no sanctions for Member States who fail to make progress and there is no basis for making recommendations to Member States on what they need to do to strengthen their efforts;

- the lack of clear quantified outcome targets (until June 2010; see below, Section 1.3) has diminished the status of the Social OMC in relation to economic and employment policies which have been dealt with separately at EU level in the context of the "Partnership for Growth and Jobs";

- the Social OMC has had a very low public visibility and (until very recently) there has been a lack of public promotion of the process;

- in most Member States, there has been a failure to integrate the Social OMC process, especially the NAPs/inclusion, into national policy making procedures;

- there has been insufficiently rigorous monitoring, evaluation and reporting of Member States' performance in part due to weak analytical tools and resources;

- the potential of the Social OMC for putting peer pressure on Member States to do more through the use of EU benchmarking and more generally transnational comparisons has been made more difficult by the lack of timely statistical evidence;

- in too many Member States, there are still weak governance arrangements (such as limited mainstreaming of social inclusion objectives, weak horizontal and vertical coordination of policies, ineffective strategic planning, poor implementation and insufficient mobilisation and involvement of actors);

- the development and dissemination of exchange of learning and good practice has been too piecemeal and not sufficiently coordinated, and too narrow a range of actors has been involved;

- the potential to use the EU Structural Funds to encourage Member States in the implementation of the EU's social inclusion objectives has not been sufficiently developed. [17]

In its recent evaluation of the impact of the Lisbon process, the European Commission's overall assessment of the OMC as a method of "soft coordination" is that "while the OMC can be used as a source of peer pressure and a forum for sharing good practice,

---

17    The European Anti-Poverty Network (EAPN) among others has been critical of the limited amount of Structural Funds available to support social inclusion measures: "Overall, EAPN was disappointed that the 2007-2013 programming period was not made a more effective instrument to combat poverty and social exclusion. The Commission's own estimates were that only 12.4% of the European Social Fund was allocated to social inclusion measures." (Harvey, 2008).

evidence suggests that in fact most Member States have used OMCs as a reporting device rather than one of policy development" (European Commission, 2010a). This is indeed borne out by the experience of the Social OMC briefly outlined above, and a major objective of this volume is to further explore the (potential) strengths and weaknesses of the Social OMC and make concrete proposals as to how future EU coordination in the social field (in particular its social inclusion strand) could be strengthened in the post-2010 period.

## 1.3 EU action on poverty and social exclusion post-2010

As will be evident from the above, the progress that has been made on the issues of child poverty and social exclusion, active inclusion, homelessness and housing exclusion and participation since 2000 has been largely because of the existence of the Social OMC and in particular its social inclusion strand. The Social OMC has provided the framework and institutional arrangements within which to develop work on these issues. The Community action programmes have then underpinned the Social OMC by providing the resources necessary to support analysis, data collection, exchange of learning and networking. As many commentators have noted (e.g. European Anti-Poverty Network (EAPN) 2009a, Platform of European Social NGOs 2009 and Spring Alliance 2009), if progress is to be continued, it is vital that the new EU arrangements that will be put in place for the post-2010 period continue to create the space for work on these issues. At the same time, it is important that these arrangements increase the political status and importance of the process and address some of the weaknesses that have been identified in the 2000-2010 process. This is necessary so that the effectiveness of EU coordination in the social field, especially in relation to social inclusion, can be further strengthened and lead to more concrete outcomes on the ground.

The need to strengthen EU coordination in the social field has become even more urgent because of the increased status given to social issues in the EU Lisbon Treaty (particularly social inclusion issues), which came into force on 1 December 2009. As we will see below (Section 1.3.4), the "horizontal social clause" in Article 9 of the Treaty is (potentially) of major importance in this respect. The need to strengthen the process is also essential because of the failure to achieve the goal of making a decisive impact on poverty and social exclusion which EU leaders set in 2000. As the Commission's own evaluation of the Lisbon process acknowledges "employment increases have not sufficiently reached those furthest away from the labour market, and jobs have not always succeeded in lifting people out of poverty. Some groups still face specific hurdles such as poor access to training for the low-skilled or lack of enabling services. Labour market segmentation persists in some Member States. So does child poverty at a high level in some Member States. Lessons need to be drawn from these facts." (European Commission, 2010a)

Drawing on the experience of recent years, and with a view to building on past successes and addressing weaknesses of the current Social OMC, we would make the following recommendations that could be considered in the development of Europe's social dimension in general and the new EU "European Platform Against Poverty" (see below, Sections 1.3.1 and 1.3.5) in particular.

### 1.3.1 Clear EU social objectives supported by EU and national social outcome targets

*Clear EU social objectives*
For social cohesion/ inclusion to have a higher political priority at EU level, it is essential that EU's political objectives include a clear statement of the interdependence and mutually reinforcing nature of economic, employment, social and environmental objectives and policies. The new *Europe 2020* Strategy must be built around these four interdependent pillars and all must be developed at the same time so that they continuously interact and reinforce each other. EU's political objectives should also contain an explicit political commitment to work both for the eradication of poverty and social exclusion (including a specific focus on child poverty and social exclusion) and for the reduction of inequalities. In our view, an effective fight against poverty and social exclusion requires that both prevention (i.e. reducing the inflow into poverty) and alleviation (i.e. lifting those in poverty out of poverty) be addressed. This means universal policies aimed at promoting the inclusion of all and then also, when necessary, targeted policies to assist those facing particular difficulties or barriers. Comprehensive social protection systems are then also needed to ensure that all citizens have access to high quality services and to an adequate income. Finally, a prerequisite for effectively combating poverty and social exclusion, and also one for achieving the Europe 2020 stated goal of "inclusive and sustainable growth", is to address (excessive) inequality.

*EU and national social outcome targets*
In its proposals for Europe 2020, issued in March 2010, the European Commission suggested that there should be five headline EU targets to be achieved by 2020. One of these was to "reduce the number of Europeans living below national poverty lines by 25%, lifting 20 million people out of poverty"[18]. The Commission also proposed that there should be 7 "flagship initiatives". One of these is a "European Platform Against Poverty", the purpose of which would be "to ensure social and territorial cohesion such that the benefits of growth and jobs are widely shared and people experiencing poverty and social exclusion are enabled to live in dignity and take an active part in society" (European Commission, 2010b).

---

18  According to the EU definition, people "at risk of poverty" are people living in a household whose total equivalised income is below 60% of the median national equivalised household income (the equivalence scale used is the *OECD modified* scale).

At their March 2010 meeting, EU leaders agreed that there should be a target on "promoting social inclusion, in particular through the reduction of poverty" but they could not agree on the appropriate indicator(s) and target(s) and decided to revert to this issue at their June 2010 meeting. (see European Council, 2010a) The EU Social Protection Committee and its Indicators Sub-Group were then asked to address the various political and scientific issues at stake and to come up with an amended proposal that would represent a compromise between the various opinions on what the nature and extent of this EU target. The compromise that was finally reached by SPC members was endorsed by the EU EPSCO Council of Ministers on 7 June 2010 and then, 10 days later, by all 27 EU Heads of State and Government. The adopted EU target is based on a combination of three indicators: the at-risk-of-poverty rate (EU definition), the material deprivation rate (EU definition but stricter[19]) and the percentage of people aged 0-59 who live in jobless households (i.e., households where none of the members aged 18-59 are working). The target will consist of lowering the number of people in the EU who are at risk of poverty and/or materially deprived and/or living in jobless households. The level of ambition has decreased significantly compared with the Commission's original proposal. Indeed, if the figure originally suggested was kept (a reduction by 20 million by 2020) the move from a target based solely on poverty risk to one based on the 3 aforementioned indicators means an increase of the targeted population from around 80 million people to around 120 million people.[20]

---

19   Originally proposed by Guio (2009), this indicator significantly improves the multi-dimensional coverage of the EU portfolio of indicators for social inclusion. Based on the limited information available from the EU-SILC data-set, it focuses on the proportion of people living in households who cannot afford at least 3 of the following 9 items: 1) coping with unexpected expenses; 2) one week annual holiday away from home; 3) avoiding arrears (in mortgage or rent, utility bills or hire purchase instalments); 4) a meal with meat, chicken or fish every second day; 5) keeping the home adequately warm; 6) a washing machine; 7) a colour TV; 8) a telephone; 9) a car. In the indicator used for the EU target, the criterion for being materially deprived is stricter as it the threshold has been put to an enforced lack of four rather than three items out of nine.
For a characterisation of the income poor and the materially deprived in 24 European countries, see Fusco, Guio and Marlier (2010).

20   At their June 2010 meeting, EU Heads of State and Government endorsed "five EU headline targets which will constitute shared objectives guiding the action of Member States and the Union as regards promoting employment; improving the conditions for innovation, research and development; meeting our climate change and energy objectives; improving education levels; and promoting social inclusion in particular through the reduction of poverty." In the words of EU leaders, the latter will consist of "promoting social inclusion, in particular through the reduction of poverty, by aiming to lift at least 20 million people out of the risk of poverty and exclusion". EU leaders have decided that "progress towards the headline targets will be regularly reviewed". (European Council, 2010b)

Despite this lower ambition, the fact that the Commission and all EU countries could agree this EU social inclusion target is a major step forward in demonstrating the political commitment of the EU. In view of the overall architecture of the Commission's proposals for the next *Europe 2020* Strategy, no target would have had the very negative political effect of making social cohesion/ inclusion appear less important than the other political priorities outlined in the Europe 2020 agenda, all of which have linked quantified targets.

The next challenge, which is both a political and scientific challenge, will be for each individual Member State to adopt one or several (sub-)national targets.[21] Under the principle of *subsidiarity*, countries will be free to set these targets on the basis of what they see as the most appropriate indicator(s) given their national circumstances and priorities. Yet, it will be important for these (sub-)national targets that they be evidence-based and that they be the result of a rigorous diagnosis. It is also important that countries be asked to explain – again, on the basis of rigorous analytical evidence – how meeting their (sub-) national targets will contribute to the achievement of the EU level target. With a view to boosting political commitment and mutual learning, we consider that countries should set their (sub-)national targets in a transparent way and in close dialogue with the Commission, and we believe that the SPC should discuss these.

## 1.3.2    *Rigorous benchmarking, monitoring and evaluation*

In our view, a major challenge that needs to be given particular attention in the post-2010 arrangements (and that is directly related to the challenge of setting targets) is that rigorous benchmarking, monitoring and evaluation should be made a central and visible feature of the EU process at both national and EU levels.

For this, we would recommend:
- instituting a process whereby the Commission and Member States would explore ways of making the EU social objectives more visible, measurable and tangible at EU level. Apart from the EU and (sub-)national targets that we have just discussed, this could *inter alia* involve a more rigorous, intensive and visible use of the commonly agreed indicators underpinning EU coordination

---

21    Setting outcome targets is essential even if it is a difficult area for a combination of political and scientific reasons. So, it is encouraging to note that the Commission's recent evaluation of the Lisbon process notes that "It seems that the effectiveness of policy learning is greater when there are clear and measurable objectives" (European Commission, 2010a). For a detailed discussion of targets, see: Marlier et al, 2007: Sections 6.2 (The role of targets in the Social Inclusion Process), 6.3 (Key issues in setting national targets) and 6.4 (Framing EU-wide targets).

in the social field and the commitment of all Member States to set the goal of improving their performance in a set of indicators covering each relevant social protection and social inclusion policy domain (including child poverty and social exclusion, active inclusion, and homelessness and housing exclusion; see below).[22]

- ensuring that progress made towards the EU and national targets and towards the improved performances in the agreed set of EU indicators are rigorously and regularly monitored and reported on. This might include the introduction of an annual report to the Spring European Council and to the European Parliament on progress towards the agreed objectives (as part of the annual *Joint Report on Social Protection and Social Inclusion*). This annual report should also be addressed to national and possible sub-national Parliaments of Member States who should be encouraged to debate progress being made by their Member State (see also Section 1.3.6);

- ensuring also that peer reviews are organised to discuss the results of this monitoring exercise with a view to boosting policy learning among Member States and the Commission.

- introducing a much more rigorous approach to monitoring and evaluation with an increased focus on results and ensure that independent critical analysis of progress made in achieving objectives is regularly carried out. Key elements could usefully include:

  o incorporating the common indicators more systematically into the Member States' national monitoring and analytical frameworks in order to improve mutual learning (see Marlier *et al*, 2007, section 2.7, pages 48-53);

  o boosting statistical capacity at EU, national and sub-national levels and in particular ensuring the production of more timely social statistics (including data on poverty and social exclusion that would allow for a better monitoring of the impact of the financial and economic crisis across the EU);

---

22  Marlier *et al* (2007) identify four respects in which the commonly agreed indicators could be used more intensively in the Social OMC. The first application is their use in a "forensic manner to identify possible explanations of differences in Member State performance". The second is in the individual National Strategy Reports on Social Protection and Social Inclusion (NSRSP-SIs). "The expectation is of course not that countries would rely solely on these common indicators in monitoring, analysing and reporting on social inclusion; rather, it is that the national indicators they develop and use for these purposes, together with in-depth multi-dimensional analysis of the underlying micro-data, should be linked back to the common indicators as far as possible, in order to facilitate mutual learning". The third application is to increase the degree of "joined-up Government". The multi-dimensioned nature of the commonly agreed indicators underlines "the need for cooperation between different agencies of Government as well as, in some countries, between different agencies belonging to different levels of Government". Finally, the fourth application is to target setting; national targets should draw as appropriate on these indicators.

o   reinforcing the analytical capacity of those people and institutions engaged
    in the new EU social process (at both country and EU levels), so as to en-
    sure that the process becomes more rigorous, more challenging and more
    comparative;

o   developing social impact assessments in all the relevant policy domains
    and using specific peer reviews and transnational exchange projects to en-
    courage mutual learning in this complex area (see below, Sections 1.3.4
    and 1.3.5);

o   requiring all Member States to have formal arrangements for truly involv-
    ing civil society organisations and independent experts in monitoring and
    assessing social inclusion policies on an ongoing basis.

We would also recommend that when monitoring each Member State's progress on an
annual basis, the Commission and the SPC, as the bodies in charge of implementing the
EU coordination in the social field, should, as necessary, make clear recommendations
to each Member State on actions it needs to take if it is to achieve the agreed national
and EU targets and the improved performances in the agreed set of EU indicators (see
above). These would then be endorsed by the Council. [23]

### 1.3.3    Social inclusion in the Integrated Guidelines for growth and jobs

The overall political decision to make combating poverty and social exclusion a key EU
priority and to set a quantified outcome target at EU level is one (important) part of the
jigsaw. The arrangements for implementation are also critical. In this regard, while the
agreement on an EU target on social inclusion is encouraging, the social dimension (not
only poverty and social exclusion but also social protection) still remains somewhat the
poor relation of economic and employment policy. On 27 April 2010, the Commission
published its proposals for *Integrated Guidelines* to deliver on the Europe 2020 Strategy
(European Commission 2010c). Ten Guidelines have been proposed, under two distinct
legal bases: six Economic and four Employment Guidelines. A Guideline on poverty
and social exclusion, which sets out policies to reach the proposed EU headline target on
poverty reduction, has been included under the Employment Guidelines.

---

23   While the Treaty does not explicitly foresee the possibility of the Commission issuing recommen-
     dations, it also does not prevent the Commission from doing so through "soft law agreements".
     For instance, Article 5 of the Treaty, as well as providing for the coordination of economic and
     employment policies, says that "The Union may take initiatives to ensure coordination of Mem-
     ber States' social policies". And Article 160 (see above), in outlining the role of the SPC includes
     among its tasks "to prepare reports, formulate opinions or undertake other work within its fields
     of competence, at the request of either the Council or the Commission or on its own initiative".

The proposed guideline is drawn in a reasonably broad manner, reflecting the main strands of the existing Social OMC and, importantly, stressing the key role of social protection systems. "*Guideline 10: Promoting social inclusion and combating poverty:*

> "Member States' efforts to reduce poverty should be aimed at promoting full participation in society and economy and extending employment opportunities, making full use of the European Social Fund. Efforts should also concentrate on ensuring equal opportunities, including through access to affordable, sustainable and high quality services and public services (…) and in particular health care. Member States should put in place effective anti-discrimination measures. Equally, to fight social exclusion, empower people and promote labour market participation, social protection systems, lifelong learning and active inclusion policies should be enhanced to create opportunities at different stages of people's lives and shield them from the risk of exclusion. Social security and pension systems must be modernised to ensure that they can be fully deployed to ensure adequate income support and access to healthcare — thus providing social cohesion — whilst at the same time remaining financially sustainable. Benefit systems should focus on ensuring income security during transitions and reducing poverty, in particular among groups most at risk from social exclusion, such as one-parent families, minorities, people with disabilities, children and young people, elderly women and men, legal migrants and the homeless. Member States should also actively promote the social economy and social innovation in support of the most vulnerable." (European Commission 2010c)

The proposed guideline has attracted some criticism from organisations concerned to strengthen the EU's focus on poverty and social exclusion. For instance, in the view of EAPN "this means that poverty and social exclusion risk remaining at the margins of EU cooperation" and calls for: "A better integration of inclusion and social cohesion objectives across all the Integrated Guidelines. The separation of the 'social inclusion and combating poverty guideline' from the Employment Guidelines to guarantee that actions on social inclusion and tackling poverty are not limited to employment related measures. Explicit reference in the 'Guideline on social inclusion and combating poverty' to ensure access to rights, resources and services in line with the already-agreed common objectives of the Social OMC." (EAPN 2010a; see also EAPN 2010)

*Social Protection Committee*
A directly related point is an "institutional" one. The pivotal role that the SPC should play in the monitoring of progress towards an EU target in the field of social protection and social inclusion and in the implementation of Guideline 10 needs to be clarified in the final set of Employment Guidelines. As mentioned in Section 1.3.1 above, we also believe that the SPC should be involved in the discussion on the (sub-)national targets

even if, under the principle of *subsidiarity*, countries will of course be free to set these targets on the basis of what they see as the most appropriate indicator(s) given their national circumstances and priorities. This role would in fact be fully in line with Article 160 of the EU Treaty.[24]

### 1.3.4   Lisbon Treaty's "horizontal social clause": a call for "social mainstreaming" and for social impact assessments

Strengthening EU coordination in the social field is even more important and urgent because of the increased status given to social issues in the EU Lisbon Treaty. Of particular significance, is Article 9 which states that: "In defining and implementing its policies and activities, the Union shall take into account requirements linked to the promotion of a high level of employment, the guarantee of adequate social protection, the fight against social exclusion, and a high level of education, training and protection of human health" (European Union, 2009). A major political and legal challenge will now be to give a concrete meaning to this new social clause. In the first instance, it is to be hoped that this new clause in the EU's objectives will provide a more solid basis for requiring the EU, that is *both* the European Commission and EU Member States, to mainstream the EU's social objectives into policy making and, for this to be effective, to systematically carry out social impact assessments of all relevant policies (see also Section 1.3.5 below).[25] Over time, it might also be taken into account in decisions of the European Court lead-

---

24   The SPC is indeed empowered under Article 160 of the EU Treaty to play an important role in this regard: "The Council, acting by a simple majority after consulting the European Parliament, shall establish a Social Protection Committee with advisory status to promote cooperation on social protection policies between Member States and with the Commission. The tasks of the Committee shall be: to monitor the social situation and the development of social protection policies in the Member States and the Union; to promote exchanges of information, experience and good practice between Member States and with the Commission; without prejudice to Article 240, to prepare reports, formulate opinions or undertake other work within its fields of competence, at the request of either the Council or the Commission or on its own initiative. In fulfilling its mandate, the Committee shall establish appropriate contacts with management and labour. Each Member State and the Commission shall appoint two members of the Committee." (European Union, 2009)

25   It is important to systematically develop poverty and social exclusion impact assessments (both *ex ante* and *ex post*) for all relevant policies and not only those specifically aimed at increasing social inclusion, so that policy proposals all take into account the potential (positive or negative) impact they may have on poverty and social exclusion. Existing policies should also regularly be reviewed for their impact on poverty and social exclusion. The ultimate goal should be to systematically work at identifying possible ways (links/ synergies) of adjusting policies to strengthen their contribution to promoting social inclusion. The European Commission, in cooperation with Member States, should develop and promote the methodology for social impact assessments at (sub-)national levels.

ing to a stronger social dimension to the Court's decisions. This important Treaty provision is usefully referred to in the Employment Guidelines ("whereas No 2"); as it is also relevant for economic policies, this reference should also be included in the preamble of the final set of the economic policies Guidelines.

### 1.3.5 Establishing the European Platform Against Poverty

The strengthening of the social dimension of the EU, and in particular the delivery of the EU's new social inclusion target will depend significantly on the proposed Europe 2020 flagship initiative, *the European Platform Against Poverty* (EPAP). Even though it is still unclear what this Platform will be, it seems likely that (much of) the existing Social OMC will, in some form, be merged into this new initiative. The shape of this will only emerge in the Autumn of 2010 when the Commission publishes its proposals on the EPAP.

In our view, the dual challenge to be met is to propose arrangements that can contribute not only to strengthening the future EU cooperation and coordination in the field of social protection and social inclusion but also to bringing together the patchwork of different strands that currently make up Social Europe to ensure that they are better coordinated, more consistent and mutually reinforcing. For this, the EPAP must become the visible symbol of this renewed Social Europe. It has to play a central role in ensuring that all other strands of EU policy making (e.g. economic, competition, education, migration, health, innovation and environmental policies) contribute to achieving the EU's social goals, including the EU target on social inclusion.

This will require explicit arrangements to better link the future EU social process (i.e., EPAP, renewed Social OMC…) with other relevant EU processes (growth, jobs, environment…) so that they are mutually reinforcing. In this regard, and in line with the Lisbon Treaty's "horizontal social clause", a key priority will be to mainstream issues of adequate social protection, the fight against poverty and social exclusion, and also children's rights across all relevant EU policy areas and programmes (including the Structural Funds) in particular through a more systematic application of the required social impact assessments (both *ex ante* and *ex post*) as part of the Commission's integrated impact assessment process.[26] The EPAP should play a central role in monitoring and reporting on the implementation of the social impact assessment process and on the extent to which the other strands of Europe 2020 are contributing to the goal of reducing poverty and social exclusion. If they are not, it could make recommendations as to how

---

26   More information on the Commission's impact assessment process can be found at http://ec.europa.eu/governance/better_regulation/impact_en.htm.

they could contribute better.[27]

### 1.3.6   *Concentrating work around thematic issues*

It is our view that future EU coordination and cooperation in the social field in the new context of the EPAP would gain a lot if it were more concentrated around the key thematic issues that have emerged from the Social OMC, which include of course child poverty and social exclusion, active inclusion, and homelessness and housing exclusion (see above, Section 1.2.1). In developing thematic work (see Chapters 2-4 of this volume for concrete ideas on the possible content of each work programme):

- clear objectives should be set on each issue and multi-annual work programmes agreed on each of them between the Commission and Member States;
- gender equality and non-discrimination should be clear cross-cutting aspects of each issue;
- Member States should be encouraged to make these themes key parts of their NAPs/inclusion;
- annual reports on progress on each key issue should be incorporated into the Joint Report on Social Protection and Social Inclusion and submitted to the Spring European Council and to the European Parliament (see above, Section 1.3.2); this annual report should also be addressed to national and possible sub-national Parliaments of Member States;
- where appropriate data are available (e.g. child poverty and social exclusion) annual scoreboards should be considered;
- as appropriate establish informal groups within the SPC to carry forward work on particular issues.[28]

---

27   In the "accompanying document" to the "Proposal for the Joint Report on Social Protection and Social Inclusion 2010" (Document SEC(2010) 98 final), the Commission very rightly emphasises that "the development of an adequate ex ante social impact assessment capacity in the context of integrated impact assessment arrangements should be encouraged. Strengthening such 'social' component can contribute to more effective and efficient social policy measures. Applied to non social policy measures, it can contribute to avoiding unintended negative social impacts and to better exploiting possibilities for positive synergies (mainstreaming). In this respect, the Social OMC can be used as a forum for exchanging know how between the Member States and between the Member States and the European Commission. The latter has recently taken initiatives to strengthen its own capacity to assess social impacts."

28   The successful outcomes of two such experiences in recent years, which could be built on in the future, are the work of the EU "Task-Force on Child Poverty and Well-Being" (Social Protection Committee, 2008) and the EU "Lisbon Task-Force" (Social Protection Committee, 2009).

### 1.3.7    Guidelines on key governance issues

An important contribution that can be played by the EPAP will be to support Member States to strengthen their governance arrangements in relation to social inclusion issues. Thus, on key governance issues where a considerable body of knowledge and good practice has been developed, the Commission together with the SPC should agree guidelines for Member States to help them to strengthen their practice. These could then become part of the EPAP acquis. Member States should then report regularly, in the context of their NAPs/inclusion, on the arrangements they have put in place to address those issues. The Commission should use such guidance notes as a basis for monitoring and reporting on Member States' performance in this regard and where necessary should make recommendations for strengthening performance. Priority areas where guidelines might be developed include:

- mainstreaming social inclusion objectives in all relevant national and sub-national policies through systematic use of poverty and social impact analysis as an essential component of the overall impact assessment of new policy initiatives;
- developing effective horizontal coordination across policy areas within and among the various policy levels involved, so as to ensure that policies are truly integrated and mutually reinforcing;
- preparing effective regional and local action plans on poverty and social exclusion and on how to ensure synergies between national and sub-national plans including, in particular, in the setting of targets;
- minimum standards on the effective involvement of stakeholders (including people experiencing poverty) in all phases of the preparation, implementation, evaluation and monitoring of social inclusion policies in general and of the Social Inclusion Process in particular.

### 1.3.8    Improving links between EU social inclusion objectives and EU Structural Funds objectives

There should be much closer alignment between the EU's and Member States' social inclusion objectives and the use of EU Structural Funds. In this context, the use of Structural Funds should become a key part of the NAPs/inclusion. In this regard, a very recent positive development should be noted. In July 2009, the European Commission issued a proposal aimed at permitting the European Regional Development Fund (ERDF) to be used for supporting housing interventions in favour of marginalised communities living in the newer Member States (European Commission, 2009b). Under the ERDF provisions adopted in 2006[29], housing interventions could only take place in the context of *urban* development operations and in the form of *renovation of existing houses*. Support to housing interventions in rural areas or for the replacement of "houses" of a very poor quality in urban or rural areas was thus not eligible whereas in the newer EU countries, the great majority of these communities live in rural areas and in shelters (in rural as well as in urban areas). On 19 May 2010, Regulation (EU) No. 437/2010 of the European Parliament and of the Council was adopted. It goes in the direction suggested by the Commission. Under specific conditions, it also extends some of the funding possibilities to all 27 EU countries (and not only to the newer Member States). This could play an important role in increasing resources for initiatives in this field.[30]

### 1.3.9    Maintaining and strengthening NAPs/inclusion

To ensure that Member States develop a strategic, comprehensive and coherent approach to translating the EU's social inclusion objectives into national policies, we consider it essential that the NAPs/inclusion are maintained and enhanced. This will require a better integration of the NAPs/inclusion into national (and also, where relevant, into subnational) policy-making processes and the development of closer links with national (and possible sub-national) parliaments. This might involve reassessing together with Member States and relevant stakeholders, the timing and structure of the NAPs/inclusion cycle so that it becomes easier for Member States to use the NAPs/inclusion as strategic planning opportunities to strengthen policies and not just as a means of reporting on existing policies to the EU.

### 1.3.10   Greater use of harder instruments

There is a need to combine the current "soft" approach of the OMC with greater use of "harder" instruments as part of the future EU coordination in the social field. This can

---

29    Article 7(2) of Regulation (EC) No 1080/2006 of the European Parliament and of the Council of 5 July 2006.

30    In a very thorough report, Barca (2009) argues for a reformed cohesion policy for the EU and that therefore a new combination of the social and territorial agendas is required. He suggests that "The social agenda needs to be "territorialised", the territorial agenda "socialised". The place-based approach to social inclusion should be the result of these two shifts". (page 36)

involve making greater use of Commission Recommendations[31] and exploring the possibilities of using legal instruments such as EU (Framework) Directives.

### *1.3.11 Enhanced exchange and learning and better communication*

Exchange and learning should be enhanced as an integral element in the EU Social Inclusion Process, *inter alia* by resourcing an increased range of opportunities for exchange and learning under the 2007-2013 *Community Programme for Employment and Social Solidarity (PROGRESS)*. The process of policy learning and exchange of good practices should be strengthened with more systematic clustering of activities (e.g. studies, peer reviews, exchange projects, EU funded networks) around specific themes. Every effort should also be made to promote a wider and more systematic involvement of regional and local actors (policy makers, stakeholders and civil society) in the process. More effective and widespread dissemination of results will be necessary.

There is also a need to build on the 2010 European Year to develop a proactive communication strategy at EU, national and sub-national levels targeting the media, which would highlight Member States' progress in achieving their social inclusion objectives.

## References

Atkinson, T., Cantillon, B., Marlier, E. and Nolan, B. (2002), *Social Indicators: The EU and Social Inclusion*, Oxford: Oxford University Press.

Barca, F. (2009), An agenda for a reformed cohesion policy: A place-based approach to meeting European Union challenges and expectations, Independent Report prepared at the request of Danuta Hübner, Commissioner for Regional Policy, Brussels: European Commission. Available from:
http://ec.europa.eu/regional_policy/policy/future/pdf/report_barca_v0306.pdf.

Council (2010), *Joint Report on Social Protection and Social Inclusion* (including related supporting document produced by the European Commission), Brussels: EU Council of Ministers and European Commission. Available from:

---

31   The Commission Communication on reinforcing the Social OMC already suggests that "The subjects that are part of the OMC could be further consolidated by formalising convergence of views whenever it arises. The Commission will contribute to this by making, where appropriate, use of Recommendations based on Article 211 of the Treaty, setting out common principles, providing a basis for monitoring and peer review." (European Commission, 2008b) In fact, a precedent for this exists within the Social OMC with the Commission's 2008 Recommendation on Active Inclusion (European Commission, 2008a).

http://ec.europa.eu/social/main.jsp?catId=757&langId=en.

Council (2005), *Joint Report on Social Protection and Social Inclusion*, Brussels: EU Council of Ministers and European Commission.

EU Network of Independent Experts on Social Inclusion:
http://www.peer-review-social-inclusion.eu/network-of-independent-experts.

European Anti-Poverty Network (2010), *EAPN proposals for New Integrated Guidelines for Europe 2020*, Brussels: EAPN.

European Anti Poverty Network (2010a), *Actions to combat Poverty and to foster Social Inclusion risk remaining at the margins of EU Cooperation*, Press Release, 30th April 2010, Brussels: EAPN.

European Anti-Poverty Network (2009a), *A Europe we can trust: Proposals on a new EU post-2010 strategy*, Brussels: EAPN.

European Anti-Poverty Network (EAPN) (2009b), *Small Steps – Big Changes*, Brussels: EAPN.

European Commission (2010a), *Lisbon Strategy evaluation document*, Commission Staff Working Document SEC(2010) 114 final, Brussels: European Commission.

European Commission (2010b), *Europe 2020: A European Strategy for smart, sustainable and inclusive growth*, Communication No. COM(2010) 2020, Brussels: European Commission.

European Commission (2010c), *Proposal for a Council Decision on guidelines for the employment policies of the Member States Part II of the Europe 2020 Integrated Guidelines*, Communication COM(2010) 193/3, European Commission, Brussels: European Commission. Available from:
http://ec.europa.eu/eu2020/pdf/proposition_en.pdf.

European Commission (2009a), *Portfolio of indicators for the monitoring of the European strategy for social protection and social inclusion – 2009 update*, Brussels: European Commission. Available from:
http://ec.europa.eu/social/main.jsp?catId=756&langId=en.

European Commission (2009b), *Proposal for a Regulation (EC) no …/2009 of the European Parliament and of the Council amending Regulation (EC) No 1080/2006 on the European Regional Development Fund as regards the eligibility of housing interventions in favour of marginalised communities*, Communication COM(2009) 382 final, Brussels: European Commission. Available from:
http://register.consilium.europa.eu/pdf/en/10/st06/st06037.en10.pdf.

European Commission (2008a), *Commission Recommendation of 3 October 2008 on the active inclusion of people excluded from the labour market*, Brussels: European Commission. Available from:
http://eur-lex.europa.eu/LexUriServ/LexUriServ.do?uri=OJ:L:2008:307:0011:0014:EN:PDF.

European Commission (2008b), *A renewed commitment to social Europe: Reinforcing the Open Method of Coordination for Social Protection and Social Inclusion*, Communication No. COM(2008) 418 final, Brussels: European Commission.

European Council (2010a), *European Council 25/26 March 2010: Conclusions*, Brussels: European Council.

European Council (2010b), *European Council 17 June 2010: Conclusions*, Brussels: European Council.

European Union (2009), *Consolidated Version of the Treaty of Lisbon*, Brussels: European Union. Available from:
http://www.consilium.europa.eu/showPage.aspx?id=1296&lang=en.

Frazer, H. (2007), *Promoting Social Inclusion: The EU Dimension*, in Administration Vol. 55, No. 2, Dublin: Institute of Public Administration.

Frazer, H. and Marlier, E. (2008), *Building a stronger EU Social Inclusion Process: Analysis and recommendations of the EU Network of independent national experts on social inclusion*, Brussels: European Commission.

Fusco, A., Guio, A.-C. and Marlier, E. (2010), "Characterising the income poor and the materially deprived in European countries", forthcoming in Atkinson A.B and Marlier E. (eds.), Comparative EU Statistics on Income and Living Conditions (provisional title), Luxembourg: OPOCE.

Guio, A.-C. (2009), *What can be learned from deprivation indicators in Europe?*, Luxembourg: Eurostat. Available from:
http://epp.eurostat.ec.europa.eu/cache/ITY_OFFPUB/KS-RA-09-007/EN/KS-RA-09-007-EN.PDF

Harvey, B. (2008), *EAPN Structural Funds Manual 2009-2011*, Brussels: EAPN.

Marlier, E., Atkinson, A.B., Cantillon, B., Nolan, B. (2007), *The EU and Social Inclusion: Facing the challenges*, Bristol: The Policy Press.

Platform of European Social NGOs (2009), *5 recommendations for an effective Open Method of Coordination on social protection and social inclusion*, Brussels: Social Platform. Available from:
http://cms.horus.be/files/99907/MediaArchive/Policies/Social_Inclusion/20090929_SP%20Social%20OMC_final.pdf.

Social Protection Committee (2009), *Growth, Jobs and Social Progress in the EU: A contribution to the evaluation of the social dimension of the Lisbon Strategy*, Brussels: European Commission. Available from:
http://ec.europa.eu/social/BlobServlet?docId=3898&langId=en.

Social Protection Committee (2008), *Child Poverty and Well-Being in the EU: Current status and way forward*, Luxembourg: office for Official Publications of the European Communities. Available from:
http://ec.europa.eu/social/main.jsp?catId=751&langId=en&pubId=74&type=2&furtherPubs=yes.

Spring Alliance (2009), *Manifesto*, Brussels: Spring Alliance. Available from:
http://www.springalliance.eu/manifesto.

Zeitlin, J. (2007), *The Open Method of Coordination and the Governance of the Lisbon Strat-*

*egy*, University of Wisconsin-Madison EUSA conference. Available from: http://aei.pitt.edu/8032/01/zeitlin-j-06e.pdf.

# 2 Child Poverty and Social Exclusion

This chapter documents and draws on the considerable body of material that has been developed on child poverty and social exclusion since the inception of the Social Open Method of Coordination (OMC) in 2000. Sections 2.1-2.4 outline the key lessons and conclusions that can be learned on tackling child poverty and social exclusion. Section 2.5 then considers child poverty and related policies in Belgium. Finally, Section 2.6 draws some conclusions and makes recommendations for strengthening European Union (EU) action on child poverty and social exclusion in the future. Children are defined here as persons aged below 18.

## 2.1 Child poverty and social exclusion in the Social OMC

### 2.1.1 An increasingly important issue

Since 2000 the issue of child poverty and social exclusion has become an increasingly important part of the Social OMC. It has featured ever more prominently in more than three quarters of the Member States' National Action Plans on social inclusion (NAPs/inclusion). Since 2002, it has been highlighted as a key issue in each of the *Joint Reports on Social Protection and Social Inclusion* (*Joint Reports on Social Inclusion* up until 2004) adopted each year by the European Commission and the EU Council of Ministers. In March 2005, EU Heads of State and Government stressed that "Social inclusion policy should be pursued by the Union and by Member States, with its multifaceted approach, focusing on target groups such as children in poverty", and one year later they called on Member States "to take necessary measures to rapidly and significantly reduce child poverty, giving all children equal opportunities, regardless of their social background".

The 2005 Luxembourg EU Presidency initiative on "Taking forward the EU Social Inclusion Process" called explicitly for *children mainstreaming* and for the adoption of at least one child well-being indicator at EU level (see Marlier *et al*, 2007). In 2006, the European Commission Communication on the rights of the child gave particular attention to the issue of children's social inclusion and to the role of the EU Social Inclusion Process. An EU Task-Force on child poverty and well-being was created in 2007, whose analytical report and recommendations were formally adopted by all Member States and the Commission in January 2008 (Social Protection Committee, 2008). In 2009 the European Parliament produced a report on promoting social inclusion and combating poverty, including child poverty, in the EU (European Parliament, 2008). In March

2010, a detailed report on *Child Poverty and Child Well-Being in the European Union* commissioned by the European Commission and produced by a consortium led by the TARKI Social Research Institute (TARKI, 2010) was published.

The Lisbon Treaty, which came into force on 1 December 2009, includes for the first time the promotion of children's rights as an explicit objective of the EU. Also at the end of 2009, the Commission Working Document on the Europe 2020 Strategy (European Commission, 2009b) recognised that child poverty and social exclusion is one of the EU's long-term social challenges which have been further exacerbated by the financial and economic crisis. The issue is also one of the key focuses of the 2010 European Year for Combating Poverty and Social Exclusion and at the opening conference of the Year in January 2010 the President of the Commission declared "Let us translate this European Year into a renewed commitment and concrete actions. Let us reduce the risk of poverty rate by 2020 for the whole population, particularly children and the elderly. Because the current figures are intolerable." (Barroso, 2010)[32] Belgium has also singled out the fight against child poverty and social exclusion as an important priority for its Presidency of the EU in the second half of 2010. Philippe Courard, Belgian Secretary of State for Social Integration and Combating Poverty, has announced that the intention is to enhance the process at EU level and contribute to moving move towards a European Commission Recommendation on Child Poverty.

### 2.1.2    Why it has become a major issue

From the preceding section it is clear that child poverty and social exclusion has emerged as an important issue for the EU and has become an increasingly high level political priority. There are six interconnected reasons which explain why this is the case and why it is likely to remain so in the future.

The first, and probably most important explanation as to why the issue has come to the fore, is that the existence of the Social OMC has created an institutional framework at EU level. This framework has made it possible to raise the issue of child poverty and social exclusion on a regular and systematic basis and to encourage cooperation between Member States on the issue. Knowledge of this issue has been deepened through im-

---

32    Authors' translation into English of the official speech by President Barroso available in French and Spanish from http://europa.eu/rapid/pressReleasesAction.do?reference=SPEECH/10/12. The French official text reads as follows:
"Traduisons cette année européenne par un engagement renouvelé et par des actions concrètes. Nous devons faire reculer le taux de risque de pauvreté d'ici à 2020 pour l'ensemble de la population, en particulier pour les enfants et les personnes âgées. Car les chiffres actuels sont intolérables."

provements in data and analysis, comparative studies and mutual exchange and learning projects, awareness and understanding of the issue and the policies necessary to prevent and tackle it. The preparation of NAPs/inclusion has encouraged many Member States to develop more strategic and comprehensive approaches. Regular monitoring and reporting have also been a stimulus to increased effort in this field.

The second reason is the growing body of evidence of the extent and persistence of child poverty and social exclusion across the EU. This evidence is elaborated in section 2.2 and shows that child poverty and social exclusion is not a peripheral or residual problem that will just disappear with economic growth. Indeed, some of the factors linked to child poverty and social exclusion such as the growth in lone parent families and the high levels of child poverty and social exclusion amongst immigrants and some ethnic minorities serve to emphasise its likely persistence unless appropriate policies to promote the social inclusion of all children are developed. Faced by this reality and under increasing pressure from civil society, from child care experts, from academics and from the general public, there has been increasing pressure on decision-makers to take concrete actions to reduce child poverty and social exclusion. Thus ensuring the social inclusion and well-being of all children has become a growing political necessity.

A third factor has been the increasing awareness of children's rights and a growing recognition that poverty and social exclusion undermine these rights (see Fernandes, 2007). The impact of the United Nations Convention on the Rights of the Child (UNCRC) has been very important in this regard as it emphasises that children's rights form part of the human rights Member States are bound to respect. The regular reporting and monitoring process linked to the UNCRC have greatly increased awareness in Member States. In addition, UNICEF has linked its work on child poverty and social exclusion to children's rights and this has further raised awareness (see UNICEF, 2007). The 2006 Commission Communication calling on Member States to establish a comprehensive EU strategy to effectively promote and safeguard the rights of the child in EU policies (European Commission, 2006) has also increased the EU's focus on children's rights and has explicitly highlighted the link with poverty and social exclusion. The recognition in the Lisbon Treaty of the protection of children's rights as one of the EU's objectives is also a very important development as previously the EU had limited competencies regarding children's rights.

The fourth reason for increasing attention being given to the fight against child poverty and social exclusion is that the demographic trends in the EU, with declining birth rates and the ageing of the EU population, mean that many Member States face serious labour constraints and a rise in dependency ratios in the future. This has led to a growing awareness of the need to maximise the EU's future human resources. The effect of this has been to create an increasingly strong social and economic argument for tackling child poverty and social exclusion. Children who grow up in poverty or social exclusion are less likely to reach their full potential when they grow up and they will have a higher risk of being unemployed and living in persistent poverty as adults. This has serious implications for future economic and social development. In an increasingly technical labour market, it is important for countries to maximise their human resources so that people can contribute fully to economic growth and development. Countries need to maximise the future potential of all their children and thus child poverty and social exclusion need to be efficiently addressed now[33].

A fifth, and closely related factor, is the long-term costs to society of children growing up in poverty or social exclusion situations. The EU Social OMC has reinforced evidence from international studies that high levels of child poverty and social exclusion lead to higher economic and social costs for countries. Growing up in poverty curtails the development of children and endangers their future well-being. As a result, children who grow up in poverty or social exclusion are likely to suffer poorer health and have a higher risk of unemployment or unskilled and low paid employment when they are adults. They will thus be likely to make more demands on welfare, health and other public services. The issue of tackling child poverty and social exclusion is thus also one of investment in the future. There is a growing body of international evidence that investing in children living in poverty leads to very real economic benefits and significant savings in social costs over the long-term.[34] It is much more costly, and less successful, to try and redress the causes of poverty and social exclusion at a later stage. Thus investing in children makes good economic and political sense.

Finally, the sixth reason why the issue of child poverty and social exclusion is receiving more attention at national and EU levels is a growing appreciation of the negative impact of child poverty and social exclusion on social cohesion in the EU. Tackling child poverty and social exclusion is not only an end in itself but is also essential to building a more inclusive society. The EU Social OMC has demonstrated that if the goal of making a decisive impact on the eradication of poverty and social exclusion is to be achieved this means breaking the recurring cycle of poverty whereby many children inherit disadvantage from their parents. It means stopping the inflow of people into poverty or social exclusion. This can only be achieved by early intervention to lift children out of poverty and social exclusion and ensure their full development and participation in society.

---

33    This is well put by Ruxton and Bennett (2002) when they argue that "the economic, social, political and cultural development of the EU depends on all its 90 million children achieving their full potential".

34    See, for instance, the UNICEF summary of evidence for the long-term advantages of high quality early childhood education and care (UNICEF, 2008).

These six reasons explain why there has been a growing recognition that it is crucial that child poverty and social exclusion is mainstreamed in the political and economic debate both nationally and in the EU. Addressing child well-being and the social inclusion of children is essential both for reasons of social justice here and now and for reasons of future well-being. As the French Conseil de l'Emploi, des Revenus et de la Cohésion sociale (2004) compellingly put it: "The question of child poverty must be considered as vital for two sets of reasons. Most theories of social justice agree upon the duty for a society to compensate for the inequalities suffered by people who are in no way responsible for the situation they are in. This applies to children more than for any other person. The second reason is that poverty suffered in one's childhood increases the risk of being poor as an adult." It is also clear that tackling child poverty and social exclusion is central to many of the key policy challenges facing the EU: challenges like demographic ageing, globalisation and the need for a skilled and qualified workforce, increased mobility and ethnic diversity, concern with political disaffection and a democratic deficit, supporting greater gender equality, reconciling work and family life, adjusting to changing family structures and promoting environmental sustainability. This explains why it has become an increasingly important political issue for the EU and national governments and will continue to be in the coming period.

### 2.1.3   *Wide range of work on child poverty and social exclusion in the Social OMC*

Since 2002, a lot has been learned about child poverty and social exclusion as a result of the wide range of work that has been undertaken under the auspices of the Social OMC. For instance, successive NAPs/inclusion have addressed the issue. While the actual coverage of the issue in the NAPs/inclusion has been rather uneven and piecemeal and in many cases lacking a comprehensive and multi-dimensional approach (Eurochild 2009b), they have provided a rich source of information about the approaches adopted by Member States and about interesting policy developments. The annual Joint Reports on Social Protection and Social Inclusion have regularly highlighted the issue, with the 2008 Joint Report analysing more specifically certain aspects of child poverty and social exclusion (an analysis that was further elaborated in a Commission services Working Document; Council, 2008). The work of the Social Protection Committee and its Indicators Sub-Group on the development of commonly agreed indicators for measuring poverty and social exclusion across the EU has also contributed to significantly increase the prominence of the issue (European Commission, 2009a).

A wide range of activities in the field of child poverty and social exclusion have been supported as part of the Social OMC under the 2002-2006 *Community action programme to combat poverty and social exclusion* and the 2007-2013 *Community Programme for Employment and Social Solidarity (PROGRESS)* and also under their predecessor, the 1998-2000

Preparatory Measures on Poverty and Social Exclusion, the results of many of which became available during the early years of the Social OMC.[35]

In terms of research and analysis there have been several reports during the course of the Social OMC that have been particularly important and influential in the development of the focus on child poverty and social exclusion and in improving understanding of the issue. These include the following:

- In 2004, a study by Petra Hölscher examined the policies to tackle child poverty in six Member States and the United States, and identified what combination of policy responses are most successful in preventing and reducing high levels of child poverty (Hölscher, 2004). It was the first thematic study commissioned as part of the Social OMC process and it did much to put child poverty and social exclusion at the heart of the EU process and to set the framework for the future development of work on this issue.[36]

- In 2005, the Luxembourg EU Presidency held a conference on *Taking Forward the EU Social Inclusion Process* which was based on a report which made children mainstreaming one of its key themes. This was subsequently updated and published as a book (Marlier *et al*, 2007). This helped to significantly advance thinking on the issue and to increase the focus on the need for better indicators (including child well-being indicators), improved data and more rigorous monitoring and evaluation.

- In 2007, the EU Network of Independent Experts on Social Inclusion wrote reports assessing policies in each Member State and this led to an overall report drawing out lessons on how best to tackle child poverty and promote the social inclusion of children in the EU (Frazer and Marlier, 2007).[37]

- In 2007, as part of the Social OMC's thematic year on child poverty an EU *Task-Force on Child Poverty and Child Well-Being* was established by the EU Social Protection Committee (SPC). The resulting report analysed child poverty and social exclusion in the EU and examined approaches to policy monitoring of child poverty and well-being in Member States. The in-depth analysis and

---

35   Some 20 out of 249 projects funded between 1998 and 2000 addressed aspects of child poverty.

36   Child poverty also was a relevant issue in other thematic studies that were commissioned such as *The situation of Roma in an enlarged European Union*, (European Commission, 2004), *Policy measures concerning disadvantaged youth* (Walther and Pohl 2006) and *Poverty and social exclusion among lone parent households* (Trifiletti *et al* 2007).

37   We would like to acknowledge the contribution of the members of this Commission funded Network as their published reports have been an important source of material when drafting this chapter. See Frazer and Marlier, 2007. For each of the 27 Member States' national independent reports on "Tackling child poverty and promoting the social inclusion of children (in expert's Member State)", see: http://www.peer-review-social-inclusion.eu/network-of-independent-experts/2007/first-semester-2007.

concrete recommendations of the report were endorsed by the Commission and Member States in January 2008 and are now part of the *EU acquis* in this area (Social Protection Committee, 2008). They thus provide an important framework for the future development of the child poverty and well-being strand of the Social OMC in general and Member States' policies in particular.[38]

- In 2008, with a view to building on all this work, the European Commission commissioned a further study on child poverty and well-being in the EU (TARKI, 2010). The findings of this research provide a concrete basis for carrying forward the EU Task-Force recommendations on measuring and monitoring child poverty and social exclusion across the EU; they also give detailed suggestions on policy priorities for individual Member State.

Apart from the NAPs/inclusion, the Joint Reports, the work of the SPC and its Indicators Sub-Group and the various major reports mentioned above, there have been many other ways in which the EU process has advanced understanding and the exchange of learning on child poverty and social exclusion. For instance, the aforementioned 1998-2000 Preparatory Measures outputs included the publication in 2002 of an important report on child poverty and social exclusion from Euronet, the European Children's Network (Ruxton and Bennett, 2002) and several more focused reports[39]. Under the 2002-2006 Community Action Programme, several transnational exchange projects examined aspects of child poverty[40] and there have been further mutual learning projects supported under PROGRESS.[41]

---

38  The recommendations adopted by the SPC cover setting quantified objectives, assessing the impact of policies on child poverty and social exclusion, monitoring child poverty and well-being, a common framework for analysing child poverty and well-being, reinforcing statistical capacity and improving governance and monitoring arrangements at all relevant policy levels.

39  See, for example, the European Forum for Child Welfare project on families under stress (Williams, 2003), a Greek led project on *Promoting the social inclusion of Roma populations* (Save the Children Greece, 2000) and a project on tackling social exclusion in families with young children (Home Start International, 2002).

40  See, for instance, the following projects: the *A Lobby for Children* project (Bohn, 2005), a project on *Promoting inclusion for unaccompanied young asylum seekers and immigrants* (European Social Network 2005), a Cyprus College led project on *Integrating children's perspectives in policy making to combat poverty and social exclusion experienced by single parent families* (Cyprus College, 2007), an Associazione Amici dei Bambini led project on *Social inclusion for out-of-family children and young people in public childcare* and an Istituto degli Innocenti project on the *Conditions of children placed in out of home care and the construction of child-oriented welfare policies*.

41  See, for instance, the Associazione Amici dei Bambini led project on *Life after Institutional Care – Equal Opportunities and Social Inclusion for Young People: Identification and Promotion of Best Practices* and the Greater London Enterprise led project on *European Cities Against Child Poverty* (see European Cities Against Child Poverty, 2008 and 2009).

Peer Reviews have been another important means of exchanging learning on child poverty and social exclusion. In April 2007, the SPC sent a questionnaire to Member States which gathered detailed information on the policies being developed by Member States to prevent child poverty and social exclusion. The responses to the questionnaires, together with the EU Task-Force Report and reports from the Network of Independent Experts on Social Inclusion, informed an SPC Peer Review on child poverty in October 2007. In the Social OMC's Peer Review programme[42], there have been several seminars on aspects of child and family poverty and social exclusion which have helped to deepen understanding of policy approaches.[43]

There has also been a core funding programme for European networks concerned with poverty and social exclusion issues, first under the Community action programme and then under PROGRESS. Child poverty and social exclusion has been a priority area for funding. From the outset, Eurochild has been a key network supported under this programme and has played an important role in focusing attention on the position of children within the EU process. It has combined a focus on influencing and analysing the NAPs/inclusion (see Eurochild, 2009b) with a wider approach to the issue of child poverty and social exclusion that ranges from working on the Commission's initiative on children's rights to developing very specific ideas in areas such as early years education and care, family and parenting support, child and youth participation and children without parental care. Two other networks also specifically concerned with children, the Confederation of Family Organisations in the EU (COFACE) and the European Foundation for Street Children are also currently funded by the EU. In addition, several of the other core funded EU networks such as the European Anti-Poverty Network (EAPN),

---

42    Peer Review seminars have been a key feature of actions under both the Community Action Programme and PROGRESS. In each seminar, the experience of the host country in a particular area is confronted with the comments and critical analysis of peer countries. The intention is that the event can serve as a useful tool to Member States to help them in the design and implementation of more effective policies. It is also hoped that this will contribute to the dialogue with stakeholders such as social partners and NGOs and where appropriate, people experiencing poverty and social exclusion. More information on peer reviews on child and family poverty can be found on the website of the EU programme on "Peer Review in Social Protection and Social Inclusion and Assessment in Social Inclusion" at: http://www.peer-review-social-inclusion.eu/key-themes/children-and-families-1.

43    For example: a 2005 peer review in Campobasso in Italy examined policies to prevent the exclusion of families with difficulties; in 2007 one in the United Kingdom looked at the Sure Start programme which helps children from disadvantaged backgrounds and their families and tries to ensure the best start in life for every child; the first peer review of 2010 in Germany examined the work of the Federal Foundation to prevent pregnant women with low incomes or in households where they are the main breadwinner from falling into poverty during pregnancy and/or following the birth of a child.

the European Social Network (ESN), the European Federation of National Organisations Working with the Homeless (FEANTSA) and Caritas Europa have also given considerable attention to the issue of child poverty and social exclusion and produced important reports.[44]

Child poverty and social exclusion has also been a key theme of the annual EU Round-Tables on poverty and social exclusion, the annual flagship event of the Social OMC, since the first one hosted by the Danish Presidency of the EU in 2002 and it has also been a recurring topic raised at the annual European Meetings of People Experiencing Poverty since the first one hosted by the Belgium Presidency of the EU in 2001. These events again have provided important opportunities to exchange learning on issues of child poverty and social exclusion. For instance, at the 2009 Round-Table in Stockholm there was an in depth discussion at one workshop on the topic of how to tackle poverty and social exclusion of children and youth.

As a result of this increased interest in the issue of child poverty and social exclusion and of all the work that has gone on since the launch of the Social OMC in 2000, a lot more is known about the issue of child poverty and social exclusion in the European Union and in particular about the policies and programmes that work best to prevent and reduce the problem. Some of the key findings are summarised in the following sections of this book.

## 2.2 Extent and nature of child poverty and social exclusion in the EU

### 2.2.1 Extent

Child poverty and social exclusion are major challenges across the European Union. However, the extent and severity varies widely from country to country and indeed in many countries from region to region. So, evidence from the 2007 wave of EU-SILC shows the following[45]:

---

44  For instance, the European Social Network has a "Policy and Practice Resources" working group on children and families and this has helped to highlight the important role played by social services in the care and protection of children experiencing poverty and social exclusion: see http://www.esn-eu.org/children-and-families/index.htm and (European Social Network, 2010). See also Caritas Europa (2004) and FEANTSA (2007). For a list of the Networks supported as part of the Social OMC and for the links to the different Networks' web-sites, see web-site of Directorate-General "Employment, Social Affairs and Equal Opportunities" of the European Commission at: http://ec.europa.eu/social/main.jsp?catId=750&langId=en.

45  See the web-site of Eurostat, the statistical office of the European Communities: http://epp.eurostat.ec.europa.eu/portal/page/portal/statistics/themes.

- 20% of children in the EU are **at** *risk of (income) poverty*[46] as compared to 16% for the total population. The risk is greater for children in all countries except Cyprus, Denmark, Estonia, Finland, Germany and Slovenia (in Latvia, the risk is identical (21%) among children and the total population). Child poverty risk is as high as 30-33% in two countries (Bulgaria and Romania), and between 23-25% in five countries (Greece, Italy, Poland, Spain and the UK), whereas it is "only" 10-12% in five countries (Cyprus, Denmark, Finland, Slovenia and Sweden).

- The national at-risk-of-poverty thresholds vary enormously across the EU. So, for a household consisting of 2 adults and 2 children, *national thresholds* (monthly amounts expressed in Purchasing Power Standards (PPS)[47]) range from less than 750 PPS in 8 countries (all these countries are newer Member States) to more than 1600 PPS in 12 countries (all older Member States, except for Cyprus). In Bulgaria and Romania, the corresponding national threshold is around 300-350 PPS, as opposed to around 2000 PPS in the UK and 3000 PPS in Luxembourg.

- The at-risk-of-poverty rate would be much higher in the EU if there were no social transfers. On average in the EU, *social transfers* (excluding pensions) reduce the proportion of children at risk of poverty by 39%, which is a higher impact than for the overall population (35%). In Finland and Sweden, social transfers reduce child poverty risk by 64-67%. On the other hand, in Bulgaria, Greece, Romania and Spain, this reduction only reaches a maximum of 20% (also for the overall population). These figures reflect both the scale of expenditure level and the extent to which transfers are targeted on children with low income.

- A national child at-risk-of-poverty rate identifies the proportion of children living under the national poverty risk threshold in a given country. It is essential to complement this information with the national poverty risk gap[48], which indicates "how poor the poor children are" – that is, the *depth* of child poverty risk. The poverty risk gap for children varies from 13% in Finland and 15% in France to 40% in Romania and 44% in Bulgaria. It should be noted that Bulgaria and Romania as well as Greece, Italy, Latvia, Lithuania, Poland, Portugal and Spain are countries where both child poverty risk *and* child poverty risk

---

46   A child "at-risk-of-poverty" is a child who lives in a household "at-risk-of-poverty", i.e. a household whose total equivalised income is below 60% of the median national equivalised household income.

47   PPS can be defined as "artificial Euros" that correct for the differences in the cost of living in the different Member States.

48   The "relative median at-risk-of-poverty gap" (here: poverty risk gap) measures the distance between the median equivalised income of people living below the poverty risk threshold and the value of that poverty risk threshold; it is expressed as a percentage of the threshold.

gap are higher than the EU average; Luxembourg and the United Kingdom are just on the border.

- The risk of poverty tends to increase with the *age* of children in most countries.

- Another key factor to look at when considering income poverty is *duration*, i.e. how long children spend living under the poverty risk threshold. As rightly emphasised in the aforementioned TARKI report, "although the risk of poverty among children in a given year gives some indication of the threat of deprivation and social exclusion they face, the threat concerned is much more serious if they have an income below this level for several years on end" (TARKI, 2010, page 30). For the 20 EU countries for which the required EU-SILC data are available, the TARKI report shows that the proportion of children living in households that have been at-risk-of-poverty for each of the years 2005-2007 ranges from 4-6% (in Austria, Cyprus, Finland, Slovenia and Sweden) up to 13-16% (in Italy, Lithuania, Luxembourg, Poland and Portugal).

- The share of children affected by *material deprivation*[49] is identical to that affected by (income) poverty risk (20%). However, material deprivation varies by a significantly larger extent across Member States: from 4-10% (in Luxembourg, the 3 Nordic countries, the Netherlands and Spain) up to 39-43% (in Hungary, Latvia and Poland), 57% (Romania) and 72% (Bulgaria) whereas the range for poverty risk rates is "only" from 10% to 33%. As put by Marlier *et al* (forthcoming), "this reflects the fact that differences in average living standards across countries as well as the distribution within them now come into play". It is therefore very useful to *complement* the picture provided by the national poverty risk rates and poverty risk thresholds with that provided by the national material deprivation rates. So, if we put in perspective poverty risk and material deprivation we can identify on the one hand a group of 7 countries where the ratio between the proportion of child material deprivation and that of child poverty risk is higher than 1.6 (Bulgaria, Cyprus, Hungary, Latvia, Poland, Slovakia and Romania; highest ratios in Bulgaria (72%/30%=2.4) and Cyprus (28%/12%=2.32.3)) and, at the other extreme, a group of 4 countries where this ratio is lower than 0.6 (Luxembourg, Netherlands, Sweden and Spain; lowest ratio in Luxembourg (4%/20%=0.2).

- At EU level, the *material deprivation rate among children at risk of poverty* is 46%, a proportion which varies significantly – from 18-28% (Denmark, Luxembourg, Netherlands, Spain, Sweden) to 72-96% (Bulgaria, Hungary, Latvia, Romania). And among children which are above the poverty risk threshold, the EU average material deprivation rate is 13%. Here again, the range is very

---

49 Originally proposed by Guio (2009), this indicator significantly improves the multi-dimensional coverage of the EU portfolio for social inclusion. For its definition, see Chapter 1, Section 1.3.1.

high: 1-6% (again: Denmark, Luxembourg, Netherlands, Spain, Sweden) and
35-62% (again: Bulgaria, Hungary, Latvia, Romania).

### 2.2.2    Main groups

Children living with lone parents and children living in large families, on the other hand,
are at highest risk in virtually all countries. Evidence from the 2007 wave of EU-SILC
indicates that at EU level, 34% of children living in *single parent families* are at risk of
poverty, with proportions varying from 17-24% (Denmark, Finland, Sweden) to 40-45%
(Estonia, Ireland, Lithuania, Luxembourg, Romania, UK) and 54% (Malta). As to children living in *large families* (i.e. households consisting of 2 adults and 3 or more children),
their poverty risk for the EU as a whole is 25%. The share ranges from 12-15% (Germany, Finland, Sweden, Denmark, Slovenia) to 41-55% (Italy, Latvia, Portugal, Romania)
and 71% (Bulgaria).

However, it should be noted that, though being at lower than average risk of poverty
(14%), children in '2 adults with 2 dependent children' households represent the largest
group of children at risk of poverty in the European Union as a whole.

### 2.2.3    Joblessness

Living in a household where no-one is in paid employment is likely to have a significant
effect on both the current living conditions of children and on their future living conditions. Joblessness not only raises the question of potential financial problems (see below,
Section 2.2.4); the absence of a working adult in the child's household can also limit current or future opportunities to participate fully in society (e.g. it could affect the future
labour market achievement of the child).

The 2007 *EU Labour Force Survey (LFS)* shows that almost 10% (9.4) of EU children
live in *jobless households*, a proportion ranging from 2.2-3.9% (in Cyprus, Greece, Luxembourg and Slovenia) to 12.0 in Belgium, 12.8% in Bulgaria, 13.9% in Hungary and
16.7% in the UK. As to the proportion of adults (18-59 year olds) living in jobless households, the EU average is almost identical (9.3%) but the range of national rates is smaller:
from 4.7% in Cyprus to 12.3% in Belgium.[50]

---

50    See Eurostat web-site: http://epp.eurostat.ec.europa.eu/portal/page/portal/statistics/themes.

## 2.2.4 Employment status a key factor

To better understand the extent to which parental employment contributes to the income of the household, one needs to look at how many adults work in the household and
whether they work part-time or full-time, and during the whole year or only part of the
year. For this, the EU has adopted a breakdown of the poverty risk by the *work intensity
(WI)* of the household. This WI only takes account of working age adults.

- A WI of 0 refers to households in which no one has been in paid employment during the income reference year. Children living in those households
  run a very high poverty risk: according to the 2007 wave of EU-SILC, the EU
  average poverty risk for these children is 70%, with the lowest risk registered
  in Denmark and Finland (47-49%) and the highest risk in Bulgaria, Czech
  Republic, Estonia, Lithuania, Portugal, Romania and Slovakia (81-90%).
- Unsurprisingly, children living in households with a WI of 1 run a much lower
  poverty risk. However, even in those households the poverty risk is not negligi-
  ble: the EU average for children living in households with *all working-age adults
  in full-time paid employment* throughout the year is still at 8% for children. This
  proportion ranges from 3-4%% (Belgium, Bulgaria, Cyprus, Czech Republic, Denmark, Finland, Malta, Slovenia) to 11-13% (Greece, Latvia, Luxembourg, Poland)
  and 24% in Romania.
- Finally, if we consider households with a WI less than 1 but higher or equal to 0.5
  (WI equal 0.5 corresponds to a couple where only one of the two partners works but
  he/she works full-time and full year), the EU average jumps to 22%, with national
  figures from 11-12% (Czech Republic, Denmark, Finland, Germany) to 31-35%
  (Italy, Portugal, Romania, Spain).

The aforementioned report on *Child Poverty and Child Well-Being in the European Union*
by TARKI (2010) has explored ways of improving the work intensity concept with a view
to allowing the Commission and Member States to better understand in-work poverty.
It has also analysed the link between income composition of households (especially low
earnings) and poverty risk.[51]

---

51   There is not enough space in the present report to elaborate on these very useful developments.
     However, more information can be found in the TARKI report.

### 2.2.5    *Multidimensional factors*

A key lesson from the EU process is that child poverty and social exclusion involve much more than surviving on a low income or in a materially deprived situation. It can also involve living in substandard housing or even being homeless (see Chapter 4 of present volume), living in a derelict and badly serviced neighbourhood experiencing high levels of crime, drug-trafficking and anti-social behaviour with a concentration of marginalised groups, suffering poor health and poor access to health services with higher risk of infant and child mortality, having limited access to social and family services, experiencing educational disadvantage and low quality educational opportunities, having limited or no access to playgrounds, sporting and recreational facilities or to cultural activities. Some children face more than one disadvantage. As different disadvantages accumulate they can interact and reinforce each other to deepen a child's experience of poverty and social exclusion and to increase the cross-generational inheritance of poverty and exclusion. (See also Frazer, 2009.)

The multi-dimensional nature of child poverty was stressed by several members of the EU Network of Independent Experts on Social Inclusion in their 2007 national reports on child poverty and social exclusion (Frazer and Marlier, 2007). For instance, the UK experts emphasised that "Child poverty matters because there is a mass of evidence, reviewed recently in an HM Treasury document, that poor children have constrained lives, poorer health, worse diets, colder and more dilapidated housing conditions, higher risks of accidents and injuries, more physical abuse, more bullying and less access to childcare. They also do less well at school and their outcomes in terms of skills and employment are worse. Recent work using data from the 1980 birth cohort survey shows that disadvantages at 22 months continue to have an impact on employment and earnings right through to later life." (Bradshaw and Bennett, 2007)

Again, there are wide variations across countries in many of these areas as can be seen for example by looking at *educational disadvantage*[52]. The low reading literacy performance among 15-year old pupils ranges from 5% (Finland) and 12% (Ireland) up to 28% (Greece and Slovakia) and 51-54% (Bulgaria and Romania). The range of children enrolled in pre-school at age 4 varies from countries where more than 98% of the 4-year-olds are enrolled in education oriented primary institutions (Belgium, France, Italy, Malta, Netherlands, Spain) to those where only 4 to 6 out of 10 children at age 4 are

---

52    Data for the 15-year olds' low reading literacy EU indicator are from the 2006 survey of the OECD Programme for International Student Assessment (PISA); see:
http://www.oecd.org/pages/0,3417,en_32252351_32235731_1_1_1_1_1,00.html.
Data on early-school leavers are from the 2007 EU LFS and those on 4-year-olds enrolment are from the "UNESCO-OECD-Eurostat data collection on education systems statistics"; see aforementioned Eurostat web-site.

enrolled (Lithuania, Greece, Finland, Ireland and Poland). Early school leaving, which do not concern children per se but young adults, also varies widely: the share of 18-24 year olds who have only lower secondary education and are not in education or training spreads between 4-9% (Czech Republic, Finland, Lithuania, Poland, Slovakia, Slovenia) and 31-38% (Malta, Portugal and Spain).

### 2.2.6 Long-term effect and intergenerational inheritance

An important theme from the EU process is that growing up in poverty limits personal development and has long term consequences for the development and well-being of children and for their future health and well-being as adults. It increases their risk of being poor and experiencing unemployment and social exclusion as adults. This was a key theme in the Social OMC's first thematic study on child poverty and social exclusion (Hölscher, 2004). In the same year, a report by France's Conseil de l'Emploi, des Revenus et de la Cohésion Sociale's (2004) stressed that "poverty affects not only the child well-being at the moment when resources are insufficient, but also the child's well-becoming. It hinders their capacity to develop, to build the required capabilities, including knowledge capital, cultural capital, social capital, health capital." More recently, this long -term impact was highlighted in the 2007 *Joint Report on Social Protection and Social Inclusion* which concludes that "Children growing up in poverty are less likely than their better-off peers to do well in school, enjoy good health, stay out of dealings with the criminal justice system, and – as young adults – to find a foothold in the labour market and in society more broadly" (Council, 2007).

The extent to which poverty is inherited from one generation to the next is a related and recurring theme. For instance, the 2007 Social Situation Report contained a first analysis of the results from the 2005 EU-SILC module on the intergenerational transmission of disadvantages. These findings are summarised in the EU Task-Force Report on child poverty and well-being (Social Protection Committee, 2008). Evidence of intergenerational inheritance in several countries is also highlighted by several members of the EU Network of Independent Experts on Social Inclusion in their 2007 reports on child poverty and social exclusion. This evidence highlights that "in a number of countries the intergenerational transmission is particularly evident in relation to education and this appears to be true in countries with both high and low levels of child poverty and social exclusion" (Frazer and Marlier 2007).

One interesting example of intergenerational inheritance is provided by Ireland where a 2006 study looked at the childhood background of adults in poverty and the social factors which impact on adult outcomes (Layte *et al*, 2006). This study shows that the risk of experiencing sustained poverty in adulthood is related to *childhood socio-economic envi-*

*ronment,* especially childhood poverty. The pathways through which such effects operate not only include the financial constraints on parental capacity to invest in their children's "human capital", but also socio-economic status, parenting styles, home environment and "role modelling". The effects of social origins work through two rather different mechanisms, with the first one involving family conditions and parental stimulation (in early childhood in particular), and the other one reflecting the decisions people make at crucial transition points in the education system and on the labour market. The study also shows that *childhood educational opportunities* impact on the likelihood of adult poverty. So, an individual whose parents have educational qualifications beyond primary level has 23 times the risk of having no formal qualification compared to someone whose parents have third level education.

### 2.2.7    Groups at risk of "extreme" poverty

The EU process has served to highlight a number of particular groups of children who are at high risk of more severe or extreme poverty. This is particularly evident from the various Member States' NAPs/inclusion and several transnational exchange projects. These groups include: children with disabilities, children from ethnic minorities (especially the Roma), young asylum seekers and immigrants (see, for instance, European Social Network, 2005), children experiencing abuse, maltreatment or neglect, children whose parents have mental health problems, children in care, homeless children and children who are the victims of domestic violence or the victims of trafficking, children living in very poor and isolated rural areas lacking many basic facilities and children living in large shanty estates on the periphery of major urban areas.[53] From the analysis of the EU Network of Independent Experts on Social Inclusion, it appears that the position of children of migrant families and some ethnic minorities is a growing issue of concern in the older Member States (Frazer and Marlier, 2007). The significance of poverty amongst these children, which is linked to discrimination, is also highlighted in the 2008 Joint Report on Social Protection which concludes that "Out of the 78 million Europeans living at risk of poverty, 19 million are children. Ensuring equal opportunities for all through well-designed social policies, and strengthening efforts aiming at successful educational outcomes for each child, is required in order to break the transmission

---

53    This pattern is reinforced in the 2007 reports from the EU Network of Independent Experts on
      Social Inclusion which led to the conclusion that "Two groups of children stand out in a signifi-
      cant number of countries as being at very high risk and of experiencing severe poverty and social
      exclusion: children living in or leaving institutions and Roma children. However, there are also
      a number of other situations that are highlighted quite often: children drawn into child labour;
      children who are victims of violence, sexual abuse, trafficking, addiction and are involved in crime;
      children with a disability; unaccompanied minors; children in homeless families and street chil-
      dren." (Frazer and Marlier, 2007)

of poverty and exclusion to the next generation. Here, inclusion and anti-discrimination policies need to be reinforced, not least in relation to immigrants and their descendants and to ethnic minorities." (Council, 2008)

## 2.3 Nine elements to prevent and tackle child poverty and social exclusion

Ultimately, preventing and tackling the poverty and social exclusion of children depends on having the right policies in place and delivering them effectively. However, it is clear from the EU experience that a number of factors are important in ensuring that this is the case. Nine such factors can be identified[54].

### 2.3.1 *Political leadership*

The countries that have the best track record on the social inclusion and well-being of children or who are currently doing most to address problems of child poverty and social exclusion are those where there is high political priority and broad public support. As highlighted by the EU Network of Independent Experts on Social Inclusion, "it is clear that some Member States have had long-term inclusive policies aimed at supporting all children and families which, in effect, have largely prevented child poverty and social exclusion arising and where child poverty levels are low. Nordic countries are typical examples of this group of countries. Austria, Belgium, France, Germany, Luxembourg, the Netherlands and Slovenia have also had a long established priority to support families with children which has promoted their social inclusion. (…) There are several Member States such as Bulgaria, Cyprus, Estonia, Hungary and Portugal where national experts note that a specific focus on child and family poverty and social exclusion has more recently become a priority and in several significant policy initiatives are becoming evident . (…) A number of Member States have been concerned about and have given a high priority to specifically tackling child poverty and social exclusion, or at least the poverty and social exclusion of families with children, for a significant period. These tend to be some of the Member States with a high level of child income poverty like Ireland, Italy, Romania and the UK." (Frazer and Marlier, 2007) The importance of giving political priority to the issue was stressed by Hölscher: "first of all make children and families in general and child poverty in particular a political priority." (Hölscher, 2004)

---

54    See Frazer and Devlin (forthcoming) for further elaboration and discussion of these factors.

### 2.3.2    *Mainstreamed and coordinated approach*

The complex and multidimensional nature of child poverty and social exclusion requires that a broad range of policy areas address this issue (see sections 2.2.5 and 2.4). This is much more likely to be the case if a concern with the well-being and social inclusion of children is systematically mainstreamed and integrated into all areas of policy making and if an assessment of all policies is made for their impact on children's social inclusion.

Several of the projects supported as part of the Social OMC have developed the understanding of "mainstreaming". The Mainstreaming Social Inclusion project's final report defines mainstreaming as "the integration of poverty and social inclusion objectives, including an equality perspective, into all areas and levels of policy-making and that is promoted through the participation of public bodies, social partners, NGOs and other relevant actors."(Mainstreaming Social Inclusion, 2006)

More specifically on children, Marlier *et al* (2007) take investment in children as the recurring case study of the academic report they wrote for the 2005 Luxembourg EU Presidency conference on *Taking Forward the EU Social Inclusion Process* (because of their key role "for today's living standards and for tomorrow's productivity and social cohesion"). In this context, they call for "children mainstreaming" and explain: "We have used the word *mainstreaming* advisedly, rather than the words "target groups" (…). Our purpose is not to single out a particular priority group; poverty and social exclusion are unacceptable for all groups in society. Rather, our aim is to suggest, as with gender mainstreaming, a perspective to approaching the general problem of poverty and social exclusion. For us *children mainstreaming* involves viewing social inclusion from a child's perspective and implies integrating a concern with the well-being and social inclusion of children into all areas of policy making." (Marlier *et al*, 2007, page 11) Eurochild have suggested that mainstreaming in relation to children means that "a children's rights perspective is used to inform policy design and implementation in relevant policy areas; policy design and implementation contribute to furthering the objective of promoting children's rights." (Eurochild, 2006) More recently, the report of the EU Task-Force on child poverty and well-being concluded that "A *children mainstreaming* approach, i.e. integrating a concern with the well-being and social inclusion of children into all relevant areas of policy-making, therefore appears as the most successful way to adequately respond to the EU political commitment to tackle child poverty and social exclusion." (Social Protection Committee, 2008)

> **Box 2.1: Examples of mechanisms used to assist children mainstreaming**
>
> - Require all Ministries to include promoting social inclusion in general and/or the social inclusion of children in particular into the objectives of their ministry.
> - Appoint an official in each Ministry who is responsible for social inclusion issues.
> - Require all policies to be proofed before they are adopted for their potential impact on the social inclusion of children and/or on children generally; and also monitor their impact subsequently.
> - Create a committee of relevant government ministers to ensure political coordination on social inclusion issues.
> - Create a high-level committee of senior officials to regularly review progress and to link a strategy on child poverty or social inclusion with other key national strategies and programmes.
> - Make child poverty a key priority in the annual budgetary process.
> - Create a committee or working group of officials from all ministries that should meet regularly to prepare a strategic approach, oversee its implementation and ensure that it is monitored and evaluated. In some countries this may also include representatives from regional and local government, social partners, NGOs and experts.

Experience across the EU suggests mainstreaming is more likely to be effective if there are formal arrangements for coordinating the efforts of all actors both horizontally (at national level) and vertically (between national and sub-national levels of governance). Where such mechanisms do not exist, policies are likely to be fragmented and less efficient; and potential synergies between them are then missed. Frazer (2006) has identified a number of different approaches that are used by Member States to enhance mainstreaming and coordination (see Box 2.1).

In their 2007 reports, the EU Network of Independent Experts on Social Inclusion assessed among other things the extent of children mainstreaming across the EU. On the basis of their analysis, it is clear that the mainstreaming of the social inclusion of children is increasing across the EU but that there remain a significant number of countries where there is little evidence of a systematic or coordinated approach. On a positive note, a general conclusion of their analysis is that "In the countries where long-term inclusive policies favouring all children are the norm, such as Finland and Sweden, it is fair to say that there is already effective mainstreaming. Many of the countries that have over the past decade or more recently prioritised child poverty and social exclusion are in the process of mainstreaming the issue and some like Ireland and the UK have developed quite elaborate arrangements." Progress is also evident in Belgium, Cyprus and Luxembourg in this regard. However, it is clear that in countries where such arrangements for mainstreaming do not exist there is a danger that a very low priority may be given to considering the impact of policies on children in many important policy areas. (Frazer and Marlier, 2007)

### 2.3.3    Commitment to promoting children's rights

The importance of linking efforts to tackle child poverty and social exclusion with the promotion of children's rights has emerged as a key theme in the Social OMC. For instance, Hölscher, in her 2004 report for the Commission, concluded that "The UN Convention on the Rights of the Child should be used as a framework for the development, implementation and monitoring of policies at EU and Member State level. The EU should integrate the principles of the UNCRC into policy and legislation in order to make children visible at EU level and to better promote children's rights and well-being" (Hölscher, 2004). The 2005 *Joint Report on Social Protection and Social Inclusion* noted that "several countries also put increasing emphasis on promoting the rights of the child as a basis for policy development." (Council, 2005) and the 2007 reports from the EU Network of Independent Experts on Social Inclusion show that there is a growing awareness in many countries of the importance of children's rights (Frazer and Marlier, 2007). The importance of adopting a children's rights perspective has also been consistently advocated by several of the EU networks active in the Social OMC such as Eurochild (Fernandes, 2007 and D'Addato, 2009), Euronet (Ruxton and Bennett, 2004) and the European Social Network (2007) and also by UNICEF (2007). The importance of a children's rights perspective was further boosted in 2006 with the EU Commission's Communication on the Rights of the Child which strongly linked the promotion of children's rights to the EU's Social Inclusion Process and to the reduction of child poverty. It stressed that "respecting and promoting the rights of all children should go hand in hand with the necessary action to address their basic needs" (European Commission, 2006). The European Parliament in its 2008 *Report on promoting social inclusion and combating poverty (including child poverty) in the EU* also highlighted "the importance of a holistic approach to the material security and well-being of children, based on the UNRC child rights-centred perspective" (European Parliament, 2008). More recently, the EU Fundamental Rights Agency (2009) has developed a series of indicators for the protection, respect and promotion of the rights of the child in the EU on the basis of EU competence in this area. This report proposes a series of indicators covering: family, environment and alternative care; protection from exploitation and violence; education, citizenship and cultural activities; and adequate standard of living.

From these various reports and initiatives, four main reasons can be identified as to why a child rights based approach based on the UN Convention on the Rights of the Child is important. First, it puts the needs of the child at the centre of policy making. Addressing their needs becomes a core political obligation and not just a possible policy choice. Secondly, it puts the focus on addressing the specific needs of the child here and now. Thirdly, it provides a useful framework for developing a comprehensive strategy to prevent and reduce child poverty and social exclusion. This view has been reinforced by evidence from the Social OMC that countries like Sweden, which have a very strong emphasis on children's rights, have been very successful in preventing child poverty and social exclusion (Halleröd, 2007). Fourthly, it puts a focus on the importance of adopting and enforcing strong legislation against discrimination as an essential element in preventing and reducing child poverty and social exclusion.

### 2.3.4 *In-depth analysis supported by quality and timely data*

In-depth analysis supported by quality and timely data is essential to develop a thorough understanding of the issue of child poverty and social exclusion. This requires putting in place a comprehensive set of indicators and data which reflect the current experience of children in its various dimensions and also data which take into account a child's perspective. This is also critical for Member States if they are to set clear objectives, establish quantified outcome targets, assess the impact of policies on the situation of children (social and also other policies) and monitor progress (see below).

The importance of good data and analysis emerges strongly from the 2007 reports by the EU Network of Independent Experts on Social Inclusion. The resulting synthesis report concludes that "Limitations in data as well as in both qualitative and quantitative analysis hinder the development and monitoring of policies in many countries, and all Member States need to ensure that they have developed effective strategies for filling gaps in this respect. In particular, they need to ensure that they develop non-monetary indicators which can be combined with existing income poverty indicators to give a deeper understanding of child well-being. More attention also needs to be given to researching the persistence and duration of child poverty and social exclusion (requiring longitudinal/ panel analysis) and to investigating the situation of children at high risk." (Frazer and Marlier, 2007)

Developing a range of indicators that are appropriate for measuring and monitoring child poverty and social exclusion has been an important issue for the Social OMC. It is clear that while general indicators and data on poverty and social exclusion broken down by age groups can be helpful they are not sufficient to give a complete picture of child poverty and exclusion. There is a need also to develop a more comprehensive set of indicators and data specifically on children's well-being which reflect the current experience of children and take into account a child's perspective (Marlier *et al*, 2007). Many organisations working with children agree. Eurochild has advocated "the development of indicators that (…) also measure the well-being and prospects for personal development of the child". (Eurochild, 2008; see also Eurochild, 2009a) This was also a conclusion of the 2005 European Round Table held under the UK Presidency which said: "We need valid indicators for defining child poverty, including indicators for the "well-being" of children". (UK Presidency of the European Union, 2005) The debate on developing a broad range of indicators on child poverty and social exclusion has also been significantly informed by other international work on child well-being (e.g., Bradshaw *et al* (2007) and UNICEF (2007)).

The need for a broad range of indicators and data analysis was stressed in the conclusions and recommendations of the EU Task-Force on child poverty and well-being, which recommended that Member States use a combination of: all relevant indicators that have already been agreed upon at EU level (these include age breakdowns of poverty risk EU indicators, children living in jobless households, indicators in the area of education and also – since 2009 – age breakdowns of material deprivation and housing indicators); the yet-to-be developed EU indicator(s) of child well-being; and relevant child well-being indicators available at country level. The Task-Force also stressed the value of longitudinal surveys implemented at national level as "Longitudinal data and their linkage with administrative/registers data are currently the most thorough and efficient way of measuring long-term impacts of events experienced during the youth on the individual socio-economic situation of adults. For example: for the inter-generational transmission of poverty to be properly analysed, such individual data collected regularly from the same people are needed." (Social Protection Committee, 2008). This work on indicators was subsequently further developed by the TARKI research project which has rightly emphasised that "a balanced and comprehensive picture can only be gained through a dedicated and separate child-indicator portfolio, with indicators reflecting all the most relevant dimensions and covering all relevant child ages" (TARKI, 2010, page 20).

Another important issue to emerge is that some groups of children with very specific problems or needs, such as children in institutions and street children, may not show up in national surveys. There is a need for special studies on the situation of such children. For example, as early as 2003, the project on the mental health of children in state care funded under the EU's Preparatory Measures on Social Inclusion, highlighted already the need to collect data which would enable policy makers and practitioners to understand the size of the group of children affected by mental health issues and the types of difficulties they experienced. (Cocker, 2003). The aforementioned EU Task-Force report also drew attention to the importance of using administrative and registers sources, specific data sources on children in vulnerable situations and data on the specific situation of the most vulnerable children (children in institutions or in foster care, children with chronic health problems or disabilities, abused children, street children, children from a migrant or minority background, etc) which cannot be monitored using the standard survey tools. (Social Protection Committee, 2008). This latter point has been reinforced by the TARKI research which concludes that datasets like EU-SILC are "not particularly well suited to issues such as the situation facing the children of migrants or of minority ethnic groups (like the Roma, in particular), or to exploring the situation of those categories of children who do not generally show up in national/ international surveys – e.g. children in institutions; victims of violence, crime and trafficking; children affected by addiction problems, etc." (TARKI, 2010, page 22)

One other important issue that has been highlighted by several actors in the Social OMC, notably Eurochild, is the need to research the views of children experiencing poverty. The EU Task-Force also noted the value of direct interviews of children which have been carried out in some countries (e.g. in Germany, Sweden and the United Kingdom) and concludes that "interviewing children on their own experience and perceptions of poverty and social exclusion allows collecting useful information on child well-being that cannot always be obtained through the parents" (Social Protection Committee, 2008). Such interviews provide a useful starting point for the active participation of children, which also requires their involvement in the evaluation of existing policies and services, and in the formulation of proposals for improvement (see also section 2.3.7 and Chapter 5).

### 2.3.5   *A strategic evidence-based approach based on clear objectives and targets*

It is clear from the Social OMC that effective strategies to tackle child poverty and social exclusion involve setting elaborated and quantified objectives for the social inclusion and well-being of children based on a rigorous analysis and diagnosis of the issue. Quantified objectives or targets are important because they provide: a significant political statement of purpose and ambition in terms of eradicating child poverty and social exclusion which can lead to increased policy effort; a goal against which to measure progress and thus a means of creating a dynamic process characterised by openness and accountability; a tool for promoting awareness of the process and thus for encouraging and mobilising all actors in support of it; a focal point around which to concentrate the efforts of policy makers and practitioners. This emphasis on objectives and targets was clear from early in the EU process (Council, 2002) and has been reinforced at regular intervals since then. For instance, a key recommendation of the 2008 *Joint Report on Social Protection and Social Inclusion* is that "Efforts to tackle poverty – of children and overall – gain leverage if underpinned by overall quantified objectives that are based on an evidence-based diagnosis of the main causes of poverty and exclusion in each Member State". (Council, 2008) However, in spite of this, the evidence from the 2007 reports from the EU Network of Independent Experts on Social Inclusion is that Member States' objectives are often too general and aspirational and that only a few countries have established quantified and realistic targets against which progress can be measured. (Frazer and Marlier, 2007) Some progress was made in the 2008-2010 NAPs/inclusion, with Eurochild noting that "An encouraging development is that the majority of Member States include quantified targets for the reduction of child poverty in their NAPs/inclusion. However, in some cases targets are not very ambitious and it is often not clear that they have been established on the basis of careful analysis. Thus, a more systematic and analytical approach is needed in order to ensure that appropriate targets which are ambitious and realistic are set for the reduction of child poverty in each country." (Eurochild, 2009b)[55]

*Objectives*

Four main types or levels of objectives that might be set in relation to child poverty can be identified: overall or general objectives, objectives relating to a specific policy domain, objectives relating to the most vulnerable groups and process objectives. A strategic approach is likely to involve a combination of these, with the objectives at the other levels being related to the achievement of the overall objective. The application of these different types of objectives is further elaborated in the synthesis of the 2007 reports on child poverty and social exclusion of the EU Network of Independent Experts on Social Inclusion (Frazer and Marlier, 2007). (See Box 2.2, which is based on the typology developed in Frazer (2006).)

---

**Box 2.2: *Typology of objectives for tackling and preventing child poverty and social exclusion***

1) *Overall* or *general* objectives might be:
   - significantly reduce the number of children at risk of poverty and social exclusion by 20XX;
   - significantly reduce the proportion of children experiencing material deprivation (or persistent income poverty) by 20XX.

2) Objectives in relation to *specific policy domains* could cover things such as:
   - ensure that all children live in households with an adequate minimum level of income;
   - reduce the number of children living in jobless households;

---

55    See Frazer and Marlier (2007), Eurochild (2009) and TARKI (2010) for summaries/ analysis of targets set by Member States.

- ensure that all children stay in education until 16 or reduce the number of children dropping out of school;
- increase healthy life expectancy at birth;
- increase access to basic health and social services;
- reduce the number of children living in substandard accommodation;
- ensure that all children have access to cultural, sporting and recreational activities.

3) Objectives in relation to particularly *vulnerable groups* of children could cover for example:
- ensure that Roma children, children from an ethnic minority, children of migrants, children with a disability, children from a lone parent family can access basic health and social services in the same way as all children in the country;
- make a decisive reduction in the number of street children;
- reduce the number of children living in institutions;
- ensure that all unaccompanied children are awarded a status in the country where they live and that they have access to a systematic programme of integration.

4) *Process objectives* could include areas such as:
- ensure that children experiencing income poverty, their families and the organisations that work with them are involved in the development, implementation and monitoring of the national strategy;
- develop arrangements to ensure that children living in income poverty have a voice in matters which affect them and that their views are given due weight in accordance with their age and maturity;
- ensure that children have the information necessary to access essential services and rights;
- strengthen the institutional arrangements for mainstreaming and coordinating efforts to eliminate child poverty and social exclusion across all areas and levels of government;
- develop effective local networks or partnerships of government agencies, social partners and NGOs to coordinate the delivery of policies and programmes to promote the well-being and social inclusion of children;
- identify and address gaps in data and analysis on child poverty and social exclusion;
- develop clear procedures for monitoring and reporting on progress on child poverty.

*Targets*

As highlighted in Chapter 1, setting outcome targets is essential even if it is a complex area for a combination of political and scientific reasons. A detailed discussion on both national and EU targets can be found in Marlier *et al* (2007; Sections 6.2, 6.3 and 6.4). The guidelines for preparing the 2006-2008 *National Reports on Strategies for Social Protection and Social Inclusion* contained a very useful annex on setting national targets (Social Protection Committee, 2006). Specifically on child poverty and social exclusion, Frazer and Devlin (forthcoming) also discuss different types of national targets.

The issue of setting targets in the area of child poverty and social exclusion was significantly advanced by the aforementioned EU Task-Force report, which concluded that "Member States who have not done so yet should consider establishing elaborated and quantified objectives for the social inclusion and well-being of children". In the light of this, the SPC (and therefore all Member States) and the Commission adopted the recommendation that: "National overall quantified objectives for the reduction of child poverty and social exclusion need to be based on a diagnosis of the causes of poverty and social exclusion in each country and have to be supplemented by specific objectives relating to the key factors identified by the diagnosis (e.g. jobless households, in-work poverty, social benefits…). In making their diagnosis, Member Sates should use the analysis and recommendations of the report prepared by the EU Task-Force (…) as part of their overall framework" (Social Protection Committee, 2008).

The issue of target setting was further advanced with the 2008 Commission Communication on strengthening the Social OMC which argues that setting targets would introduce a new dynamism in the EU Social OMC as a whole and that they could be set for the reduction of poverty in general "as well as for specific forms of poverty, such as child poverty". The Communication argues that at national level "The introduction of these quantified targets, supported by the commonly agreed indicators, based on robust analytical tools, will help Member States to sustain commitment and work more concretely towards the achievement of common objectives. In order to take account of their diversity, particular national context and different points of departure, Member States could define national targets." (European Commission, 2008) The issue of target setting has now achieved much higher political prominence with the developments in relation to Europe 2020 (see Section 1.3.1).

### 2.3.6    *Balance between universal and targeted approaches and between prevention and alleviation*

Most Member States seem to combine both universal policies aimed at promoting the well-being of all children and preventing child poverty and social exclusion arising with more targeted policies aimed at alleviating poverty and social exclusion. While the balance between the two changes depending on the situation in different countries, it would seem that the most successful Member States are those that adopt a predominantly universal approach based on a strong belief in preventing problems arising and in ensuring equal opportunities for all children backed up as necessary by targeted policies to address particular extreme situations – a sort of *tailored universalism* (Frazer and Marlier, 2007)[56]. While there may be pressure in Member States with the most severe problems to focus on alleviation, it is nevertheless true that the structural nature of the phenomenon makes it urgent to combat child poverty and social exclusion under a more preventative approach as well. As the 2008 *Joint Report on Social Protection and Social Inclusion*, stresses in one of its key messages, "the best performers target the most disadvantaged children within a broader universal approach". (Council, 2008)

The balance between prevention and poverty alleviation varies significantly across Member States[57]:

- At the one end of the continuum, one can identify countries where there is a very strong emphasis on universal provision aimed at all children; this is the case in Finland, the Netherlands and Sweden where this universal approach is nevertheless often complemented with targeted measures for the most vulnerable individuals (see for instance Halleröd, 2007). In some Member States, a predominantly universal approach is based around a focus that is put primarily on the family rather than on children; this is particular true in the cases of France and Luxembourg.

- At the other end of the spectrum some countries, such as Portugal, appear to put more emphasis on alleviating poverty and social exclusion and on remedial action compared to a more universal and preventive approach.

- There are several Member States such as Belgium, Denmark and Luxembourg where the tendency is to supplement universal services and measures targeting all children with a more targeted approach addressing children at risk. Italy and the Czech Republic also seem to have a mixed or balanced approach. In fact, even the UK, which is often seen as having an overwhelmingly targeted strategy, has a strategy of "progressive universalism" which combines universal and targeted elements even if overall it is rather complex due to its emphasis on targeting.

(For a more detailed analysis, see Frazer and Marlier, 2007; see also the 2007

---

56   The strengths and weaknesses of universal and targeted approaches are discussed in more detail in Frazer and Devlin (forthcoming).

57   In this continuum we do not identify actual "groups of countries" but rather some common characteristics shared by countries; i.e., we do not suggest mutually exclusive groups. Thus Luxembourg appears twice because of the different characteristics we are looking at.

national reports prepared by the EU Network of Independent Experts on Social Inclusion.)

### 2.3.7 Involvement of key actors (including children themselves)

A key learning point from the Social OMC is that efforts to promote the well-being and social inclusion of children are greatly strengthened when effective arrangements are in place for involving all actors, particularly national, regional and local authorities as well as social partners and NGOs in the preparation, implementation and monitoring of national strategies. It is also important to seek ways of directly involving children in the process for two main reasons. First, they have a right to be heard; giving children the possibility to express their views in matters that concern them is a requirement under the UN CRC. Secondly, involving children enables the issues that matter to them to be better identified and should contribute to developing policy responses that meet children's needs more effectively. For instance, their input into the design of services can help make these more relevant, more appropriate and more effective.

Over the course of the Social OMC, Member States' NAPs/inclusion and other documents have demonstrated that in many countries NGOs and, to a lesser extent, social partners are increasingly involved in the development of policies to promote the well-being and social inclusion of children. However, the direct involvement of children has been quite limited although the importance of doing so has been advocated by a range of organisations and projects active in the EU process[58].

There are at least three key arguments for mobilising and involving a wide range of actors that can be deduced from the experience of the Social OMC. These are: first, that it leads to better and more informed policy making; secondly, that it mobilises a broader range of resources and actors who can contribute to implementing policies; and thirdly, that it leads to better monitoring of policies.

### 2.3.8 Effective delivery arrangements at local level

Having the right policies is essential but it is only part of what is required. How they are implemented and delivered is also a key to their effectiveness. The range of activities supported as part of the Social OMC have been a rich source of learning about what works (and also what does not work) in delivering policies and programmes for children.

---

58　See for instance: EAPN, 2009; Eurochild, 2008; UK EU Presidency, 2005; European Social Network, 2005; Williams, 2003; Home Start International, 2002; Ruxton and Bennett, 2002.

For instance, the first Joint Report on Social Inclusion identified ten key principles for inclusive services and policies. (Council, 2002) More particularly, the European Forum for Child Welfare (EFCW) project on *Families under stress* has produced a set of Good Practice Principles which highlights a series of key principles in relation to services for children (Williams, 2003).

Drawing on all the sources mentioned above, some of the key principles for effective delivery that seem to be generally transferable and relevant in all countries when addressing child poverty are summarised below.

First, effective delivery of national strategies requires effective coordination between the different levels and departments of government and thus a clear definition of their respective roles and responsibilities to ensure that they are mutually reinforcing. This point was made strongly by Martin Hirsch, French High Commissioner for Active Solidarity, speaking at an EAPN conference when he said that it is essential "to establish links between local and national measures and to avoid clashes between the two" and when he highlighted French efforts in this regard. (Frazer, 2008) In the UK, for example, this issue is addressed since 2006 through the *Child Poverty Accord* between the central and local governments which involves regular meetings and liaison and which is proving useful in getting more 'buy-in' to the child poverty strategy from local government.

Secondly, an integrated approach at local level, which promotes cross sectoral collaboration and networking and which brings together all relevant actors in partnership arrangements, is essential to deliver services in a holistic manner. Partnerships help to ensure a comprehensive assessment of needs. They enable a coordinated approach to meeting needs and thus overcome the compartmentalisation and fragmentation of services. They promote more tailor-made responses to particular situations. They maximise the use of resources. They facilitate the participation of those experiencing poverty and social exclusion in the development and delivery of social inclusion policies and programmes.[59] The *European Cities Against Child Poverty* project's final report summarises well the importance of coordination when it concludes that "the most successful projects bring together professionals from a range of sectors and establish a network that is focused on the family's well-being. Roles are clearly defined and joined-up working is made easier through the involvement of intermediaries and information sharing. Again, this approach is not necessarily costly; rather it makes better use of the expertise and resources available." (European Cities Against Child Poverty, 2009).

Thirdly, services need to be delivered in ways that respond to the needs of each child and their family and thus they need to be flexible and delivered in a way that is tailored to

---

59    For more on partnership, see for instance: Eurochild, 2006; Walter and Pohl, 2006; Bohn, 2005.

meet their particular needs. This point is well made in a thematic study on disadvantaged youth which concludes that access depends on support being "flexible or unconditional as this helps to ensure that individuals do not remain excluded due to bureaucratic rules" (Walther and Pohl, 2006). While some families and children may only need particular help and assistance intermittently or in the short term, others will need longer-term and consistent support which fosters their personal growth and development over time. This of course means ensuring that services are developed with a long-term perspective. (Williams, 2003)

Fourthly, a community development approach which ensures that policies and programmes are delivered in ways which empower children, respects their dignity and rights and avoids stigmatising them is essential. The importance of empowering children and respecting their dignity and rights is highlighted by many of the projects supported under the Social OMC.[60] Community development can contribute significantly to "strengthening the quality of community life in disadvantaged communities by promoting strong family, social and community networks and a healthy infrastructure of community and voluntary organisations. It is also an important means of empowering individuals and groups who are at risk of exclusion and isolation. It can help them to act together to change their situation and to work together with others to overcome barriers to their active participation in society such as poverty, lack of access to resources, rights, goods and services and discrimination. Community development must thus be a core element in any strategy to overcome poverty and social exclusion and to building more inclusive and cohesive societies. That is true whether one is talking of the European, national, regional or local level" (Frazer, 2005).

### 2.3.9    *Effective monitoring and reporting arrangements*

The development of effective policies is a continuous process which requires the regular monitoring of policies to ensure their effectiveness. Countries that are successful in preventing and tackling child poverty and social exclusion tend to have well developed systems for evaluation and monitoring. The importance of such monitoring has been strongly emphasised in a number of key publications, notably the report for the Luxembourg EU Presidency conference on Taking Forward the EU Social Inclusion Process (Marlier *et al*, 2007), the EU Task-Force report on child poverty and well-being (Social Protection Committee, 2008) and the reports of the EU Network of Independent Experts on Social Inclusion's on child poverty and social exclusion (Frazer and Marlier, 2007). The 2008 *Joint Report on Social Protection and Social Inclusion* sums this evidence up well when it concludes that "Efforts to tackle poverty – of children and overall – gain

---

60    See for instance: European Cities Against Child Poverty, 2009; European Social Network, 2007; Walter and Pohl, 2006; Williams, 2003.

leverage (…) by the regular monitoring of policies' impact and effectiveness, possibly in relation to specific targets; and, where needed, by a reinforcement of the statistical capacity." (Council, 2008) However, the extent and quality of monitoring remains very uneven across Member States (see Frazer and Marlier, 2007).

Key elements for effective systems that emerge from the Social OMC include: having clear objectives and targets; ensuring an evidence-based approach that builds *inter alia* on *ex ante* impact assessments of policies; using appropriate indicators covering all the dimensions of poverty and social exclusion; collecting quality and timely data also on populations not living in private households (e.g. on people living in institutions); establishing a focus on the link between specific policy measures and outcomes and undertaking regular *ex post* impact assessments of policies; establishing good links between the policy and research communities (which requires *inter alia* a wide access to quality data by the research community); involving all relevant actors, including organisations working with children and children themselves; reporting regularly on findings. The most crucial challenge is to make the link between the specific policy measures implemented by governments and the expected related social outcomes. (See Section 1.3.2.)

## 2.4 A comprehensive policy framework

A key lesson for policy makers from the Social OMC is the need to develop a comprehensive and multidimensional approach, involving integrated and coordinated actions across a range of policy areas. As the EU Transnational Exchange Project *A lobby for children* concluded, "there is no "one and only" solution for all target groups and all national contexts. (…) child centred poverty prevention must be holistic" (Bohn, 2005). This view is emphasised by the EU Network of Independent Experts on Social Inclusion who stresses that "given the multi-dimensional nature of the problem no single policy is sufficient to ensure the social inclusion of children" (Frazer and Marlier, 2007). Similarly, the EU Task-Force on child poverty and well-being concluded that "given the multi-dimensional nature of the phenomena at stake, no single policy is sufficient to ensure the social inclusion and well-being of children and their families." (Social Protection Committee, 2008) More recently, the TARKI study concluded that "improving both the present well-being of children and their future prospects requires multi-dimensional policy combinations. These include income support, promoting the labour-market participation of parents, facilitating access to enabling services, and creating opportunities to participate in social, cultural, recreational and sporting activities" (TARKI, 2010, page 184). Thus, Member States that are effective in preventing high levels of child poverty and social exclusion tend to be those which develop comprehensive and integrated policy frameworks that address the multidimensional nature of children's needs. (See also Frazer and Devlin (forthcoming).)

In particular, these frameworks combine increasing access to adequately paid work for parents with ensuring effective income support for all families with children and increasing access to key enabling services (child care, education, housing, health and social services, etc.) and to services which support their active participation in social, recreational, cultural and sporting life. In other words, an "active inclusion type" approach which combines in a balanced way employment activation, adequate income support and access to high quality services – is essential. However, Member States who are most successful do not just focus on the most disadvantaged children but develop policies that are universal (i.e., intended to promote the social inclusion of all children and their families). They then supplement these with specific additional supports for those children and parents facing particular difficulties – i.e., what we referred to as "tailored universalism". It is also important that an effective approach to tackling child poverty and social exclusion is closely linked to tackling the poverty and social exclusion of parents. One cannot successfully tackle the one without tackling the other. Thus policies to promote the social inclusion and well-being of children need to be part of a wider approach to building an inclusive society for all generations.

### 2.4.1    Ensuring an adequate income

Ensuring that children grow up in homes with an adequate level of income is fundamental for their well-being and personal development. The most effective approaches to ensuring an adequate income involve a combination of policies which increase parents' access to work and which provide generous child income support and income support for all parents. These are then often also supplemented, to a greater or lesser extent, by subsidising the costs of key services. Neither employment nor income support measures on their own are sufficient. The two need to go hand in hand.

- *Ensuring access to paid work*: Four main priorities can be identified for effective policies in this area. These are: developing a comprehensive approach with a mix of policies which allow for effective family-work combination and aim to increase employment of both parents and also to give special attention to increasing and supporting the participation of mothers in paid work; reconciling work and family life (particularly through effective equality legislation and the provision of accessible and affordable child care); promoting flexible working; and developing active inclusion measures which particularly target the parents of children at high risk of poverty and social exclusion such as lone parents and parents in jobless households (i.e. a combination of quality job opportunities allowing parents to integrate and progress in the labour market, adequate and well-designed income support and the provision of necessary services for children and their families).

- *Ensuring work lifts families out of poverty and avoiding "in-work" poverty*: Key policies to provide an adequate income from work to families with children while at the same time avoiding disincentives or barriers to taking up employment can include: providing affordable / free access to high-quality child care (often a more effective solution than just raising the gap between wages and benefits); ensuring a relatively high minimum wage; allowing parents on lower income to retain social benefits for a period when moving into work to ensure that there is a real increase in income; providing benefits to parents on a low income who are in work and/or reduce their tax burden; ensuring the difference between wages and unemployment benefits increases relatively more for small income earners; reducing costs associated with employment such as public transport; and tackling the problem of inadequate income from insecure employment.

- *Providing effective income support*: Effective income support systems for children and families play a vital role in countering poverty amongst children whose parents are both working and not working. On average (see above, Section 2.2.1), social transfers other than pensions reduce the risk of poverty for children by 39% across the EU and in the best performing countries by over 60%. The countries with the lowest child poverty rates are often those who spend most on social benefits (excluding pensions).

### An EU minimum income for children?

In relation to an adequate income for all children, it is worth noting a proposal by A.B. Atkinson (2010) that the EU should agree on a Basic Income for Children. He proposes that "Each Member State would be required to guarantee unconditionally to every child a basic income, defined as a percentage of the Member State median equivalised income (and possibly age-related)". He points out that the implications of such a proposal have been modelled by Levy, Lietz and Sutherland (2007) using the EU tax benefit model, EU-ROMOD. They show that a Child Basic Income set at 25% of national median income would halve child poverty in all EU-15 Member States except Italy and the UK. He suggests that "implementation would be left to Member States, who could employ different instruments. The minimum could be provided via child benefit, via tax allowances, via tax credits, via benefits in kind, or via employer-mandated benefits. The only restriction is that the set of instruments selected must be capable of reaching the entire population. In view of the problem of incomplete take-up, this requirement in my view rules out use of income-tested schemes that rely on families claiming."

### 2.4.2    Ensuring access to and participation in services

Access to quality basic services is particularly important for children's development and to ensure that they receive the support necessary to reach their full potential. They are also essential to combat the negative consequences of poverty and social exclusion on the child's development. As already emphasised in Section 2.3.7, it is vital that children themselves are also directly involved in the development, delivery and monitoring of services so that these are tailored to their needs and so that they have a voice in the things that affect them.

- *Housing:* The importance of children being brought up in decent housing with good basic services and in a safe environment is widely recognised as being essential for their long-term development. Thus, housing policies need to give particular attention to the situation of families with children. Special attention needs to be given to the situation of children who are currently in high risk situations: policies such as eradicating slum areas, subsidising more social housing, promoting more efficient land use, developing measures to prevent the eviction of children from their homes, reducing the number of households in temporary accommodation and providing temporary shelters for families with children who have lost their homes are all important. (See also Chapter 4.)
- *Education:* Tackling educational disadvantage and improving access to education is particularly important both in order to combat the negative consequences of poverty and social exclusion on the child's development and in order to empower children and break the intergenerational inheritance of disadvantage. In this regard, four aspects stand out for policy attention: the importance of early childhood education and development; the need to develop strategies to tackle school drop outs and educational disadvantage; the importance of integrating minorities (e.g. ethnic minorities, migrants, children with a disability) in the school system; and the need to reduce costs and financial barriers to participating in education.
- *Early childhood education and development:* Access to affordable pre-school provision and good quality child care, as well as being important for participation of parents in work (see above, Section 2.4.1), is key in promoting the development of the child and preventing later problems of educational disadvantage. A twofold approach is important: providing for learning opportunities for all, in particular children from disadvantaged backgrounds, and early identification and removal of obstacles which may have a negative effect on children's full development.
- *Health services*: Children born in low-income families are more likely to experience unhealthy lifestyles and have poorer access to health services. It is therefore important to develop policies which overcome access barriers, reduce health inequalities, adjust care to the needs of specific groups and improve/ widen health promotion and disease prevention programmes. Universal coverage of health insurance has a strong influence on access to health care and a key challenge is how to tackle those who may not be covered by health insurance such as recipients of social assistance and migrants.

- *Transport:* Ensuring access to affordable and efficient transport is especially important in the context of child poverty and social exclusion, as it should contribute to making it economically worthwhile for parents to work and to better reconciling work and family responsibilities (through facilitating flexible working). It is also important in terms of enabling families with children to access essential services, enabling children to take part in social, sporting and cultural activities and overcoming social isolation, especially in remote rural areas. A particular issue is also the availability of suitably adapted transport to enable children with disabilities to access services and social activities.

### 2.4.3   Developing effective care and protection policies

The third group of policies emphasises the importance of effective child protection systems and social services. These services are essential to ensure high levels of protection for children who are vulnerable and marginalised as a result of discrimination, maltreatment, neglect, sexual abuse, drugs and alcohol, mental health problems or other reasons. Such services often employ early intervention and prevention methods with parents-to-be and with families whose lives are complicated by drug abuse, alcoholism or indebtedness. They develop projects which divert from criminal activity, provide alternative housing and care. They work across public agencies and service providers (health, schools, police, psychosocial support) to ensure that children with potential problems are identified early and get the full range of support they need. They manage fostering and adoption services, residential day care, sheltered accommodation and provide associated support services for vulnerable children and parents, including victims of abuse and children whose parents have an alcohol problem. They work with children with disabilities and learning difficulties to improve their life chances. Thus a critical challenge in developing effective responses to child poverty and social exclusion (in particular the more extreme situations) is to improve the quality and standards of social services, to improve local coordination and to increase their capacity for early intervention.

While the best interest of the child must be at the heart of child care and protection services, it is important to avoid excessive intervention and the undue use of residential in-care placement. For most children, the family provides the best setting in which to develop and care and protection services should, as far as possible, focus on supporting children in their families. Thus, one important theme that has emerged in the Social OMC has been the need in several Member States to move away from institutionalised provision for children and to put more focus on families and on care in the community. This is especially, but not exclusively, evident in several of the newer central and eastern EU countries.

### 2.4.4    *Promoting access to and participation in social, cultural and recreational activities*

A key element of the well-being and personal development of children and also for their active inclusion in society is the opportunity for them to participate in the social, recreational, sporting and cultural activities that their peers do. For instance, participation in sport and recreational activities creates opportunities for participation in social life, for personal development and promotes better health. Participation in cultural activities contributes to building skills and self-confidence, enhancing self-esteem and identity, promoting respect for cultural diversity and thus countering discrimination. Thus, policies which increase the access of young people at high risk of poverty and social exclusion to such activities are particularly important.

## 2.5 Child poverty and related policies in Belgium

The choice of child poverty as one of the policy priorities in the Belgian NAP/inclusion illustrates the growing influence of Europe and the Open Method of Coordination on the Belgian social inclusion agenda (Steenssens *et al*, 2008). Unlike in Anglo-Saxon countries, where child poverty is often alarmingly high and consequently has received a great deal of attention over many years, children living in poverty were almost invisible in the Belgian social inclusion discourse – until they were put in the spotlight at EU level. This section starts with an overview of the groups where children are most at risk of poverty, and subsequently discusses selected areas that we consider most relevant to children.

### 2.5.1    *The poverty risks of children*

The EU-SILC figures suggest, as for the EU as a whole, that the poverty risk in Belgium is slightly higher among children (15-18%) than among the population at large (14-15%). It is much more serious in the Walloon Region (19-21%) than in Flanders (10-12%) despite the fact that all regions share the same (federal) tax and social protection system.[61] There is no distinct trend in the figures.

Table 2.1 displays at-risk-of-poverty rates for different household types. As far as households with children are concerned, the table shows that children in jobless households, large households, and single-parent families are particularly vulnerable.

---

61    The figures for Brussels are less reliable

**Table 2.1: At-risk-of-poverty rate by work intensity and household type (in %, 2007)**

|  | Flemish Region | Walloon Region | Belgium | EU-15 | EU-27 |
|---|---|---|---|---|---|
| **Work intensity** | | | | | |
| Jobless households without dependent children | 22.8 | 36.3 | 31.8 | 31.0 | 30.0 |
| Jobless households with dependent children | 67.4 | 73.8 | 74.5 | 64.0 | 65.0 |
| Households with dependent children and full-time working parents | 3.3 | 4.7 | 3.8 | 6.0 | 7.0 |
| **Household type** | | | | | |
| Single parents with at least 1 dependent child | 27.6 | 43.8 | 35.8 | 34.0 | 34.0 |
| 2 adults with 1 dependent child | 5.9 | 12.0 | 9.3 | 11.0 | 12.0 |
| 2 adults with 2 dependent children | 5.0 | 12.0 | 8.2 | 14.0 | 14.0 |
| 2 adult with 3+ children | 12.5 | 21.3 | 17.8 | 22.0 | 25.0 |

*Source: EU-SILC 2007.*

In Belgium, more than elsewhere in Europe, the *joblessness of parents* appears to be the number one risk factor for children: three-quarters of the children living in jobless households in Belgium are at risk of poverty. Not only the poverty risk, but also the proportion of children in jobless households is alarmingly high. In 2006, Nearly one in seven (13.5%) of all Belgian (poor and non-poor) children lived in a jobless household, with only Bulgaria and the UK having higher shares. The EU25 average is 9.5%. A further analysis shows that this problem is concentrated in metropolitan areas (in Brussels, for example, the corresponding share is estimated around 30%)[62], and in single-parent families (which make up 55% of the jobless households). The presence of children in jobless households appears to constitute in itself an additional barrier to employment, as child care is scarce and priority is often granted to families with working parents. Moreover, the cost of child care (especially when there are several children under age three) increases unemployment traps. We will come back to child-care issues in section 2.5.4 of this chapter.

*Single parents* were identified in Table 2.1 as the second major at-risk group. Moreover,

---

62    29% according to the 2005 Labour Force Survey, 31% according to the 2006 "Barometer of well-being" (Welzijnsbarometer, 2006).

their number has increased by 60% in 15 years (Morissens and Nicaise 2007). It is also worth noting that single-motherhood is on the increase among the immigrant popula-tion. The consequences of a marital break-up further aggravate the vulnerable economic situation of many migrant households. Cultural practices can also result in isolation of single parents from their communities. Research on single mothers (Solera 2003; Moris-sens 1999) has indicated that the combination of employment and generous family ben-efits offers the best protection against poverty for this group. Whereas the supplementary child allowance for single parents is a step in the right direction to improve single parents' income situation, employment rates for single mothers remain far below the average, suggesting that there is much room for improvement.

*Families with three or more children* face a higher risk of poverty than families with one or two dependent children. Not only the direct cost of children, but also their indirect costs (the need to spend more time on domestic tasks) appear to have a negative impact on the family's budget and contribute to increased poverty risks. This suggests that the child-friendly reputation of the Belgian welfare state in previous decades is gradually being eroded.[63]

Other studies (Van Robaeys *et al*, 2007; SPC, 2008) have pointed to a fourth at-risk group, namely, children with an immigrant background, whose poverty risk (60%) is five times higher than for the average child in Belgium. Immigrant families often have more children than Belgians. The Belgian NAP/inclusion does not refer to this group, for which additional measures may well be needed. Indeed, cultural and language bar-riers put an additional burden on the educational opportunities of poor children from immigrant families, compared with 'native' poor children.

### 2.5.2    Financial support to families with children

Immervoll, Sutherland and de Vos (2003) calculated that *family related benefits* accounted for 6.6% of a household's income in Belgium in 1994. This was the highest score among the European countries in their study. If these family benefits were to be removed, the child poverty rate would increase by 10 percentage points. In 2003, Belgium spent 2.7% of its GDP on family benefits and thus occupied a middle position in an OECD ranking (OECD Family Database 2007). Bradshaw (2006) also compared the child poverty rate

---

63    Cattoir and Jacobs (1998) found a favourable impact of child benefits on the income security of
       families with three or more children and single parent households. Looking at the current poverty
       rates for those family types, it seems that a deterioration has taken place. Discontinuities in data
       sources make it difficult to assess whether there is a data issue or a genuine deterioration, but the
       recent trends in the EU-SILC data point to a worsening situation, especially among single par-
       ents, compared to the mid-1990s.

before and after transfers, based on EU-SILC data for 2003. The data suggest that child poverty is halved thanks to family-related benefits.

Besides *universal*[64] cash benefits, which make up the largest share of the family policies expenditure, there are a few *targeted* allowances such as supplementary child benefits for the long-term unemployed, disabled and social assistance recipients. A third type of family-related transfers consists of *tax deductions* which are more likely to benefit the middle and higher income groups, such as substantial tax deductions for all children. The tax deductibility of child-care costs is definitely a measure that can help overcome barriers to work, but for low-income families, access to affordable child care may remain problematic – and the advantage of tax deductions is modest or useless.[65] In other words, one must admit that the Belgian child-friendly welfare state is still biased in favour of children from better-off families.

With the inclusion of child poverty issues in the social inclusion strategy, the existing policies are being extended or targeted to specific groups in order to play a preventive or alleviating role in child poverty. Nevertheless, targeting is still more the exception than the rule. The (federal) *back-to-school bonus*, introduced in 2006 to help cover extra costs at the start of the school year, is a universal measure. A higher, means-tested benefit targeted to low-income families would have had a stronger impact for this group. The supplementary €20 child allowance for single parents is the only recent example of a targeted family-related transfer.

In 2004, the *Alimony Fund* became operational; this fund was created to pay a cash advance in the event of the other parent failing to pay alimony. Prior to the creation of this fund, parents could ask the public centres for social welfare for an advance payment. The functioning of this fund has not been very successful so far. It was estimated that in 2006, 120,000 people were eligible for an advance payment; whereas the Fund received only 25,000 applications. This points to a problem of information: many entitled persons do not know that the Fund exists.

### 2.5.3    *Maternity and early childhood services*

In Belgium, two governmental agencies are responsible for support to young children and their families. They are actively providing advice and help to mothers and their young children (up to age three). They are the Office de la Naissance et de l'Enfance

---

64    In theory, family allowances are linked to the parents' (previous) employment status, however there are guaranteed family allowances for uninsured households.

65    Tax credits for children are in principle reimbursable (i.e. they can be transferred as 'negative taxes' to low-income households. However the amount of the transfer is limited to a fraction of the total tax deduction.

(ONE) in the French Community and Kind en Gezin (K&G) in Flanders. Both organisations are important actors in the implementation of policies related to child well-being. They cover a wide range of activities, including information sessions for future parents, pamphlets with information about childrearing and nutrition, visits after childbirth – both in the hospital and at home – and free (medical) consultations allowing for babies to be inoculated. Kind en Gezin also screens all newborns for hearing problems in order to detect them at an early stage. Both agencies also play a coordinating and controlling role in child-care provision in Belgium.

With regard to child poverty, visits by nurses just after childbirth and free consultations are activities that reach all families, including the most disadvantaged. These visits are also helpful in the sense that nurses can detect family or financial problems and provide help at an early stage or refer cases to specialised authorities.

Kind en Gezin has explicitly integrated "attention to poor families" in its approach and provides extra help for this group. The organisation has also developed its own, relatively sophisticated poverty registration system in order to gather the necessary information to offer appropriate help to low-income families with young children. Kind en Gezin also works with '*ervaringsdeskundigen*', i.e. mediators with a personal experience of poverty, who have an advantage in building trust. Poor families have often had negative experiences with public services and therefore tend to be suspicious vis-à-vis social workers. In 2005, the triple P (Positive Parenting Programme, a counselling service for parents in difficult educational circumstances) was introduced with support from the Flemish government. As the pilot projects proved to be successful, the programme should now be mainstreamed in Flanders. Kind and Gezin has also launched a new antenatal programme for vulnerable pregnant women. The latter measures in particular can be seen as steps forward from a preventive point of view.

### 2.5.4    *Child care and the reconciliation of work and family responsibilities*

In the welfare state literature (Esping-Andersen 1990, 1999) Belgium is classified as an example of a conservative-corporatist welfare state. One of the characteristics of this welfare state is that it leaves caring tasks to families, with the state offering little support in terms of daycare. However, Belgium deviates in this regard since subsidised daycare provisions are fairly well developed. The main objective of daycare provision is to lower the barriers to female employment. The above-average female employment rates among women in the childbearing age cohorts (71% in 2005) indicate that the policies to combine work and family life are quite successful. In recent years, Belgium has also improved the conditions for parental leave for both mothers and fathers and has increased the tax rebates for child-care costs. How do these policies affect low-income families?

Better and more generous parental leave conditions are a commendable initiative but, as explained above, it is unlikely that low-income families are the main beneficiaries of these measures. They often cannot afford to reduce their working hours or may be employed in precarious jobs that do not allow them to take up parental leave. As concerns tax deductions for child-care costs, high-income families gain more from such measures than families whose income is below the tax-free minimum threshold. Parents with limited budgets may benefit more from direct financial support instead of a future tax rebate from which they only have limited gains.

When child-care costs are high, low-income families will have modest financial gains from being in employment. But provision of affordable daycare alone is not necessarily sufficient to allow low-income families to increase their income through employment. Immervoll and Barber (2005) have examined the impact of child-care provision and tax benefits on work incentives. The main findings for Belgium can be summarised as follows:

- the average monthly fee for child care in Belgium was estimated at 16% of the gross earnings of the average production worker (APW). Belgium occupies a middle position compared with other OECD countries;
- single parents in Belgium gain little from low-wage employment as a consequence of the relatively high tax burden. The introduction of the work bonus should have a positive impact on their gains from work.

Raising the number of child-care places is seen as a key measure to lower barriers for women's employment, but in the NAP/inclusion 2006-2008, it is also promoted as a measure to combat child poverty. All regions announced an increase in the number of daycare places in the years to come, though with slightly different emphases. In the French Community, centre-based types of child-care provision are now being extended with 'co-accueillantes', a familial type of daycare with 8-10 children supervised by two carers.

However, all these measures must be seen against the backdrop of a well-developed system with a good quality of services, but highly unequal access. Hedebouw and Pepermans (2009) show that, despite means-tested fees, groups with a low socio-economic status (SES) in general make far less use of formal child-care services than the rest of the population (see Table 2.2). This is due, in the first place, to the fact that priority is given to two-earner families as the number of available places is limited. The level of the fees, and distrust of formal care providers, appear to be the main barriers for poor families (Vanpée *et al*, 2000). It is therefore important to widen access to existing provision, in addition to the specific measures included in the NAP/inclusion.

**Table 2.2: Use of child-care services among native Flemish households with children aged 3 months – 2 ½ years, by socio-economic status (%)**

| Use of child-care services | Non-poor households | Native poor households* | Immigrant households |
|---|---|---|---|
| Regularly | 65.7 | 21.0 | 32.6 |
| Seldom or never | 35.3 | 79.0 | 67.4 |

\*      Poverty is defined here using the multi-dimensional definition of Kind en Gezin (De Cock & Buysse, 1999).
        *Source: Hedebouw and Pepermans (2009, pages 43-45).*

### 2.5.5    Education

According to PISA research (OECD, 2007), education in Belgium – in all three communities – treats pupils from different socio-economic backgrounds very unequally, although average performance is good. And nowhere in the OECD is the performance gap between native and immigrant young people as wide as in Belgium (OECD 2006). According to UNICEF, Belgium comes last (out of 24 countries) in terms of inequality at the bottom of the education ladder (the gap between the 5th and 50th percentiles in PISA), and 14th out of 24 in terms of a composite indicator of "educational disadvantage" (UNICEF 2002).

The education system in Belgium is the responsibility of the three language communities (Flemish, French and German-speaking). After more than 15 years of autonomy, the differences between the three education systems are visible at various levels. However, two common challenges become evident. One raft of measures relates to the financial barriers for pupils and the financing of schools. At macro level, a new financing structure is outlined for education and, at the same time, at household level, the aim is to curb increasing school costs. A second raft of measures corrects the social segregation in education. In particular, this means increasing participation in nursery education, more transparent enrolment procedures, and lowering school drop-out rates.

#### 2.5.5.1 School funding
*New financing system in the Flemish Community*
One structural step forward in the equal opportunities policy was the decision of the Flemish Government to thoroughly reform the financing system in elementary and secondary education (Vandenbroucke, 2007a). The support policy for equal opportunities before the reform only provided additional staff and had no effect on operating resources

and the basic staffing of the school. Since September 2008, the size of all regular staff and operating resources per school is being calculated on the basis of "pupil and school characteristics". The initial phase covers elementary education and the first level of secondary education. Schools that have to help relatively high numbers of children cross socio-cultural barriers will receive a relatively higher operating budget and more staff. For some schools, this means a stepping up of the present policy; for others, it means a financial incentive which can encourage them to attract pupils with lower educational opportunities. The additional resources are above all an incentive to develop a strong(er) equal opportunities policy in the school. The intention is to make the schools accountable for this.

The differentiated financing is based on a set of four pupil characteristics: mother's level of education, parental income (whether or not the family is entitled to a study grant), mother tongue and the social environment from which schools draw pupils. In addition, the school size, the level and type of education provided – nursery, elementary education, study programme and form of education at secondary level – remain the main "drivers" for calculating financing.

*Reducing school costs*
The government of the French Community has in recent years been able to invest more in education. In anticipation of further structural measures, a number of smaller, concrete measures are in force, in particular reimbursement for books in parts of elementary education, free school agendas and limiting the costs of photocopies.

The education budget in Flanders has more financial room. Steps have been taken tangibly to reduce school costs in compulsory education (Vandenbroucke, 2006a). This involves a combination of *free* elementary education, *cost control* in secondary education and a selective expansion of the system of *study grants*. It is important to mention that these measures are accompanied by an increase in the operating budgets of the schools.

In contrast to the means-tested grants, the federal government decided to allocate a lump-sum school subsidy to everyone in the short run.

*2.5.5.2 Preventing social segregation*
A meritocratic education system, such as in Belgium, to a certain extent implies equal opportunities but in practice also accepts unequal treatment and unequal outcomes (Hirtt, Nicaise and De Zutter, 2007). In the infamous "waterfall", the "less talented" and underachieving pupils are allowed to drop out of general education and into technical and vocational education and, within the latter, into weaker education programmes resulting in early school-leaving. The selectivity and performance focus of education can to a large extent explain how children from poor families are excluded within education. From the

very start of the school career, the education system works as a filter and facilitates social division (Groenez *et al*, 2003).

In Belgium, the waterfall effect goes hand in hand with quasi market forces in education. The combination of free school choice (by parents) with the free organisation of schools and a large degree of pedagogical freedom (e.g. the absence of a national curriculum) has produced a very competitive system that performs well on average but has also clearly facilitated selective admission rules and social segregation. After Hungary, Belgium is the OECD country with the widest between-school variance in performance (OECD, 2004). This between-school variance is for the most part explained by social segregation.

In francophone Belgium, the aim is to achieve a general increase in the competence level of the overall pupil population, combined with a clear focus on improving the results of the weaker pupils. In order to achieve this, one ideal means is envisaged: ensuring greater social diversity in schools. Within this context, we refer to the publication of a survey commissioned by the minister regarding the so-called *bassins scolaires* (school districts) (Delvaux *et al*, 2005). There is a proposal to achieve a better social mix in schools within a *bassin scolaire* through a collective registration policy for all the schools. Although, at policy level, no action has been taken on this potential instrument, failing to mention this long-awaited study would ignore the dynamism it has since generated in francophone education.

*Reform of enrolment procedures*
In order to avoid schools being able to reject pupils unlawfully, the enrolment procedure has been adjusted in both Flanders and the French Community.

Since 2008, a fixed registration date is being introduced in the French Community for all schools. In addition, changing schools during a (two-year) grade cycle are forbidden. Schools that register excluded pupils are also no longer financially penalised. With these measures, the government is aiming for transparency, a more stable school career and freedom of choice for all parents. Opponents doubt whether the new arrangement will actually help in the struggle against "concentration schools" (schools with a high concentration of disadvantaged or ethnic minority children).

In Dutch-speaking Belgium, the 'right to register' is part of the decree regarding equal educational opportunities. Pupils can only be rejected or referred on the basis of precisely defined grounds and procedures. In order to close some loopholes, the scheme was fairly quickly – too quickly for some – changed in 2005. However, complex mechanisms lurk behind the segregation of the education landscape, which means that the right to enrol will not necessarily prevent pupils being refused access to certain schools. Direct discrimination will perhaps largely disappear but may be partially replaced by indirect discrimination (such as the ban on wearing headscarves).

*Restrictions on referrals to special education*
As far as referrals to special education are concerned, the number of pupils making the switch to special education is still rising. With 6.4% of pupils in special elementary education, Flanders in particular is among the leaders at world level in terms of the segregation of pupils with special educational needs. This segregation is strongly socially determined: the chance of a pupil being referred to special education is much higher if the father is unemployed or the mother is poorly educated, as well as within ethnic minority families (Ruelens and Nicaise, 2004). The Centres for Student Guidance (CLBs) can turn this tide by involving parents at an early stage and in an appropriate manner in the guidance, by offering staff plenty of opportunities for training about poverty and by collaborating with mediators with a personal experience of poverty (VLOR, 2006a).

High expectations are placed on the draft decree regarding 'learncare' (leerzorg), where the aim is to achieve one coherent care framework for all adjustments in ordinary education as well as the specialist settings in special education. This involves a comprehensive reorganisation with an extended timeline until 2016. By imposing stricter rules on referrals to special education, social selection upon referral should be counteracted or even neutralised. It is noticeable here that the accent is on better cooperation between support services and parents.

### 2.5.5.3 Other measures
*Increasing pre-school participation*
In anticipation of a possible reduction in the compulsory school age at federal level, the Flemish government gave its approval to an action plan to increase the participation of underprivileged children in pre-school education. The plan includes increased support for pre-schools, measures to improve the transition from child care to education and an awareness campaign.

The French community decided right from the start of the legislative session to strengthen pre-school education. Besides a substantial increase in funding for elementary education, the strategic plan also provided for the recruitment of an additional 320 pre-school teachers over two years.

*Combating learning deprivation*
According to UNESCO, under-achieving pupils in Belgium are approximately five terms behind (relative to the average pupil) by the end of the first level of secondary education, compared to 3.5 terms in Finland or Spain (UNICEF, 2002). The risks of school fatigue or of leaving school without qualification for children from vulnerable families are

genuine. Children of poorly educated mothers are 5.5 times more likely to leave higher secondary education without qualifications than children of well-educated mothers.

In a recommendation concerning poverty in education, the Flemish Education Council stipulates that, when tackling poverty, attention must be devoted above all to social integration and the prevention of school fatigue and unqualified school-leaving (VLOR, 2006a). We mention three policy priorities in this respect: reform of the first grade of secondary education, boosting on-the-job training and language policy.

1.  In francophone education in recent years, the *reform of the first (two-year) grade* of secondary education has been the central focus. At the same time as expanding the joint timetable to 27 or 28 hours, the minister is aiming primarily at teaching the basic skills of reading, writing and arithmetic. Remedial measures should be strengthened as soon as difficulties become tangible. In order to facilitate the transition from elementary to secondary education, pupils will be given the opportunity of spreading the first cycle over three years, rather than the current two years. In addition, it appears that a considerable proportion of underprivileged children have inadequate skills for dealing with new information and communication technology (ICT). The French Community has taken a step forward through the strategic plan for the integration of ICT into educational establishments – also described as good practice in the latest National Action Plan on Social Inclusion (Federal Government, 2006).

2.  Improved links between education and work are sought in an effort to improve the systems of *on-the-job training*. The key aspect is the choice to convert part-time compulsory education into a full-time commitment, combined if possible with part-time work, or where this is not possible with other activities such as preparatory pathways (voortrajecten) and bridge projects.

3.  Last but not least, we focus on one aspect of the problematic school careers of many ethnic minority children. In line with the assimilation policy pursued by the Flemish government, the present minister is investing in a *language policy for education*, among other things. Since language difficulties are associated with school difficulties, the emphasis is on acquiring a command of Dutch, for both pupils and parents – and the minister also wishes to impose minimum obligations in terms of parental involvement. Pupils will be tested on their knowledge of Dutch and the language policy of the school must be upheld by all teachers. The reception classes for foreign language-speaking newcomers will also be expanded.

### 2.5.6    *Specialised youth care*

Among the essential services for poor children, specialised youth care is undoubtedly the most controversial type of provision. For many generations, in Belgium as well as in other countries around the world, in-care placement of children from poor families has been common practice, and still is a major source of distress for both children and parents.

The Belgian NAP/inclusion emphasises that forced placement is the last resort and that measures to support families with difficulties are preferred over placement. Measures to support parents in their educational role are important in this regard, as well as initiatives organised for or by poor families themselves.

According to Nicaise and De Wilde (1995), 80% of all persistently poor families [66] have been in touch with some provision from the sector of specialised youth care or youth protection. Roughly half of the parents and half of the children had a personal experience of 'placement', which points to the vicious circle of deprivation of one's normal affective family ties. Across the board, the relationship between poor families and services is characterised by tensions. A closer analysis revealed the following reasons:

- A systematic *confusion between social and judicial approaches*. Specialised youth care is the common denominator for specialised social services for children, while youth protection refers to the judicial approach. The former supposedly operate on a voluntary basis and aim to support families and children in 'problematic educational circumstances' (including, of course, poverty). Judicial interventions are, in principle, confined to cases of delinquency, neglect or abuse of children, *or 'acute risk' in problematic educational circumstances*. In practice, workers from social services tend to resort to this notion of 'acute risk' in order to impose measures on their clients whenever they feel that the latter resist the 'support' on offer. This means that the voluntary character of the 'support' from the social services (mainly in-care placement) is often violated (at the time of the research, the majority of parents and young people completely disagreed with the intervention).
- The support was traditionally confined to *residential placements*, which are mostly experienced as extremely traumatic by parents as well as children. Over the last decades, semi-residential and ambulant care has gradually been developed (day centres, counselling, home support, parenting courses etc.). Paradoxically, the first effect of this widened scope of services has been an extension of social control over poor families, resulting in a further increase in in-care placements, in parallel with the rise of alternative types of support.
- There has been wide controversy about the *relationship between poverty and (interventions in) problematic educational circumstances*. Statistics undeniably demonstrate a strong social bias in interventions (with disproportionately high risks

---

66   The research by Nicaise and De Wilde (1995) was based on a study of the literature and a survey of 100 Belgian families (including 350 individuals) characterised by multiple deprivation (at least three indicators of severe deprivation in distinct dimensions of life).

of placement among children from the lowest socio-economic strata). Whereas parents tend to attribute the problems to their material deprivation (poor housing, financial hardship, health problems etc.), social services tend to deny these elements and to emphasise the (individual) educational disfunctioning of parents as the key problem. This perception is in turn rejected by parents as 'a condemnation for their poverty'.

- Although most reforms since the mid-1960s were meant to be more *'family-focused'*, parents often felt that their views were ignored as measures were taken for their children (such as the choice of school, health care, religious education etc.). The remote location of institutions, the long duration of placements, the lack of communication, tensions surrounding visits etc. tended to foster alienation rather than restoration of family ties.

This diagnosis, documented by Nicaise and De Wilde (1995), was also made in the General Report on Poverty (ATD-Quart Monde *et al*, 1995) and has been endorsed in subsequent memoranda issued by associations of poor people (Associations-Partenaires du RGP 1998; SLPPES, 2005a-b).

*Recent tendencies*
Although policy-makers seem to have recognised the problems, recent policy options do not seem to reflect a will to radically reform the system. On the contrary, some elements have contributed to a tightening of social control of educational relationships and increased interventionism:
- the Dutroux affair and subsequent paedophilia scandals;
- increased public attention on problems of domestic violence;
- the continued weakening of family ties in general; and
- the rise of juvenile violence, dramatically symbolised by murders in Brussels central station and in the streets of Antwerp in 2006.

All these elements have led to increased interventionism and stricter rules, for example, regarding the obligation to report any truancy, risk of violence, neglect or child abuse. The systematic confusion between judicial issues and problematic educational circumstances has thus reinforced the climate of suspicion as well as the stigma resting on poor families.

It must be admitted that efforts have been made to differentiate services, to make them more 'family-focused' and to limit in particular the number of residential placements of children. New types of services have been developed – apparently with greater success in the French than in the Flemish Community. In the French Community, the number of children placed in custody decreased by 10% in the period 1997-2002. However, as regards the Flemish Community, it increased by 24% between 1995 and 2004 (SLPPES

2005a; Vervotte 2006). The main 'push factor' in this trend appears to be the explosive growth of judicial interventions in the sphere of 'acute risk' (+50% in four years).

The Flemish Minister of Well-being and the Family has launched a master plan for youth care in which a number of measures reflect the priorities of associations of poor people. Services will be further diversified. For example, 'education shops' providing individual counselling as well as group-wise training sessions will be accessible in all main cities; 'support families' liaising with poor families and providing informal educational support will be encouraged; parenting support at home will be fostered, etc. More flexible combinations of services will also be facilitated. Further, the role of the 'Committees for specialised youth care' (the main gatekeepers, often feared by families) will be reduced as some services will become directly accessible. (Vervotte 2006).

On the other hand, the master plan goes diametrically against the two key demands of the associations of poor people (reducing the number of residential placements, and suppressing judicial interventions in problematic education circumstances). Indeed, the plan involves a new increase in residential provision, 'dictated' by the sharp increase in placements initiated by juvenile courts. Admittedly, the link between the rising number of placements and poverty remains to be examined.

*The quest for further reform*

All in all, it seems that the policy agenda of grassroots associations, as summarised in SLPPES (2005a) remains up-to-date:

- a radical *separation between judicial and social 'support'* is necessary to restore the confidence of poor families in specialised youth care services. This is seen as a prerequisite for families to address the services without fear of 'sanctions';
- the fundamental *right of children to be educated within their family* must be seen as the cornerstone of youth care policies. This means a shift from a 'youth care' approach to a 'family care' approach. Parents must be enabled and empowered to assume their role as educators;
- as poverty appears to remain a major cause of problematic educational circumstances, a preventive strategy should include measures to *support the material, social and cultural security of families*. Some well-intended recent measures that aim to protect atypical families may indirectly undermine traditional families: for example, specific support to single parents may discourage them from re-uniting or engaging in a new relationship. Similarly, the reduction or suppression of family allowances when children are placed in care prevents families from investing in regular contacts with their children. As regards measures to promote access to regular child-care services, tax deductions benefit high-income parents and have no effect on poor families;
- apart from more diversified and flexible services, the associations also demand

*more and better trained staff* in those services in order to ensure high-quality support;

- in the event of in-care placement, *pathways and action plans* should be designed that lead to the restoration of family ties at some point in the future. Appropriate guidance is required, also after children return to their families, in order to support their re-integration;
- specific attention is required for *homeless families*, as the crisis in the housing sector appears to boost their number, while shelters for complete families are nearly non-existent in Belgium;
- representative associations of parents in the sphere of youth care should be recognised as partners in the preparation of policies, and subsidised for this purpose. Although one organisation has gained some recognition in Flanders (Raad van Ouders in de Jeugdzorg – Council of Parents in Youth Care), the legal framework for its participation in negotiations and financial support is still lacking.

The French Community has set up the multidisciplinary 'AGORA' group in which youth-care representatives and the responsible administrations consult monthly with grassroots organisations active in the field (ATD Quart Monde) about the fears of poor families and the notion of 'risk'.

### 2.5.7    Children's rights and participation, a blind spot

The measures described above are strongly geared toward families, and the same is true for the measures announced in the Belgian NAP/inclusion. These measures are an important support for families with children, not only financially but also in providing services that facilitate the combination of work and family life. These measures obviously benefit the well-being of children. However, it must be admitted that they are not explicitly inspired by children's rights. No explicit reference is made to children's rights or the UN Convention on children's rights, which Belgium ratified. As regards children's participation, children experiencing poverty were not consulted about the draft of the NAP/inclusion. Poor people's organisations have been consulted during the NAP/inclusion process but within these organisations, the opportunities for children to participate are also limited. This remains a point of attention for the future.

Some tools are available to promote children's rights and participation. For example, Flanders has introduced the means to assess the effects of new legislation on children. It offers the opportunity to test Flemish decrees against the UN Convention on children's rights and to check whether children's rights are respected by the legislative powers. Unfortunately, this option has remained under-utilised so far.

In 2006, the Regions agreed to step up cooperation and to coordinate their policies in implementing the requirements of the UN Convention on children's rights. This agreement should result in a National Commission for children's rights that will be entrusted with coordination between the different actors and reporting to the UN.

Children may experience poverty in a different way to their parents. Financial poverty is generally seen as a key indicator, but this indicator is likely to be inadequate to capture children's experience of poverty. Poor children are likely to have their own indicators. They may experience exclusion at school, when they cannot participate in extra-curricular activities or when they do not have access to the same toys or clothes as their non-poor counterparts. And yet it is very uncommon to discuss poverty and social exclusion from a children's perspective in Belgium. Knowledge about children's experience of poverty is still very limited. A better insight into children's own experience would be useful to detect poor children's primary needs and examine how they can be fulfilled. If child poverty is a policy priority, children's voices need to be heard as well.

### 2.5.8    Concluding remarks

Even if Belgium is among the European countries where overall children poverty is not at an alarmingly high level, there are nonetheless indications that call for policy attention and action to prevent a deterioration in the situation of specific groups.

First, there are a growing number of single parents who – together with their children – face a much higher poverty risk than their married or cohabiting counterparts. Employment, in combination with family benefits, is regarded as the most effective manner to keep poverty low among this group.

Employment rates among single mothers are far below the average female employment rate. Improving daycare possibilities has been the main remedy so far: a measure that is also targeted at mothers in general. However, there are indications that specific measures for single mothers are being implemented. This is a new shift in Belgian family policies that hitherto had a universal character. Better insights into what exactly makes employment more difficult for single parents can help to adjust policies and improve their employment situation.

A second group of children at risk of poverty is the group of children living in jobless households. Belgium has one of the worst records, in a European perspective, both as regards the share of children living in such households and the poverty level among these households. Here again, employment is promoted as the main remedy. In the last couple of years, Belgium has made considerable efforts to make work pay and it is too early to evaluate the impact of these measures on the outcomes for children in jobless households. However, an increase in employment does not automatically result in less poverty if the new jobs do not reach this group. As for the single parents, more knowledge about the characteristics of this group and their problems is desirable.

Looking at the measures to combat child poverty, we find several initiatives to support parents in their role as educators. However, the actual impact of recent policies appears to be mixed. Access to child-care services is improving, but remains strongly biased in favour of middle-class families, and two-earner families in particular, leaving little room for the poorest. In the area of youth care, grassroots organisations keep demanding more radical reforms in order to restore the confidence between social workers and families. More ambitious measures have been taken in the education sector, to tackle educational disadvantage. Achieving universal participation in kindergartens, pulling down financial barriers, and combating segregation emerge as key objectives in this field.

Children's rights and perspectives are rather weakly reflected in the proposed package of measures in the NAP/inclusion.

Summing up, we can say that the social security system, in combination with the (mostly) universal family benefits and child allowances, protect most families and children against extreme poverty. Nevertheless, there are also clear shortcomings. Families in which no one works are not sufficiently protected, partly due to the low benefit level of the guaranteed minimum income.

How the proposed measures to tackle child poverty will be implemented, and what their impact on children's poverty in Belgium will be, remains to be seen. The current monitoring system can be improved and a stronger linkage between the measures and their outcomes is recommendable as well. As regards indicators for child poverty, an extension of the current set is desirable. The intention to increase knowledge in certain areas is likely to stimulate this discussion.

## 2.6  Conclusions and recommendations for strengthening EU action on child poverty and social exclusion

The experience of the Social OMC has shown that, while responsibility for addressing issues of child poverty and social exclusion rests primarily with Member States, the Social OMC has added value to Member States' efforts and is likely to continue to do so. There are at least six aspects to this. First, the Social OMC has raised public and political awareness of the importance of the issue and of the need to invest in preventing and reducing child poverty and social exclusion. This is evidenced by the steadily growing number of Member States who have prioritised the issue in their NAPs/inclusion. Continued focus by the EU on this issue will provide further encouragement to and pressure on Member States to continue to make it a political priority. Secondly, the requirement to prepare regular NAPs/inclusion has encouraged and helped many Member States to move towards more comprehensive and coordinated efforts to address child poverty and social exclusion. Thirdly, by identifying indicators and improving the availability of comparable data, particularly through supporting the *Community Statistics on Income and Living Conditions (EU-SILC)* instrument, the Social OMC has enabled Member States to make use of comparisons with other countries as a way of deepening the understanding of the issue in their own country. Fourthly, the EU focus on the issue and the improvement in data availability has increased awareness in Member States of the need to monitor and report on the outcome of policies and has also enhanced the possibility of doing so. While there is a long way still to go, this is encouraging and is helping Member States to develop a more evidenced based and analytical approach to the issue. Fifthly, the Social OMC has led to a wealth of learning and analysis about the nature and extent of child poverty and social exclusion and about the policies and programmes that work best to combat them. This is particularly helpful for those Member States who have lagged behind in this area and most need to develop effective policies and programmes to ensure the well-being and social inclusion of all children. Sixthly, the Social OMC has resourced and fostered the development of networking between all those actors concerned with developing policies and programmes to support children. The wide range of policy makers, social services deliverers, NGOs and academics who have been enabled to meet and discuss the issues is proving an important resource of contacts and information for Member States when developing their own policies.

On the other hand, although significant progress has been made between 2000 and 2010 in putting child poverty and social exclusion on the EU agenda and also on a growing number of national agendas, the data show clearly that there is still a long way to go to make a decisive impact on the eradication of child poverty and social exclusion. While most of what needs to be done requires effective actions at both national and sub-national levels, evidence from the Social OMC clearly highlights the added value of having the fight against child poverty and social exclusion as a key priority on the EU social agenda, and the need for continued and intensified efforts at EU level to encourage and support Member States' efforts. This is all the more so in the light of the new objectives on social inclusion and children's rights in the Lisbon Treaty. The challenge is thus to build on the solid basis that has been developed for action at EU level and to consolidate and deepen the EU dimension in the future.

In Chapter 1, we highlighted some of the weaknesses that have been evident in the Social OMC and that need to be addressed if the EU's effectiveness in tackling poverty and social exclusion is to be significantly improved. These weaknesses also apply in the area of child poverty and social exclusion and have to be taken into account in enhancing work on this issue in the future. The following recommendations build on the general recommendations at the end of Chapter 1 and concentrate specifically on identifying what actions need to be put in place to ensure that the indispensable strong focus on child poverty and social exclusion be maintained and strengthened as a key component of the social pillar of the Europe 2020 agenda.

### 2.6.1    Clearly stated political priority in Europe 2020 agenda

In an area of "soft" law such as social inclusion policy, effective action at EU level is not possible without strong political commitment and leadership and without a clearly artic-ulated agreement between Member States concerning the way forward. A key challenge is thus to ensure that by the end of 2010 such a clear political commitment on poverty and social exclusion in general, and child poverty and social exclusion in particular, is in place. This would then underpin all the work on the issue up to 2020. For creating the required policy dynamic, we would recommend:

- that the Conclusions of one of the 2010 European Councils include a strong com-mitment to tackling poverty and social exclusion in general and child poverty and social exclusion in particular as a key component of the Europe 2020 agenda;
- that by the end of 2010 a renewed and strengthened EU coordination in the social field is formally agreed upon at EU level (by the European Council and/ or the EU Council of Ministers) with tackling child poverty and social exclu-sion specified as one of its cornerstones[67];
- that enhanced NAPs/inclusion are the central part of the post-2010 EU coor-dination in the social field arrangements, with child poverty and social exclu-sion a "required" topic in each Member States' NAPs/inclusion;
- that the recently agreed EU social inclusion target (see Sections 1.3.1 and 1.3.2) should, as soon as possible, be complemented with a specific EU target for the reduction of child poverty and social inclusion and that countries should be encouraged to set (sub-)national targets in relation to children[68];

---

67    Other key designated themes that could form key parts of the social pillar of the EU2020 strategy might include active inclusion (especially adequate minimum income), homelessness and housing exclusion, and the integration of ethnic minorities and migrants.

68    A constructive way to make progress on this could be for the Commission and the SPC to insti-tute a process whereby the Commission and Member States would explore ways of making the EU child poverty and social exclusion objectives more visible, measurable and tangible at EU level. For instance, this could involve a more rigorous and visible use of the commonly agreed indicators for the Social OMC and the commitment of all Member States to set the goal of improving their performance in a set of indicators covering each relevant social policy domain including child poverty and social exclusion.

- that a political commitment is made at EU level during 2010 that there will be an annual report to the Spring European Council and to the European Parliament on progress towards the agreed objectives (as part of the annual *Joint Report on Social Protection and Social Inclusion*). This annual report should also be addressed to national and possible sub-national Parliaments of Member States.


### 2.6.2   Multi-annual work programme for EU action

To date, the work on child poverty and social exclusion has evolved in a rather ad hoc and piecemeal manner. The challenge now is to build on the work done to date and to develop, as an integral part of a renewed EU coordination in the social field, a more systematic and structured approach to achieving the overall 2020 political objectives in a series of incremental steps. It would thus be helpful if the Commission and Member States, in the context of the Social Protection Committee (SPC) and as part of the renewed EU coordination in the social field, would draw up a multi-annual work programme on child poverty and social exclusion.

The first work programme, which ought to reflect the recommendations outlined below could have a series of highlights such as:
- an annual scoreboard on child poverty and social exclusion which reflects the multi-dimensional nature of the issue and also includes indicators on child well-being;
- a Commission Communication or Working Document followed by a Commission Recommendation (see below, Section 2.6.3);
- NAPs/inclusion with a required section on strategies to prevent and tackle child poverty and social exclusion;
- a series of declarations/communications/high profile events on specific issues (e.g. early years, deinstitutionalisation, Roma children, discrimination, consultation/ participation of children).

It might also cover:
- a work programme on indicators, data collection and further policy analysis;
- an ongoing monitoring programme resulting in an annual report on progress;
- a programme of enhanced mutual learning;
- joint actions with the EU Strategy on the Rights of the Child;
- action to better embed child poverty objectives in Structural Funds;
- action to deepen child inclusion mainstreaming across EU policies.

### 2.6.3    Recommendation on child poverty and well-being

Given the considerable work that has been undertaken on child poverty and social exclusion over the past decade it will be important to move the process to a new level
of effectiveness by consolidating in one overarching political document all the learning
to-date and by setting out clearly in that document the range of actions that need to be
taken to make further progress in the future. It is thus recommended that, following the
precedent established with the Commission's 2008 Recommendation on Active Inclusion and in line with the 2008 Commission Communication on reinforcing the Social
OMC, a priority should now be given to working towards a European Commission
Recommendation on child poverty and well-being.[69]

### 2.6.4    Mainstreaming across EU policy making

Child poverty and social exclusion cut across many different policy areas at EU as well
as at national levels. Any programme of work should therefore aim not only to develop
a strong focus on the social inclusion and well-being of children within the renewed
EU coordination in the social field but also a clear plan for ensuring that the issue of
child poverty and social exclusion is fully taken into account in all EU policy making. To
achieve this, it will be necessary to ensure that:

- arrangements are in place that require all EU policies to be systematically
  proofed for their potential impact on child poverty and social exclusion;
- clearer institutional links are created between the EU's Strategy on the Rights
  of the Child and the work on the social inclusion of children so that they are
  mutually reinforcing;
- the arrangements for implementing the Europe 2020 agenda guarantee closer
  and more effective links between social, employment and growth policies, and
  especially between the renewed EU coordination in the social field and the
  future arrangements to promote growth and jobs;
- the goal of promoting social inclusion, especially of children, is fully integrated
  into the EU's sustainable development agenda and environmental policies are
  based on the principle of environmental justice with a particular concern for
  their impact on children;
- links between other policy areas with a high relevance to the social inclusion

---

69    The Commission Communication on reinforcing the Social OMC suggests that "The subjects
      that are part of the OMC could be further consolidated by formalising convergence of views
      whenever it arises. The Commission will contribute to this by making, where appropriate, use of
      Recommendations based on Article 211 of the Treaty, setting out common principles, providing a
      basis for monitoring and peer review." (European Commission, 2008)

and well-being of children are explored and made more regular and systematic. These might include policies and initiatives in the area of immigration, discrimination, gender equality (e.g. revived declaration on early years with emphasis on quality and monitoring), active inclusion, flexible working, housing, health (e.g. the work of the Commission's Directorate-General for "Health and Consumers (SANCO)" on child and adolescence mental health) and education (especially early education). A first step could be to launch a reflection on how to achieve better synergies between policy areas affecting children on a consistent basis – in the longer term, the children's rights agenda could provide a framework for linking the different policy areas;

- tackling child poverty and social exclusion are included as a priority in the use of EU Structural Funds.

### 2.6.5 *Strengthening data, targets, monitoring and evaluation*

It is clear from the experience between 2000 and 2010 that a key way that the EU level can add value is through encouraging the systematic setting of targets and benchmarks, enhancing data and developing indicators, ensuring regular monitoring and reporting, and making recommendations. While progress has been made much remains to be done in this area. Priorities in this area should include establishing:

- a clear system whereby the Commission would work with each Member State to agree appropriate outcome targets on child poverty and social exclusion for that Member State;
- a work programme to develop further the agreed indicators on child poverty and social exclusion as well as on child well-being and to improve the timeliness, coverage and relevance of related data (which should then also cover children who are not living in private households, such as those in institutions);
- an enhanced system for regular monitoring and reporting on child poverty and social exclusion and on child well-being including:
  - o implement the EU Task-Force recommendations which are already part of the EU *social acquis* (Social Protection Committee, 2008);
  - o introduce an annual scoreboard on child poverty and social exclusion which reflects the multi-dimensional nature of the issue and thus also includes indicators covering key aspects of child well-being;
  - o carry out regular properly *contextualised benchmarking*, which is indispensable for policy learning (see Social Protection Committee (2008); Marlier

and Atkinson (2010));[70]
- o   develop social impact assessments (e.g., child poverty proofing) in all the relevant policy domains and use specific peer reviews and transnational exchange projects to boost mutual learning;
- a process for monitoring the impact of the financial and economic crisis on children;
- an agreed basis for making annual/regular recommendations to Member States for strengthening their policies on child poverty and social exclusion and for regularly monitoring their progress;[71]
- a further programme of in-depth policy orientated research into:
  - o   intergenerational aspects of child poverty;
  - o   multidimensionality;
  - o   children in "extreme" situations;
  - o   links between socio-economic/political systems and impact on child poverty.

### 2.6.6   Maintaining and deepening exchange of learning

One of the successes of the Social OMC has been to promote the exchange of learning and good practice. However, often the different initiatives (exchange projects, thematic studies, peer reviews, reports from networks etc.) have taken place in a rather disjointed

---

70   League tables of social indicators can provide very useful insights into the determinants of poverty and social exclusion and can serve as a spur to political action. For this to be made possible, a key requirement is the proper "contextualisation" of the interpretation of indicators when conducting international comparisons. Even for indicators that have been commonly agreed at EU level and that therefore comply satisfactorily with the various methodological criteria required by the Social OMC monitoring framework (in terms of robustness, international comparability...; see European Commission (2009a)), it is essential to always keep in mind the need for contextualised benchmarking. Indeed, as Atkinson and Marlier (2010) have put it "specific policies and their impacts measured through indicators can be properly understood only in the context of the broad institutional setting in which they operate. For example, measures of labour market participation or unemployment may have different meanings in different labour-markets depending, inter alia, on the national and/or sub-national labour-market regulations and collective bargaining arrangements. A 'system-wide analysis' is required for proper international benchmarking." (Atkinson and Marlier, 2010)

71   The EU Task-Force report (Social Protection Committee 2008) which included an evidence-based typology of countries and highlighted the key areas in which each Member State most needs to make progress (joblessness, in-work poverty, and level and impact of social transfers) demonstrates how it is possible, through careful analysis, to come up with practical recommendations that are helpful and acceptable to Member States.

and unconnected fashion, and dissemination of results has often been limited to a rather narrow circle. Thus the Member States and the Commission should explore how to best ensure that the suggested multi-annual work programme for EU action to tackle child poverty and social exclusion promotes:

- a more systematic approach to work on child poverty and social exclusion and to the dissemination of learning;
- focussed work around specific issues (e.g. deinstitutionalisation, migrant children, homeless children).

### 2.6.7  Improving governance and involving children

The Social OMC has done much to promote the participation of different actors. However, in the area of child poverty and social exclusion the direct involvement of children experiencing poverty in the development, implementation and monitoring of policies has remained weak. The importance of such involvement is clear (see 2.3.7) thus every effort should be made to:

- put the involvement of children at the heart of future EU coordination in the social field and then build this as a theme into the proposed work programme;
- promote the direct involvement of children in the issues that concern them and involve then in developing policy responses which will meet their needs more effectively;
- deepen the involvement of other actors defending children's needs, such as NGOs and local social services in the policy-making process.

## References

Alter Educ (2005), La lutte contre les inégalités dans le Contrat pour l'école: refuser les « écoles ghettos », no. 105.

Alter Educ (2006), Trois mesures de lutte contre le marché scolaire et les écoles ghettos, no. 126.

Alter Educ (2007a), Débats passionnés autour du décret inscription, no. 140.

Alter Educ (2007b), Décret relatif aux manuels scolaires: le point de vue des acteurs de terrain, no. 140.

Arena, M. (2005), Le Contrat pour l'Ecole, Ministre-Présidente de la Communauté française en charge de l'Enseignement.

ATD-Quart Monde, Fondation Roi Baudouin, Union des Villes et des Communes Belges (1995), Rapport général sur la pauvreté, Bruxelles: FRB

Atkinson, A.B. (2010), *Poverty and the EU: The New Decade*, Macerata Lectures on European Economic Policy, Dipartimento di Studi sullo Sviluppo Economico, Working Paper 24, University of Macerata, May 2010.

Atkinson, A.B. and Marlier, E. (2010), *Analysing and measuring social inclusion in a global context*, New-York: UNDESA. Available from: http://www.un.org/esa/socdev/publications/measuring-social-inclusion.pdf.

Barroso, J.M. (2010), *2010 European Year for Combating Poverty and Social Exclusion: Working together towards a society in line with our values*, Speech delivered at the Opening Conference of the 2010 European Year for Combating Poverty and Social Exclusion, Madrid, 21 January 2010. Available from: http://europa.eu/rapid/pressReleasesAction.do?reference=SPEECH/10/12&format=HTML&aged=0&language=ES&guiLanguage=en.

Bohn, I. (2005), *A Lobby for Children: Final Report*, Germany: Arbeiterwohlfahrt (AWO) Bezikesverband Ostwestfalen-Lippe eV.

Bollens, J., De Vos, H., Vleugels, I., Verhaeghe, J.P. (2000). Studiekosten in het basisonderwijs, Wat het kost om schoolgaande kinderen te hebben. Leuven: HIVA.

Bradshaw, J. and Bennett, F. (2007), *Tackling child poverty and promoting the social inclusion of children: a study of national policies*, Brussels: European Commission.

Bradshaw, J., Hoelscher, P. and Richardson, D. (2007), *An index of child well-being in the European Union*, in *Social Indicators Research*, Volume 80, No. 1, Netherlands.

Bradshaw, J. (2006) 'Child Poverty and Child Well-Being' Paper to the Social Policy Association Conference, University of Birmingham.

Caritas Europa (2004), *Poverty Has Faces in Europe – The Need for Family-Oriented Policies*, 2nd Report on Poverty in Europe, Brussels: Caritas.

Cattoir, P. en Jacobs, D. (1998) 'Het gezinsbeleid in België: welke instrumenten voor welke doelstellingen?' in *Belgisch Tijdschrift voor Sociale Zekerheid*.

Cocker, C. (2003), *The Mental Health of Children in State Care: a European Study – Final Report*, NCH – The Bridge Child Care Development Service, UK.

Conseil de l'Emploi, des Revenus et de la Cohésion sociale (CERC) (2004*)*, *Les enfants pauvres en France*, Rapport No. 4, France. Available from: http://www.cerc.gouv.fr/rapports/rapport4/rapport4cerc.pdf.

Council (2002), *Joint Report on Social Inclusion*, Brussels: EU Council of Ministers and European Commission.

Council (2005), *Joint Report on Social Protection and Social Inclusion*, Brussels: EU Council of Ministers and European Commission.

Council (2007), *Joint Report on Social Protection and Social Inclusion* (including related supporting document produced by the European Commission), Brussels: EU Council of Ministers and European Commission.

Council (2008), *Joint Report on Social Protection and Social Inclusion* (including related supporting document produced by the European Commission), Brussels: EU Council of Ministers and European Commission. Available from: http://ec.europa.eu/social/main.jsp?catId=757&langId=en.

Cyprus College (2007), *Integrating children's perspectives in policy making to combat poverty*

*and social exclusion experienced by single parent families*, Final report on the implementation of the action. Available from:
http://www.csca.org.cy/UserFiles/File/very%20final%20report,%20TOC.pdf.

D'Addato, A. (2009), *Measuring and monitoring: a child-rights perspective,* Paper delivered at the December 2009 Paris Peer Review meeting on "Measuring the impact of active inclusion and other policies to combat poverty and social exclusion", Brussels: Eurochild. Available from:
http://www.eurochild.org/fileadmin/user_upload/Publications/Eurochild_Reports/EUROCHILD_paper_peer_review_France.pdf.

De Cock, R., Buysse, B. (1999), *Kansarmoede-atlas van gezinnen met jonge kinderen 1999*, Brussels: Kind & Gezin.

Delvaux, B., Demeuse, M., Dupriez, V., Fagnant, A., Guisset, C., Lafontaine, D., Marissal, P. and Maroy, C. (2005), *Les bassins scolaires : de l'idée au projet. Propositions relatives aux domaines d'intervention, aux instances et aux territoires*, Research financed by the French Community, final report.

Dewilde, C. and Levecque, K. (2002) De mobiliteit in en uit armoede:' Wie is arm en voor hoe lang? VRANKEN, J., *et al* (eds.) (2002), Armoede en Sociale Uitsluiting. Jaarboek 2002, Leuven-Leusden: Acco, 85-104.

Dupriez, V. and Dumay, X., *L'égalité dans les systèmes scolaires: effet d'école ou effet de société ?*, Cahier du Girsef, no. 31 October 2004.

Duquet, N., Glorieux, I., Laurijssen, I., Van Dorsselaer, Y. (2006), Wit krijt schrijft beter. Schoolloopbanen van allochtone jongeren in beeld. Antwerp-Apeldoorn: Garant.

Esping-Andersen, G. (1990) *The Three Worlds of Welfare Capitalism.* Cambridge: Polity Press.

EU Network of Independent Experts on Social Inclusion:
http://www.peer-review-social-inclusion.eu/network-of-independent-experts.

Eurochild (2006), *Position Paper on the Guidelines for Preparing National Reports on Strategies for Social Protection and Social Inclusion*, Brussels: Eurochild.

Eurochild (2008), Seminar Report, *Members' Exchange Seminar on Child and Youth Participation*, Brussels: Eurochild. Available from:
http://www.eurochild.org/index.php?id=394&L=0&tx_ttnews[backPid]=287&tx_ttnews[pS]=1245799660&tx_ttnews[tt_news]=33&cHash=1a86c651f8

Eurochild (2009a), *Indicators: an important tool for advancing child well-being*, Policy Briefing No. 5, Brussels: Eurochild. Available from:
http://www.eurochild.org/fileadmin/user_upload/Policy/Policy_briefing/PB05_Indicators_LAST.pdf.

Eurochild (2009b), *Ending child poverty within the EU? A review of the 2008-2010 National Strategy Reports on Social Protection and Social* Inclusion, Brussels: Eurochild.

European Anti-Poverty Network (EAPN), (2009), *Small Steps Big Changes: Building Participation of People Experiencing Poverty*, EAPN, Brussels: EAPN.

European Cities against Child Poverty (2008), *Tackling child poverty: parental Employ-*

*ment*, Policy Bulletin, Brussels. Available from:
http://www.againstchildpoverty.com/newsandevents.php.

European Cities Against Child Poverty (2009), *Improving life chances for children in poverty: lessons from across Europe*, Brussels. Available from:
http://www.againstchildpoverty.com/newsandevents.php.

European Commission (2004), *The Situation of Roma in an Enlarged European Union*, Brussels: European Commission.

European Commission (2006), *Towards an EU Strategy on the Rights of the Child*, Communication No. COM(2006) 367 final, Brussels: European Commission.

European Commission (2008), *A renewed commitment to social Europe: Reinforcing the Open Method of Coordination for Social Protection and Social Inclusion*, Communication No. COM(2008) 418 final, Brussels: European Commission.

European Commission (2009a), *Portfolio of indicators for the monitoring of the European strategy for social protection and social inclusion – 2009 update*, Brussels: European Commission. Available from:
http://ec.europa.eu/social/main.jsp?catId=756&langId=en.

European Commission (2009b), *Consultation on the Future "EU 2020" Strategy*, Commission Working Document No. COM(2009)647 final, Brussels: European Commission.

European Parliament (2008), *Report on promoting social inclusion and combating poverty (including child poverty) in the EU (Rapporteur: Gabriele Zimmer)*, Brussels: European Parliament. Available from:
http://www.europarl.europa.eu/sides/getDoc.do?language=EN&reference=A6-036 4/2008.

European Social Network (2005), *Promoting inclusion for unaccompanied young asylum seekers and immigrants: a duty of justice and care*, Brighton: ESN.

European Social Network (2007), *Child Poverty and Welfare in Europe: the message from Social Services*, Brighton: ESN.

FEANTSA (European Federation of National Organisations Working with the Homeless) (2007), *Child homelessness in Europe – an overview of emerging trends*, Brussels: FEANTSA.

Federal Government of Belgium (2006), National Action Plan on Social Inclusion 2006-2008, Brussels: Federal Government.

Federale Overheidsdienst Werkgelegenheid, Arbeid en Sociaal Overleg (FOD WASO) (2006) ' De Immigratie in België: aantallen, stromen en arbeidsmarkt', Brussels.

Fernandes, R. (2007), *A child rights approach to child poverty*, Brussels: Eurochild.

Flemish Education Council (2006a), Recommendation of the General Council on the report, "Armoede uitbannen, een bijdrage aan politiek debat en politieke actie" (Banning poverty; a contribution to political debate and political action), AR/PCA/ADV/001.

Flemish Education Council (2006b), Recommendation on the "Leren en Werken"

(Learning and Working) discussion paper, RSO/GCO/ADV/002.

Frazer, H. (2005), *Setting the scene Europe-wide: The challenge of poverty and social exclusion*, Community Development Journal, Oxford: Oxford University Press.

Frazer, H. (2006), *Lessons learned on child poverty: Why and how to tackle child poverty*, UNICEF Regional Office for CEE/CIS/Baltics, Geneva.

Frazer, H. (2008), *Yes to an Active Inclusion based on rights! Promoting EAPN Principles on Active Inclusion*, Report of EAPN seminar on Active Inclusion held in Paris on 13 June 2008, Brussels: EAPN.

Frazer, H. (2009), *Combating child poverty and social exclusion in European Union countries: Lessons for policy and practice*, Paper presented at the African Child Policy Forum (Addis Ababa, May 2008) and subsequently published in: J.E. Doek, A.K. Kumar, D. Mugawe, and S. Tsegaye. (Eds.). Child poverty: African and international perspectives (pp. 219–236). Antwerp, Belgium: Intersentia.

Frazer, H. and Devlin, M. (forthcoming), *A Comparative Study of Policies to Tackle and Prevent Poverty and Social Exclusion among Children*, Maynooth: NUI Maynooth.

Frazer, H. and Marlier, E. (2007), *Tackling child poverty and promoting the social inclusion of children in the EU – Key lessons*, Independent overview based on the 2007 first semester national reports of the national independent experts on social inclusion, Brussels: European Commission. Available from:
http://www.peer-review-social-inclusion.eu/network-of-independent-experts/2007/reports/first-semester-2007/synthesis-report-2007-1.

Fundamental Rights Agency (FRA) (2009), *Developing indicators for the protection, respect and promotion of the rights of the child in the European Union*, Vienna: FRA. Available from:
http://fra.europa.eu/fraWebsite/products/publications_reports/pub-rightsofchild-summary_en.htm.

Groenez, S., Van den Brande, K., Nicaise, I. (2003). Cijferboek sociale ongelijkheid in het Vlaamse Onderwijs. Een verkennend onderzoek op de Panelstudies van Belgische Huishoudens, LOA report no. 10, Leuven: Steunpunt LOA 'Loopbanen doorheen onderwijs naar de arbeidsmarkt'.

Guio, A.-C. (2009), *What can be learned from deprivation indicators in Europe?*, Luxembourg: Eurostat. Available from:
http://epp.eurostat.ec.europa.eu/cache/ITY_OFFPUB/KS-RA-09-007/EN/KS-RA-09-007-EN.PDF

Halleröd, B. (2007), *Tackling child poverty and promoting the social inclusion of children: A Study of National Policies in Sweden*, Brussels: European Commission.

Hedebouw, G. and Pepermans, A. (2009), *Het gebruik van opvang voor kinderen jonger dan 3 jaar in het Vlaamse Gewest*, Leuven: HIVA / Steunpunt Welzijn, Volksgezondheid en Gezin

Hölscher, P. (2004), *A Thematic Study using transnational comparisons to analyse and identify what combination of policy responses are most successful in preventing and reducing high levels of child poverty*, Brussels: European Commission.

Home Start International (2002), *Tackling Social Exclusion in Families with Young Children: Final Report*, UK: Home Start International.

Immervoll, H. and Barber, D. (2005), 'Can parents afford to work? Childcare costs, tax-benefit policies and work incentive.' OECD Social Employment and Migration Working Papers No. 31. OECD, Paris

Kamerman, S., Neuman, M., Waldfogel, J. and Brooks-Gunn, J. (2003), Social Policies, Family Types and Child Outcomes in selected OECD countries;' OECD Social Employment and Migration Working Papers No.6. OECD, Paris

Layte, R., Maître, B., Nolan, B. and Whelan, C.T. (2006), *Day in, Day out: Understanding the Dynamics of Child Poverty*, Dublin: Institute of Public Administration/Combat Poverty Agency.

Lejeune, A. (2007), Le coût scolaire, l'école et des familles : Pratiques de communication et réduction des frais, Family Association.

Lejeune, A., Lacroix, J. (2006), sous la direction d'Emily Hoyos, Le coût scolaire à charge des familles. Survey 2004-2005, Family Association

Levy, H., Lietz, C. and Sutherland, H. (2007), "A guaranteed income for Europe's children?" in Jenkins, S.P. and Micklewright, J. editors, *Inequality and poverty re-examined*, Oxford: Oxford University Press.

Mahieu, P. and Desmedt, E., Van arbeiderszoon tot allochtoon, Een overzicht van het kansenbeleid in het Vlaams onderwijs, in: Vranken, J., De Boyser, K. and Dierckx, D. (eds.) (2006), *Armoede en Sociale Uitsluiting. Jaarboek 2006*, Leuven-Voorburg: Acco, 239-256.

Mainstreaming Social Inclusion (2006), *Better Policies, Better Outcomes – Promoting the Mainstreaming of Social Inclusion*. Available from:
http://www.combatpoverty.ie/publications/BetterPoliciesBetterOutcomes-MSI_2006.pdf

Mangez, E., Joseph, M. and Delvaux, B. (2002), Les familles défavorisées à l'épreuve de l'école maternelle, CERISIS, UCL.

Marlier, E. and, Atkinson, A.B. (2010), *Indicators of Poverty and Social Exclusion in a Global Context*, in Journal of Policy Analysis and Management.

Marlier, E., Atkinson, A.B., Cantillon, B. and Nolan, B. (2007), *The EU and Social Inclusion: Facing the challenges*, Bristol: The Policy Press.

Marlier, E., Cantillon, B., Nolan, B., Van den Bosch, K., and Van Rie, T. (forthcoming), *Developing and learning from measures of social inclusion in the EU*, in D.J. Besharov and K.A. Couch (Vol. Eds.), D.J. Besharov and N. Gilbert (Series Eds.), International policy exchange series. New York: Oxford University Press.

Morissens, A. and Nicaise, I. (2006) Assessment of the Social Inclusion strand of the Belgian National Strategy Report on Social Protection and Social Inclusion.

Morissens, Ann (1999) *Solo Mothers and Poverty: Do Policies Matter? A Comparative Case Study of Belgium and Sweden*. LIS working paper series no.210.

Nicaise, I., De Wilde, C. (1995), *Het zwaard van Damocles. Arme gezinnen over de bijzondere jeugdzorg*, Leuven – Apeldoorn: Garant

Nicaise, I. (2001), Onderwijs en armoedebestrijding: op zoek naar een nieuwe adem. In: Vranken, J. *et al*, *Armoede en sociale uitsluiting. Jaarboek 2001*. Leuven: Acco.

Nicaise, I. (ed.) (2000), *The right to learn. Educational strategies for socially excluded youth in Europe*. Bristol: The Policy Press.

Observatorium van Welzijn en Gezondheid Brussel-Hoofdstad (2006), Welzijnsbarometer, Brussels Armoederapport.

OECD (2006), Where immigrants students succeed? A comparative review of performance and engagement in PISA 2003, Paris Cedex: OECD Publications.

OECD (2007), *PISA 2006. Science compentencies for Tomorrow's World,* Paris: OECD, 2 vol. (383 + 310p.).

OECD Family Database (2007) www.oecd.org/els/social/family/database

Paasch, O. (2007), Bildungspolitisches Gesamtkonzept, Antwort auf die Interpellation des Herrn G. PALM, Minister for Education and Scientific Research, Government of the German-speaking Community of Belgium.

Peer Review in Social Inclusion and Social Protection (2009), *Short Report: The City Strategy for tackling unemployment and child poverty*, Vienna: ÖSB.

Ruelens, L. and Nicaise, I. (2004), Expertennota 'Gelijke Onderwijskansen', in: Vlaams Netwerk van Verenigingen waar Armen het woord nemen and Team Armoede Vlaamse Gemeenschap (eds.), Final Report of Progress and Future of Poverty Conference, 6 May 2004, Brussels, Ministry of the Flemish Community.

Rijksdienst voor Kinderbijslag voor Werknemers (2003), 'Gezinsbeleid, een literatuurstudie', Brussels.

Ritakallio, V.M. and Bradshaw, J. (2005) 'Child Poverty in the European Union' SPRU Working Papers.

Ruelens, L., Dehandschutter, R., Ghesquière, P., Douterlungne, M., Maes, B., Vandenberghe, R. (2001), De overgang van het gewoon naar het buitengewoon basisonderwijs. Analyse van de verwijzingspraktijk in PMS/centra. Leuven: KULeuven / HIVA.

Ruxton, S. and Bennett, F. (2002), *Including Children? Developing a coherent approach to Child Poverty and Social Exclusion across Europe*, Brussels: Euronet.

Save the Children Greece (2000), *Promoting the Social Inclusion of Roma Populations*, ASOUN MAN project, SCG.

Service de lutte contre la pauvreté, la précarité et l'exclusion sociale (SLPPES – 2005a), *Lance-débat: 10 ans après le Rapport Général sur la Pauvreté*, Bruxelles: Centre pour l'Egalité des Chances et de Lutte contre le Racisme / SLPPES

SLPPES (2005b), *Abolir la pauvreté: une contribution au débat et à l'action politiques*, Bruxelles: Centre pour l'Egalité des Chances et de Lutte contre le Racisme / SLPPES / Chancellerie du Premier Ministre, 113p.

Social Protection Committee (2006), *Guidelines for preparing National Reports on Strate-*

*gies for Social Protection and Social Inclusion*, Brussels: European Commission.

Social Protection Committee (2008), *Child Poverty and Well-Being in the EU: Current status and way forward*, Luxembourg: office for Official Publications of the European Communities. Available from:
http://ec.europa.eu/social/main.jsp?catId=751&langId=en&pubId=74&type=2&furtherPubs=yes.

Solera, C. (1999), 'Income Transfers and Support for Mothers' Employment: The Link to Child Poverty Risks: A Comparison between Italy, Sweden and the UK' LIS Working Paper No. 192.

Steenssens, K., Agauilar, L.-M., Demeyer, B., Fontaine, P., Corveleyn, J., Van Regenmortel, T., *Enfants et pauvreté. Situation de la recherche scientifique en Belgique*, Leuven: GIREP/IGOA, 133 p.

TARKI (2010), *Child Poverty and Child Well-Being in the European Union*, Report prepared for the European Commission (Directorate-General "Employment, Social Affairs and Equal Opportunities"; Unit E.2), Budapest. Available from:
http://www.tarki.hu/en/research/childpoverty/index.html.

Trifiletti, R. *et al* (2007), Study on Poverty and Social Exclusion among Lone Parent Households, Brussels: European Commission.

UK Presidency of the European Union (2005), Event Summary Document, European Round Table Conference, UK Government.

UNICEF (2007), *Child poverty in perspective: an overview of child well-being in rich countries,* Report Card 7, Florence: UNICEF Innocenti Research Centre.

UNICEF Innocenti Research Centre (2002), A league table of educational disadvantage in rich nations (Report Card 4).

Van Robbaeys and Perrin (2006) *Armoede bij personen van vreemde herkomst becijferd.* Oases/Cedem.

Vandenbroucke, F. (2006a), Schoolkosten: voorstellen voor een nieuw Vlaams beleid, Brussels: Flemish Minister for Education, Training and Work.

Vandenbroucke, F. (2006b), Leren en werken (discussion paper), Brussels: Flemish Minister for Education, Training and Work.

Vandenbroucke, F. (2007a), Een nieuw financieringssysteem voor basis- en secundair onderwijs: helder, voorspelbaar en effectief, Speech given in Leuven on 2 February 2007, Flemish Minister for Education, Training and Work.

Vandenbroucke, F. (2007b), Conceptnota Leerzorg, Brussels: Flemish Minister of Education, Training and Work.

Vanpée, K., Sannen, L., Hedebouw, G. (2000), Kinderopvang in Vlaanderen. Gebruik, keuze van de opvangvorm en evaluatie door de ouders, Leuven: HIVA, 348p.

Vervotte, I. (2006), *Globaal plan jeugdzorg. De kwetsbaarheid voorbij... opnieuw verbinding maken*, Brussels: Office of the Flemish Minister of Well-being, Health Care and the Family.

Vleminckx, Koen and Smeeding, Timothy (eds.) (2000), *Child Well-Being, Child Poverty and Child Policy in Modern Nations. What Do We Know?* Bristol: The Policy Press.

Vranken, J. De Boyser, K. and Dierckx, D. (red.) (2006) *Jaarboek Armoede en Sociale Uit-sluiting 2006.* Leuven-Leusden: Acco.

Walther, A. and Pohl, A. (2006), *Thematic study on policy measures concerning disadvan-taged youth*, Brussels: European Commission.

Williams, A. (2003), *Families under stress: supporting services in Europe*, Brussels: European Forum for Child Welfare (EFCW).

# 3 Active Inclusion

This chapter documents and analyses most of the reports that have emerged on Active Inclusion since it became a key issue in the Social OMC in about 2006. Sections 3.1 and 3.2 summarise some of the key lessons and conclusions that can be learned on active inclusion from the experience of the Social Open Method of Coordination (OMC) between 2000 and 2010. Section 3.3 then considers active inclusion policies in Belgium. Finally, Section 3.4 draws some conclusions and makes recommendations for strengthening EU action on active inclusion in the future.

## 3.1 Active inclusion in the EU Social OMC

### 3.1.1 What is active inclusion?

"Active Inclusion" can be seen as a "concept" or "approach" aimed at promoting the greater social inclusion and participation in the labour market and in society of those of working age who are experiencing poverty and social exclusion. The concept was developed and agreed by the European Commission and Member States as a means to strengthen the effectiveness of the social inclusion strand of the Social OMC. More particularly, the aim of the EU's Active Inclusion initiative is to encourage all Member States to design and implement a comprehensive and integrated set of social inclusion policies which "should facilitate the integration into sustainable, quality employment of those who can work and provide resources which are sufficient to live in dignity, together with support for social participation, for those who cannot" (European Commission, 2008a). In other words, it is aimed **both** at supporting the inclusion and participation of those who can work into the labour market **and** the inclusion and participation of those who cannot work (either temporarily or in the longer term) into society.

The active inclusion approach is built around three key policy "pillars": adequate income support, inclusive labour markets and access to quality services. It is based on the understanding that "the active inclusion of people excluded from the labour market requires the design and implementation of a comprehensive strategy combining in an integrated way adequate income support, inclusive labour markets and access to quality services" (European Commission, 2008c).

### 3.1.2    Why is active inclusion a priority in the Social OMC?

There are five main reasons why active inclusion has become an important element of
the Social OMC since 2006:

- Learning from the Social OMC in its first phase (2000-2005) reinforced understanding of the multidimensional nature of poverty and social exclusion and
thus of the need to develop comprehensive policy responses that combine employment, income support and access to services in an integrated manner. At
the same time, it was clear that many Member States lacked such integrated
approaches and that many had rather unbalanced approaches overemphasising
employment policies at the expense of income support and/or access to services.

- Between 2000 and 2005, the social strand of the Lisbon Strategy had been
much weaker than the economic and employment strands, and there was a danger that with the refocusing of the Lisbon Strategy on growth and jobs in 2005
it would be further downgraded. Thus, in part, the development of active inclusion as a concept was an effort to reinforce the social inclusion strand within
the newly streamlined Social OMC (see Chapter 1) and to create stronger
linkages between employment and social inclusion policies.

- From the very beginning of the Social OMC in 2000, there had been a major
emphasis on employment as the best means of countering poverty and social
exclusion. However, by 2005 it had become clear that the European Employment Strategy had been less successful in reaching those most distant from the
labour market and that additional and more comprehensive efforts were needed
to help those people who are most distant to access employment. It was also
clear that for some people access to employment is not a realistic solution and
that they need a range of supports for them to be integrated into and able to
lead an active life in society.

- There was a long-standing commitment to advance the 1992 EU Council of
Ministers' Recommendation on common criteria concerning sufficient resources and social assistance in social protection systems[72] in the context of
the Social OMC. However, in practice relatively little attention was given to
this issue in the 2000-2005 period. This led to considerable pressure from key
actors in the EU Social OMC (notably the various EU poverty networks and
the European Parliament) to give more attention to the question of adequate
minimum income. There was also a growing awareness that in many Member
States existing schemes were not effective enough. While the Commission (or

---

72    This Recommendation urged EU Member States "to recognise the basic right of a person to sufficient resources and social assistance to live in a manner compatible with human dignity as part
of a comprehensive and consistent drive to combat social exclusion" (Council, 1992).

more particularly Directorate-General "Employment, Social Affairs and Equal Opportunities") was keen to advance this issue, there was a reluctance among several Member States to give much focus to minimum income issues. The development of the Active Inclusion approach, by linking income support to employment and services, created a framework within which it was easier for Member States, in the context of the Social Protection Committee (SPC), to address the question of adequate income support and in particular to address the issues raised in the 1992 Recommendation.

- Up until the adoption in 2008 of the EU Active Inclusion approach, there was a tendency for labour market, income support and access to services policies to be treated separately both in the Lisbon Strategy generally and in the Social OMC in particular. The development of the Active Inclusion approach has created a framework in which the Commission and Member States can handle these three pillars in a more coherent manner.

### 3.1.3 What have been the main developments at EU level?

Active inclusion only emerged as an issue in the EU Social OMC in 2006. Indeed, there is still no reference to active inclusion as late as the 2006 *Joint Report on Social Protection and Social Inclusion* or any earlier such reports. However, during the period 2000-2005 much of the learning that underpins the concept of active inclusion was developed in the context of the Social OMC and the three pillars of active inclusion were highlighted consistently in earlier Joint Reports.

The following is a summary of some the key events in the development of the Active Inclusion concept since 2005:

- 2005: In its *New Social Agenda 2005-2010*, the Commission outlines its intention to instigate "a Community initiative on Minimum Income Schemes and the integration of people excluded from the labour market". (European Commission, 2005)
- 2006: The Commission develops the idea of active inclusion[73] and launches a

---

73    It concludes that the "evidence suggests that a comprehensive policy mix combining three elements is justified: (i) a link to the labour market through job opportunities or vocational training; (ii) income support at a level that is sufficient for people to have a dignified life; and (iii) better access to services that may help remove some of the hurdles encountered by some individuals and their families in entering mainstream society, thereby supporting their re-insertion into employment (through, for instance, counselling, healthcare, child-care, lifelong learning to remedy educational disadvantages, ICT training to help would-be workers, including people with disabilities, take advantage of new technologies and more flexible work arrangements, psychological and social rehabilitation). Such an approach may be termed *active inclusion*." (European Commission, 2006a)

public consultation on possible guidelines for action at EU level with a view to promoting the active inclusion of people furthest from the labour market. Many Member States and stakeholders in the EU Social OMC make submissions. (European Commission, 2006a and 2006b)

- 2007: The *Joint Report on Social Protection and Social Inclusion* stresses in its Key Messages that "Active inclusion emerges as a powerful means of promoting the social and labour market integration of the most disadvantaged. Increased conditionality in accessing benefits is a major component, but this must not push those unable to work further into social exclusion. While most Member States champion a balanced approach combining personalised labour market support, including skills training, for those who have the potential to work, and accessible, high-quality social services, more attention needs to be given to ensuring adequate levels of minimum resources for all, balanced with making work pay." (Council, 2007)

- 2007: The Commission draws on the results of the 2006 consultation and the initiatives that followed[74] to set out proposals for deepening the OMC in this area through the adoption of common principles and their subsequent monitoring and evaluation and to launch a second consultation. Many Member States and stakeholders in the Social OMC make submissions. (European Commission, 2007)

- 2007: The Presidency Conclusions of the Brussels European Council (14 December) stress that "active inclusion policies should combine integration in the labour markets, mobility of the workforce, motivation to actively search for a job, adequate income support and quality, accessible and effective social services". It also "reaffirms its commitment with the decent work agenda as a global instrument to promote employment, better labour standards and foster development".

- 2008 (March): The *Joint Report on Social Protection and Social Inclusion* stresses that "comprehensive active inclusion policies for those furthest away from the labour market enhance human capital and labour supply while also strengthening society's cohesiveness". (Council, 2008)

- 2008 (July): The Commission announces that it will in 2008/2009 "propose a Recommendation on active inclusion covering questions of income support, links with the labour market and better access to quality services." And it continues: "The planned 2010 Year of inclusion and the fight against poverty will provide the opportunity for a renewed political commitment on the part of the EU and its Member States to those fundamental goals of the EC Treaty." (European Commission, 2008b)

---

74   For instance, an in-depth peer review by the Social Protection Committee of the NAPs/inclusion, the sixth conference of people experiencing poverty (4-5 May 2007) and the stakeholders' conference on active inclusion (15 June 2007).

- 2008 (October): The Commission adopts a Recommendation on the active inclusion of people excluded from the labour market, containing common principles and practical guidelines on a comprehensive strategy based on the integration of three policy pillars, namely: adequate income support, inclusive labour markets and access to quality services. This Recommendation is accompanied by a Commission Communication. (European Commission, 2008a and 2008c)

- 2008 (June): Martin Hirsch, French High Commissioner for Active Solidarity addresses a European Anti-Poverty Network (EAPN) seminar in Paris on active inclusion and stresses the great importance that the future French Presidency of the EU attaches to the concept of active inclusion (see Frazer, 2008b).

- 2008 (October): The *EU Round Table on Poverty and Social Exclusion* organised under the auspices of the French Presidency of the EU focuses on active inclusion.

- 2008 (December): The *EU Council of Ministers* endorses "the aim of designing and implementing comprehensive and integrated national strategies to promote the active inclusion of people excluded from the labour market, combining adequate income support, inclusive labour markets and access to quality services on the basis of the common principles and guidelines identified in the European Commission Recommendation".

- 2009 (March): The *Joint Report on Social Protection and Social Inclusion* stresses that "comprehensive active inclusion measures are needed to address the situation of those furthest from the labour market". (Council, 2009)

- 2009 (May): The European Parliament adopts a (non-legislative) resolution welcoming the Commission's Recommendation and endorsing the proposed common principles and practical guidelines on the three pillar active inclusion strategy. It points out in particular that "any active inclusion strategy has to be built on the principles of individual rights, respect for human dignity and non-discrimination, equality of opportunities and gender equality, on the promotion of labour market integration combined with full participation in society, and on the realisation of the principles of quality, adequacy and accessibility across all three pillars". The Parliament also states that "the implementation of Recommendation 92/441/EEC needs to be improved in relation to minimum income and social transfers" and that "social assistance should provide an adequate minimum income for a dignified life, at least at a level which is above the "at risk of poverty" level and sufficient to lift people out of poverty". (European Parliament, 2009)

- 2009 (throughout the year): the Commission instigates the first steps in monitoring and evaluating active inclusion strategies in Member States. As a contribution to this process, the EU Network of Independent Experts on Social

Inclusion produces national reports assessing Member States' minimum income schemes as well as an overall Synthesis Report with policy conclusions and concrete suggestions on the way forward (Frazer and Marlier, 2009).[75]

- 2010: Promoting integrated approaches to active inclusion is a priority theme in the European Year for Combating Poverty and Social Exclusion and at the opening conference for the Year the President of the Commission stressed that "for the "Europe 2020" strategy to have a real impact on poverty and social exclusion it can not be confined to the more traditional measures. While employment is usually the best safeguard against poverty and exclusion, for 8% of Europeans having a job has not been enough to escape poverty. This situation is clearly unacceptable. Work must be a way out of poverty. It is now time to get a new political consensus on this issue in Europe. Part of this political consensus must be "active inclusion" policies that guarantee citizens a minimum additional income supplement and access to quality services (for example in child care or housing), with everything they need to be able to contribute to society. Needless to say, those for whom work is not a realistic option should also have an adequate minimum income that allows them to live a decent life. For this reason, the "Europe 2020" strategy should adopt a very ambitious approach, using the various instruments required for reaching as many people as possible. The goal should be a society that does not leave anyone on the road." (Barroso, 2010)[76]

- 2010: The *Joint Report on Social Protection and Social Inclusion* stresses that "Balanced active inclusion strategies, combining adequate income support, access to the labour market and to social services, can reconcile the goals of fighting

---

75  We would like to acknowledge the contribution of the members of this EU Network, which is funded by the European Commission, as their published reports have been an important source of material when drafting this chapter. See Frazer and Marlier, 2009. And for each Member State's national independent reports on "Minimum Income Schemes", see: http://www.peer-review-social-inclusion.eu/network-of-independent-experts/2009/minimum-income-schemes.

76  Authors' translation into English of the official speech by President Barroso available in French and Spanish from http://europa.eu/rapid/pressReleasesAction.do?reference=SPEECH/10/12. The French official text reads as follows:
"Pour influer réellement sur la pauvreté et l'exclusion sociale, la stratégie «UE 2020» devra sortir du cadre des mesures classiques. Bien que l'emploi offre généralement la meilleure protection contre la pauvreté et l'exclusion, le simple fait d'avoir un emploi n'a pas permis à quelque 8 % des Européens d'échapper à la pauvreté. Cette situation est clairement inadmissible. Le travail doit être un moyen de sortir de la pauvreté. Le moment est venu de dégager un nouveau consensus politique sur cette question en Europe. Ce consensus politique doit englober les politiques d'«inclusion active», qui garantissent aux citoyens un revenu complémentaire minimum et l'accès à des services de qualité, par exemple en matière de garde d'enfants ou de logement, avec tous les éléments dont ils ont besoin pour pouvoir apporter leur contribution à la société."

poverty, increasing labour market participation, and enhancing efficiency of social spending" (Council, 2010).

In addition to the key political moments identified above, there is a growing body of work which examines active inclusion in more detail and highlights some of the practical realities of implementing such an approach. These can be found in particular in various peer reviews, in the work of various EU Networks (such as COFACE, EAPN, ESN and Eurochild[77]) and in several of the reports of the EU Network of Independent Experts on Social Inclusion. Finally, it should also be mentioned that the Indicators Sub-Group of the SPC is working towards a comprehensive set of indicators to ensure a proper follow-up to the implementation of the various dimensions of the 2008 Recommendation.

## 3.2 Extent of active inclusion approach in the EU

As highlighted in the preceding section, active inclusion is still a relatively new concept in the EU's policy armoury. The full implementation of the principles identified in the 2008 Commission's Recommendation remains to be achieved in many countries and especially the effective balanced integration of the three pillars. Thus the *2009 Joint Report on Social Protection and Social Inclusion*, in assessing Member States 2008-2010 National Strategy Reports on Social Protection and Social Inclusion (NSRSPSIs), notes that "As in the 2006 National Strategy Reports, most Member States have active inclusion among their priorities. However, inclusive labour markets, access to quality services and adequate income are dealt with separately in most cases, whereas most disadvantaged people suffer from multiple disadvantages and integrated responses are essential. Several countries have taken steps to ensure that the purchasing power of minimum incomes is maintained. It remains essential to design better links between out-of-work benefits and in-work support, in order to create the right incentives, while at the same time ensuring adequate income support and prevent in-work poverty. Coordinated social and employment services are needed to tackle obstacles to full and lasting participation in society and the labour market. So more attention must be paid to optimising the interaction between the three strands and ensuring that due account is given to each."

Overall, there is some evidence that linkages between minimum income schemes (MISs) and inclusive labour market policies are more often evident than specific linkages ensuring access to quality services. (Frazer and Marlier, 2009)

---

77    EAPN played a prominent role in pushing forward the concept of Active Inclusion (see for instance EAPN 2008 and Frazer 2008b) and the European Social Network have had a Policy to Practice Working Group on the topic (see European Social Network, 2008 and 2009). See also COFACE (2009).

### 3.2.1    *Adequate minimum income*

Evidence from the Social OMC suggests at least six main reasons why minimum income schemes are an essential element in the struggle against poverty and social exclusion in general and in promoting active inclusion in particular:

- minimum income schemes give substance and reality to the right of all to a life of dignity and they have a role in embedding solidarity as a core societal value;
- if well organised, they can help to support the transition from unemployment to work and, together with minimum wage and tax reliefs, ensure that those who are working have an income sufficient to lift them and their families out of poverty;
- they can provide the security needed by people distant from the labour market to engage in active labour market programmes and to start on paths of progression towards employment;
- they can contribute to efficiency by improving the functioning of the labour market through supporting increased acceptance of flexibility and facilitating greater mobility in the labour force through job search and re-skilling;
- they enhance social equity and social solidarity by supporting those who do not have the capacity or possibility to work and by enabling them to be included and active in society; and
- they can prevent people falling into extreme poverty and their problems becoming deep-seated and intractable. (See also Frazer 2008a.)

In spite of the importance of ensuring an adequate minimum income for all, the minimum income pillar of the Recommendation on active inclusion remains very underdeveloped. For instance, it is striking that in their 2008-2010 NAPs/inclusion most Member States did not prioritise the issue of an adequate income (both for those at work and those not at work, whether looking for a job or unable to work). This is not because most MISs are adequate. Indeed, as highlighted in the aforementioned analysis by the EU Network of Independent Experts on Social Inclusion: even if they "do play a very important role in reducing the intensity of poverty" across the EU, "most countries' MISs fall short of allowing all people to live life with dignity and many fall far short" (see below, Figures 3.1a-3.1c). This leads the Network to suggest that "urgent action is required if the minimum income pillar of the Commission's October 2008 Recommendation on active inclusion, the Council Conclusions of December 2008 and indeed the 1992 Council Recommendation are to become a reality." (Frazer and Marlier, 2009)

While most Member States have some form of MIS these vary widely in their coverage, comprehensiveness (i.e. to the extent to which schemes are non categorical and apply to the generality of the low income population) and effectiveness. In many countries, they play an important role in reducing the intensity of poverty but do not actually lift people out of poverty. Key issues that need to be addressed in many schemes are:

- the lack of clarity as to what constitutes an adequate income to live life with dignity;
- a lack of transparency and consistency in how levels of payments are established leading to inadequate levels of payments;
- a lack of clear mechanisms for uprating payments over time leading to a decline in the value of payments;
- an undue focus on reducing financial disincentives to work at the expense of ensuring the adequacy of benefits;
- limited or partial coverage of some low income groups;
- high levels of non-take up arising from poor delivery arrangements, the complexity of schemes, inadequate income, excessive use of discretion and fear of stigmatisation.

The important role played by MISs has come into sharper focus with the current economic and financial crisis. Monitoring of social impact of the crisis has highlighted in many Member States they have significantly contributed to limiting the poverty and social exclusion impacts of the crisis. It has also highlighted the key role that MISs play as automatic stabilisers at a time of economic crisis. Indeed, as emphasised in the *2010 Joint Report on Social Protection and Social Inclusion* "firm policy intervention and the automatic stabilisers embedded in European welfare systems have limited the economic and social impact of the worst recession in decades." (Council, 2010). However, at the same time, this monitoring of the crisis has revealed that the effectiveness of MISs varies widely across the EU and that some Member States have large gaps in their schemes that will need to be addressed in the future. It is also striking that, in spite of growing demand, many Member States have maintained and in some cases increased levels of income support during the crisis. On the other hand, in a significant minority of Member States governments are restricting or failing to uprate their income support systems, thus deepening the poverty impacts of the crisis.

*Cross-country comparisons*
An in-depth EU comparative study of the generosity and adequacy of social assistance schemes in the different Member States is beyond the scope of this study. However, before moving to the next section whose focus is on the second pillar of the active inclusion approach (Inclusive labour markets), we find it useful to present some statistical evidence on this for a number of countries.[78]

Figures 3.1a and 3.1b show the value of social assistance as a proportion of the average

---

78 We would like to thank Jonathan Bradshaw for providing us with Figures 3.1a-3.1c and also for very useful related discussions. See also Bradshaw and Bennett (2009).

wage; they are based on the *OECD Benefits and Wages* data base. The results show a very wide disparity between the countries covered and also between different family types within countries. The OECD assumes a rent of 20% of the average wage which is probably too high for most social assistance recipients so Figure 3.1a includes the housing benefit paid on this rent and Figure 3.1b excludes it. Among the EU countries covered by this analysis, the most generous social assistance levels including housing benefit are in Ireland and the Czech Republic. In contrast, Italy has no nationally-organised MIS and Greece has very low payments only for the families with children (see Frazer and Marlier 2009 for more detailed information). The rank order of the countries changes somewhat if housing benefit is excluded.

**Figure 3.1a: Net incomes on social assistance (including housing benefit) as a % of the average wage – 2007**

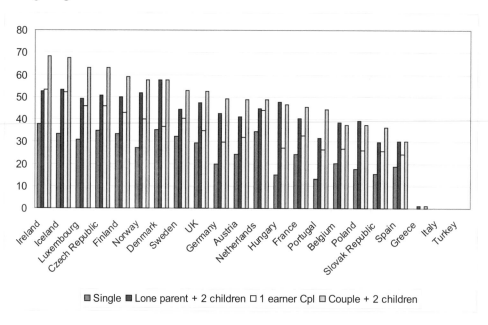

*Source: Bradshaw's analysis of OECD Benefits and Wages data base.*

**Figure 3.1b: Net incomes on social assistance (excluding housing benefit) as a % of the average wage – 2007**

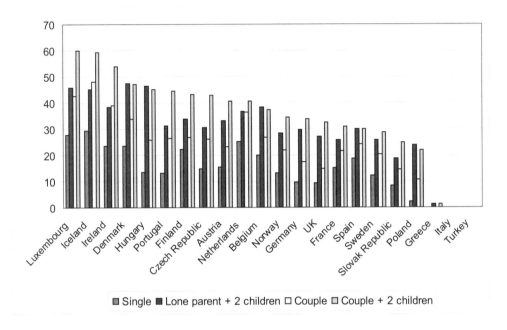

*Source: Bradshaw's' analysis of OECD Benefits and Wages data base.*

Figure 3.1c (next page) replicates and updates the comparative analysis of social assistance by Bradshaw and Finch (2002). It provides the monthly amount of out of work social assistance for two family types, as at January 2004 (Bradshaw, 2006).[79] This again shows very wide variations for the EU countries included, with the Czech Republic and Slovakia at the bottom and Austria and Denmark at the top.

---

79  Bradshaw, J. (2006) 'Child benefit packages in fifteen countries', in Lewis, J. (ed.), *Children, Changing Families and Welfare States*, Cheltenham: Edward Elgar.

**Figure 3.1c: Monthly amount of out of work social assistance for two family types (in Purchasing Power Standards (PPS)[80], 2004)**

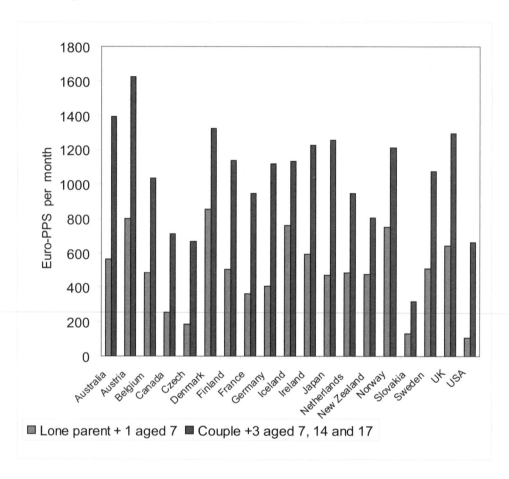

*Source: Bradshaw, 2006 and http://www.york.ac.uk/inst/spru/research/nordic/childben-efit2004%2018%20countries.pdf*

### Limited impact of MISs in reducing poverty levels

In the absence of clear definitions of adequacy and what is necessary to ensure the right to live in dignity, looking at the levels of income against poverty lines, and in particular

---

80   PPS can be defined as "artificial Euros" that correct for the differences in the cost of living in the different Member States.

against the national at-risk-of poverty lines[81], provides some basis for assessment as was also suggested by the European Parliament in its May 2009 Resolution (see above, Section 3.1.3). The analysis of national MISs in the 27 EU countries carried out in 2009 by the EU Network of Independent Experts on Social Inclusion (Op. Cit.) largely bear out the European Commission's assessment a year before which emphasises that "in most Member States and for most family types, social assistance alone is not sufficient to lift beneficiaries out of poverty." (European Commission, 2008c) Quite in line with the Commission's analysis, even though some of them question the statistical evidence on which it is based[82], the experts' reports suggest that the countries which come closest to achieving the at-risk-of-poverty threshold with their MISs are Ireland, Sweden, The Netherlands and Denmark.

### 3.2.2 Inclusive labour markets

In most Member States, the most developed of the three active inclusion pillars is the inclusive labour market pillar. Virtually all Member States prioritised an inclusive labour market in their 2008-2010 NAPs/inclusion. The plans provide some evidence that a growing number of countries are developing a more multidimensional approach, which reflects to some extent an active inclusion approach, even if the adequacy and comprehensiveness of the measures under some pillars is sometimes questioned. However, in many Member States there is a rather narrow approach to increasing access to employment which fails to take into account the important contribution that the minimum income and services pillars can make to achieving this goal.

While in most Member States there is a trend to strengthen activation measures, these are often not sufficiently targeted at or tailored to meet the needs of the most vulnerable

---

81  As mentioned above, for each country the agreed EU definition sets the at-risk-of-poverty line at 60% of the country's national median equivalised household income.

82  The Commission's analysis is based on a statistic which is part of the portfolio of "context statistics" (as opposed to "indicators" per se) that have been adopted at EU level for monitoring the Social OMC. For each country and for 3 different types of household (one-person households, single-parents with 2 children and couples with 2 children), this statistic provides the ratio between the net income of social assistance recipients (drawn from simulations based on model families) and the national poverty threshold (calculated from the "Community Statistics on Income and Living Conditions (EU-SILC)" micro-data). Even though this statistic provides useful information on the adequacy of MISs in the different Member States, this information needs to be interpreted cautiously in view of the very wide range of possible benefit entitlements than can be available in some countries. A clear illustration of this is provided for most OECD countries in Immervoll (2009).

groups and those who are most distant from the labour market.[83] There is some evidence beginning to emerge that this problem is becoming more acute in the context of the current economic and financial crisis.[84] This limited adoption of an active inclusion approach when promoting an inclusive labour market is also evident in Member States' 2008-2010 National Reform Programmes for Growth and Jobs where the active inclusion agenda is only taken into account in a fairly limited number of Programmes.

### 3.2.3    Access to quality services

The importance of access to quality public services (particularly health, education and training, housing and social services) as a critical element in preventing and tackling poverty and social exclusion has emerged as a key theme in the Social OMC since 2000.[85] However, to date access to quality public services is probably the pillar of active inclusion which has received the least attention. This needs to change as it is clear that people who are furthest from the labour market and who are most excluded require intensive well-coordinated support from social, employment, health, education, housing and income services. Public services and especially social services supporting people furthest from the labour market play (or at least should play) a key role in helping people to move towards the labour market or, for those for whom this is not a realistic option, alternative forms of participation in society. To ensure that this is the case there is a need to integrate the experience and expertise of local public services providers into the Social OMC as their

---

83    There are, however, a growing number of good examples from the Social OMC process of more tailored and targeted programmes to reach the most vulnerable. See, for example, the Peer Review reports on *Developing well-targeted tools for the active inclusion of vulnerable people, Initiatives by the social partners for improving the labour market access of disadvantaged groups, The social economy from the perspective of active inclusion* and *Integrated Services in Rehabilitation – On Coordination of Organisation and Financing* (Peer Review in Social Protection and Social Inclusion, 2009, 2008a, 2008b and 2006). See also the 2006 (Begg *et al*, 2006) and 2009 reports of the EU Network of Independent Experts on Social Inclusion (Frazer and Marlier, 2009: Section 4.1 on *Minimum income schemes and inclusive labour markets*), the Nicis Institute examples of good practice (Nicis Institute, 2008) and Urbact projects (Urbact 11, 2008).

84    See, for instance: Immervoll 2009.

85    In this regard, the establishment of a regular Forum on social services of general interest (SSGI) has been an important development. The first Forum was held in September 2007 under the Portuguese Presidency of the EU and the second one under the French Presidency in October 2008. These conferences have provided an important framework for Member States to discuss issues such as access to quality services and how to enhance legal certainty in the field of SSGI (i.e. acknowledgement by the internal market and competition regulations of the specificities of SSGI). A third Forum will be organised in October 2010 under the Belgian Presidency; it will *inter alia* receive and discuss the European Commission Second Biennial Report on SSGI.

direct experience on the ground of working with those who are most vulnerable can provide valuable direction for effective policy-making.

The importance of local services in providing support to people has become increasingly evident during the financial and economic crisis. In many Member States, there is growing pressure on services, particularly at local level, where funding of services is often becoming an increasing problem. However, while services in some countries are being restricted because of the economic crisis, it is encouraging that in several countries economic stimulus packages are being used to invest in and upgrade their education, health and social services and housing infrastructures and that there are new initiatives to counter the negative impacts of the crisis which are particularly evident in the area of housing, education and training and financial advice and counselling.

## 3.3 Active inclusion in Belgium

In this section, Belgium's active inclusion policy will be discussed from the perspective of minimum income schemes. As in the European sections, the text will deal with the three key elements of active inclusion, namely (1) the guarantee of a minimum standard of living, (2) the access to employment, and (3) the access to affordable quality services. We start with a brief discussion of the general context of the Belgian minimum income schemes.

Belgian minimum income schemes are part of a broader institutional design referred to as the 'right to social integration', formalised in the law of 26 May 2002 regarding the right to social integration which replaced the former (1974) law on 'subsistence minimum'. As such, this law also formalised the paradigm shift to a more emancipatory and active welfare state approach to minimum income schemes, developed since the mid-1990s. In fact, it was feared that the mere provision of a financial minimum benefit – the 'living wage' – would push people into a powerless acquiescence. As a consequence, the right to social integration has been conceived not only as an individual right, but also an individual goal. To achieve this goal, the legislation provides three important instruments, namely (1) the living wage and/or (2) employment, embedded in (3) an 'individualised project for social integration'. In other words, the right to social integration takes up two important challenges: (1) adequate income protection (through the living wage) and (2) integration into the labour market (through employment and the individualised project).

For a full picture of the Belgian minimum income schemes, a formal distinction must be made between the 'right to social integration' (RSI) and the 'right to social assistance' (RSA). Although interrelated, they can be considered to some extent as separate schemes. Since the RSI is embedded in a universal, comprehensive legal framework, its approach to minimum income and poverty is structural in nature. The RSA lacks this comprehensive framework and the approach is contingent on very specific social conditions and social needs that differ from municipality to municipality and from person to person. Furthermore, the RSI is limited to essentially two forms of support – i.e. employment and the living wage, while the RSA includes various forms of support:

- for households benefiting from the RSI it may include *additional* financial support;
- those ineligible for 'social integration' still have a legal right to social assistance. This may mean financial support equivalent to the living wage, or in-kind help. For example, it may include urgent medical assistance (for undocumented immigrants), financial support for medical and housing costs, additional child support, etc.

The effective delivery of the RSI and RSA is guaranteed by the municipal Public Centres for Social Welfare (PCSW). Due to the existence of a uniform legislative framework, the PCSWs have little discretionary competence in the field of social integration. In the field of social assistance, on the contrary, practice differs widely. As such, the increased discretionary competence allows for differentiated support according the specific social conditions and needs. However, it may also result in unequal treatment of beneficiaries and legal insecurity (Van Mechelen and Bogaerts, 2008; Steenssens *et al*, 2007).

### 3.3.1    Minimum income: coverage, (non-)take-up, and adequacy

Applicants for the RSI have to reside in Belgium and be aged over 18, have a Belgian or European nationality, or be a foreigner registered in the national register, a recognised refugee, or displaced person; they need to demonstrate insufficient (financial) resources, show their willingness to work (unless prevented by health or equity reasons); and have exhausted their rights to any other (social) benefit.

In theory, the *coverage* of the RSI (and the RSA) is quasi-universal. Moreover, the eligibility conditions are interpreted with some flexibility: the residence criterion is interpreted in terms of 'affinity' (with Belgium) rather than in geographical terms, the adulthood criterion does not exclude 'unaccompanied minors'. Whereas the nationality criterion is rather strict and excludes undocumented migrants who, strictly speaking, are only entitled to urgent medical care and education for their children, the 'willingness to work' criterion should be interpreted as an 'effort commitment' rather than a 'result commitment' on the part of the applicant. The last condition indicates the primarily residual nature of the RSI. The other sources of income refer to the societal as well as the family level (e.g. unemployment benefits, disability benefits as well as alimony).

In practice, the coverage can be more problematic, for example, for roof- and homeless people, because applicants need to be enrolled in the national register. The roof- and homeless have often been removed from the municipal register of their previous residence, thereby closing the door on application for a minimum income. Since 1994, however, roof- and homeless people with no legal address can apply for a 'reference address' (i.e., an address where the person concerned will receive his/her mail and administrative documents) which is equivalent to enrolling in the national register. In spite of this measure, the access to minimum income remains problematic. This is partly due to the lack of information on the reference address, but to some extent also to the unwillingness of some PCSWs to handle a reference address.

**Table 3.1: The average monthly number of beneficiaries of the RSI and the RSA**

|  | RSI | | | RSA | | |
|---|---|---|---|---|---|---|
|  | 1999 | 2004 | 2008 | 1999 | 2004 | 2008 |
| Flemish Region | 28,148 | 25,509 | 25,620 | 17,138 | 23,038 | 10,760 |
| Walloon Region | 39,196 | 37,784 | 41,276 | 8,197 | 13,065 | 7,536 |
| Brussels Capital Region | 13,981 | 20,596 | 25,284 | 6,536 | 10,382 | 10,760 |
| Belgium | 81,325 | 83,890 | **92,181** | 31,871 | 46,484 | **31,125** |

*Source: PPS Social Integration; http://www.mi-is.be*

Table 3.1 displays trends in the case load of both the RSI and the RSA. The rise in the overall number of RSI beneficiaries can be attributed to the 2002 law on social integration, which put citizens of foreign origin on equal footing with Belgian nationals. As a consequence of this law, many foreigners were transferred from the RSA to the RSI. The sharp decline in the RSA caseload between 2004 and 2008 can also be explained by the replacement of financial with in-kind support to asylum seekers (which discouraged them to apply). Note also that the national figures conceal strongly diverging trends between the regions: whereas Flanders shows a favourable evolution, the number of beneficiaries in Brussels has almost doubled in a decade.

The vast majority of RSI beneficiaries (90%) receive a living wage. Almost half of the living-wage beneficiaries appear to be single persons (46%), 28% are cohabitants, while 27% draw a benefit as a household head. The majority of the beneficiaries are women – 56% in 1999 and 59% in 2008. More than one third (35%) are below age 30. Non-EU citizens make up 20%. Finally, more and more beneficiaries tend to depend fully on the living wage, with roughly 60% receiving the full amount in 1999, as against approximately 70% in 2008.

Compared to the RSI benefit, the RSA benefit is less substantial and is decreasing – see Table 3.1. The majority of RSA-recipients (62%) receive financial aid (also known as the living-wage equivalent). Contrary to the 'regular' living wage, the living-wage equivalent is more often handed out to men (53% in 2008), youngsters (below age 30 – 38%), and more often to single persons (47%) than cohabitants (23%) or families (30%).

Although the theoretical coverage by the RSI and RSA is quasi-universal, the *lack of effective recipiency* remains an important issue. Note that lack of protection by the minimum income system as the 'last safety net' should be clearly distinguished from non-take-up, as there are many possible reasons why households living below the MI-level do not draw the (full) benefit:
- they may not be entitled due to legal restrictions;
- they may be entitled without applying (non-take-up, properly speaking);
- they may be denied access or receive less than the due amount by mistake;
- they may refuse to comply with additional discretionary conditions, such as activation requirements, enforced sale of property, debt management, etc.;
- they may have lost their benefit due to sanctions or suspension;
- they may draw a partial benefit due to seizure for debt reimbursement.

Research concerning the lack of effective protection is limited and somewhat dated (e.g. Groenez and Nicaise, 2002; Nicaise *et al*, 2004 – both on the basis of panel data from the 1990s). According to these studies the proportion of individuals falling through the safety net – i.e. the rate of 'under-protection' in the population – (3.9%) was larger than the proportion of individuals rescued by the safety net (1.2%) (Groenez and Nicaise, 2002). The 'quasi-universal coverage' would thus be a rather biased picture of reality. Furthermore, from an international perspective, the issue of 'under-protection' in minimum income systems is similar in the neighbour countries (Nicaise *et al*, 2004). The likelihood of falling below the national minimum income threshold without receiving financial assistance (in Belgium) is greater for women, couples, individuals with an education level below the second stage of secondary, and the -24 age cohort (Groenez and Nicaise, 2002). Note that the gender and age characteristics are common to RSI beneficiaries and under-protected individuals.

The reasons for *non-take-up* have been the subject of some further research (e.g. Vercauteren and Daems, 1995; Steenssens *et al*, 2007). In fact, every applicant has to overcome a number of consecutive barriers before effectively applying for the RSI. A first cluster of barriers can be summarised as the perceived need of financial help. The applicant first needs to identify his own situation as one of need and of insecurity. Knowledge forms a second barrier. This knowledge does not only comprise basic knowledge about the minimum income schemes and the existence of PCSWs, but also the identification of the personal situation as one that gives right to the RSI or RSA. Since every PCSW has the obligation to inform potential beneficiaries, the former problem should be limited. Resistance against the social system as a whole, or the PCSW in particular (for example, due to prior conflicts) may constitute a third barrier. Fourthly, some households may perceive financial assistance as useless in their situation. Finally, psycho-social barriers such as feelings of shame or pride must be mentioned. In general, non-take-up originates from a complex combination of different barriers. Overall, social assistance is a very complex intervention. Some grassroots organisations therefore call for a more proactive approach on the part of PCSWs – and indeed, wherever possible, the automatic assignment of social rights such as the RSI. Lack of information is a major problem leading to the non-take-up of social rights. The law of 2002 has tried to tackle this deficiency by mandating the PCSWs with an extensive information duty. Since there are no more recent figures about non-take-up of social rights, we cannot assess the effectiveness of this measure.

Although the 'living wage' is not the only minimum income scheme, it is the only structural financial benefit provided by the RSI. Overall, there are three standard amounts according to the specific household type[86]:
- Category 1: Cohabitant person (approx. € 485 in 2009);
- Category 2: Single person (approx. € 725);
- Category 3: Family (approx. € 970).

The PCSW examines to what category the applicant belongs. In calculating the amount of the benefit, the PCSW takes into account all the applicant's possible resources, as well as those of applicants' cohabitees. There is wide agreement that in general the living wage is insufficient to lift beneficiaries out of poverty. Research indicates that the degree of inadequacy depends on the composition of the household[87] (e.g. Van Mechelen and Bogaerts, 2008). More precisely, the gap between the living wage and the European risk-of-poverty threshold is smaller for singles and lone parents, whereas couples with or

---

86   These are the amounts indexed June 1, 2009 (http://mi-is.be).
87   Households with dependent children, for example, can also rely on guaranteed child allowances, thereby substantially increasing their financial resources, but the combined amount remains below the risk-of-poverty threshold.

without children receive considerably less than the threshold. The same study has also revealed a relative deterioration between 1992 and 2005 – while the situation has stabilised in recent years. This evolution was worst for couples, whereas conditions improved slightly for lone parents. (See Table 3.2.)

Table 3.2: The living wage and the risk-of-poverty threshold (ROPT) (€/month)

|  | Single | | | | 2 adults with 2 children | | | |
|---|---|---|---|---|---|---|---|---|
|  | 2004 | 2005 | 2006 | 2007 | 2004 | 2005 | 2006 | 2007 |
| Living wage | 613 | 626 | 644 | 657 | 716 | 834 | 859 | 877 |
| ROPT | 777 | 829 | 860 | 878 | 1632 | 1740 | 1805 | 1844 |
| Gap in % | 21.1 | 24.5 | 25.1 | 25.2 | 56.1 | 52.1 | 52.4 | 52.4 |

*Source: EU–SILC, http://www.mi-is.be*

Other research has compared the living wage with the national income per capita and the minimum wage (e.g. Cantillon *et al*, 2003; 2004). These studies revealed that Belgium has not succeeded in linking the living wage to the overall standard of living – apart from the regular price-indexations of the living wage and some real increases since 2002. The degree of inadequacy also depends on the composition of the household. Singles and especially single parents find themselves in a more favourable situation than couples (with or without children).

Actually, the erosion of the minimum income level should not come as a surprise. Since 1999, as in other EU countries, Belgian social protection policy has been strongly influenced by the *making-work-pay* paradigm. This specific policy perspective helps to understand the inadequacy of the living wage in terms of the fight against poverty. In order to encourage the take-up of work, there has been an explicit strategy to raise low wages while containing benefit increases, so as to increase the gap between the two. Yet, as Table 3.3 shows, the transition from minimum income to employment has never been poorly rewarded. There is obviously a sufficient incentive to take up work. It is strongest for singles and single-earners without children and weakest for single parents. Admittedly, the transition to full-time employment is more rewarding than to part-time employment. As such, this makes perfect sense, but single parents often face obstacles to full-time employment – e.g. due to child care responsibilities. The correct policy response is probably to make child care more accessible and affordable, rather than keeping benefits low.

Table 3.3: Net gain from employment compared to the unemployment benefit and the living wage, 1999-2008 (in %)

| | Max. unemployment benefit | | | Min. unemployment benefit | | | Living wage | | |
|---|---|---|---|---|---|---|---|---|---|
| | 1999 | 2008 | Dif. | 1999 | 2008 | Dif. | 1999 | 2008 | Dif. |
| **Full-time Employment** | | | | | | | | | |
| Single | 42 | 19 | -23 | 58 | 45 | -13 | 66 | 70 | 4 |
| Single parent | -3 | 10 | 13 | 7 | 23 | 16 | 15 | 21 | 6 |
| One earner no kids | 12 | 23 | 11 | 27 | 43 | 16 | 40 | 49 | 8 |
| One earner with kids | 9 | 19 | 10 | 21 | 33 | 12 | 29 | 37 | 7 |
| **Part-time Employment** | | | | | | | | | |
| Single | 27 | 8 | -20 | 31 | 16 | -15 | 38 | 34 | -5 |
| Single parent | 15 | 8 | -6 | 18 | 15 | -3 | 13 | 18 | 4 |
| One earner no kids | 26 | 13 | -13 | 30 | 22 | -8 | 30 | 2 | -28 |
| One earner with kids | 23 | 11 | -12 | 25 | 16 | -10 | 15 | 2 | -13 |

*Source: Bogaerts, 2008, page 21.*

The overview of recent trends in the Belgian minimum income system shows that Belgium, like many other EU countries, has a long way to go in achieving an effective minimum security for its citizens. Apart from a gradual increase in the real level of benefit, there is a need for a more proactive policy reaching out to households living in poverty. Both options require a paradigm shift away from the dependency culture hypothesis towards recognition of the right to a minimum income as one of the most fundamental conditions for genuine participation in social life.

### 3.3.2   *Access to inclusive employment*

The way PCSWs handle the transition to employment can be subdivided into three approaches:
- the centre acts as an employer or a coach;
- the centre co-finances the individual's employment through 'activation of the minimum income benefit'; or
- the centre mediates for other (subsidised or unsubsidised) jobs.

According to art. 60, § 7 of the law on PCSWs[88], the centre can itself act as the employer, or mediate with a third party to hire the beneficiary. In both cases, the job is subsidised by the federal government. The aim of the measure is to reintegrate excluded persons into the labour market and to restore their social security rights. In the case of full-time employment, the subsidy is equivalent to the full amount of the living wage. If the beneficiary is hired in a social economy initiative, the subsidy equals the gross wage cost with a ceiling of € 22 665/year[89]. The problem with art. 60 is that the subsidy expires as soon as the individual's eligibility for unemployment benefits is restored. More than half of the beneficiaries used to fall back into unemployment at that moment. Art. 61 of the PCSWs law (Op. Cit.) therefore aims to facilitate the transition into the regular labour market after a period of employment within the PCSW. The subsidy – also paid by the federal government – amounts to a maximum of € 250/month (for full-time employment) and can be granted for at most 12 months over a period of 24 months.

RSI beneficiaries also have access to other, mainstream employment programmes: the ACTIVA plan, SINE employment, transitional employment programmes, and 'insertion interim'. The PCSW can also engage in a partnership with the regional employment service and/or one or more accredited partners.

- The ACTIVA plan is a programme that promotes the employment of (long-term) unemployed individuals through hiring subsidies. The employer who recruits a (long-term) unemployed person is entitled to a temporary exemption from employer contributions as well as a wage subsidy from the PCSW. The amounts of the exemption and the subsidy depend on the age of the beneficiary, the duration of unemployment, and the type of ACTIVA measure – three in total.

- SINE is an employment programme targeted at particularly vulnerable groups. They are employed in recognised social enterprises. After building up enough work experience, they can move into the regular labour market – although the possibility of failure to reintegrate into the regular labour market is accounted for as well. The programme promotes employment through para-fiscal and financial benefits for the employer. In particular, the employer is entitled to an exemption from employer contributions and a wage subsidy by the PCSW – *not* necessarily limited in time. This financial contribution depends mainly on the type of employment (full-time or part-time).

- The so-called 'transitional employment programmes' have a limited duration and are essentially designed for the non-profit (socio-cultural, sports, leisure or environment) sector. Work experience, combined with training and guidance, explicitly prepares beneficiaries to move into the regular labour market. Employers are entitled to an agreed exemption from employer contributions and a financial

---

88    Organic law of 8 July 1976 regarding the Public Centres for Social Welfare (PCSWs).
89    http://www.socialeconomy.be. These are 2009 amounts.

contribution from the PCSW. The contribution is limited to two or three years. This financial contribution also depends on the type of employment, the employee's previous activities, and the unemployment rate in the municipality.

- A fourth measure, called 'insertion interim', is based on agreements between temp work agencies and the Minister of Social Integration. The agency commits itself to provide a person entitled to the right to social integration or financial social assistance with work experience through interim assignments, and eventually a contract of indefinite duration (with a third employer). The agency also has to guarantee the necessary training and guidance. In return, the agency receives an agreed wage subsidy for two years.

In 2008, the employment programmes of the PCSWs created a total of more than 20 000 jobs (see Table 3.4). Between 2004 and 2008, job creation in various employment programmes more or less stagnated after it had doubled between 1999 and 2004. The change in government in 1999, accompanied by a new policy approach – the active welfare state – is the most plausible explanation for the strong expansion in the first half of the decade. The recent financial and economic crisis has revealed how sensitive these employment programmes are to economic trends. In fact, since the end of 2008, the number of people employed in these programmes has declined[90].

Of all activation measures, art. 60, § 7 is the most important one. With approximately 19 000 individuals entering work in the course of one year, this type of activation is far more important than any other activation measure. Insertion interim, on the other hand, appears to be the least successful (the figures even indicate a dwindling of this measure). Whereas the number of individuals employed in the SINE system is growing continuously, this does not fully compensate for the decrease in employment in the other programmes.

**Table 3.4: The number of individuals entering work in the course of one year through the employment programmes**

|  | 1999 (2002) | 2004 | 2008 |
|---|---|---|---|
| Art. 60, § 7 | 9,917 | 19,879 | 19,121 |
| Art. 61 | 447 | 786 | 504 |
| ACTIVA* | 291 | 968 | 809 |
| SINE | 1 | 250 | 422 |
| Transitional employment programmes | 19 | 631 | 363 |
| Insertion interim | 38 | 101 | 8 |

* The first year for which we have data on the ACTIVA-programme is 2002 and not 1999.
*Source: PPS Social Integration; http://mi-is.be*

---

90 Source: PPS Social Integration – http://www.mi-is.be.

Tempera and Agence Alter (2006) evaluated the programmes and found that nearly half (49.6%) of the activated individuals remained employed after the end of the activation programme, with some variation between the measures. Programmes whose main objective is to restore access to social insurance –such as art. 60, § 7, art. 61 – show less sustainable employment effects (46% as against 58% in other measures). Of the beneficiaries who stayed in employment, 77% remained in the same job, while 23% found a different job after the activation programme. Roughly one third hopes to find a new job. The activation programmes thus seem to achieve their goal to a large extent. Yet, the situation of the beneficiaries remains precarious. To begin with, after one year of activation, only 26.8% have a contract of indefinite duration. A second problem is the persistent need for intensive guidance. The activated individuals have trouble finding jobs on their own and often need help from the PCSW. It also appears that individuals who have not found a job one month after the end of their activation programme remain unemployed for at least another year.

All in all, the recent experience has shown that a voluntaristic policy can boost the labour market integration of minimum income recipients (and socially excluded groups in general). Admittedly, a 50% retention rate after completion of the programme is far from perfect – and given the absence of control groups in the evaluation, the net effect remains uncertain. However, an earlier evaluation showed that the outflow from minimum income into work among non-participants in activation programmes did not exceed 25%, which suggests that the net effect is substantial (Nicaise, 2002). The same study showed that a net employment gain of 10% can be sufficient to recover the full cost of the programme for the government budget.

The relationship between the minimum income system (and related activation programmes) on the one hand, and mainstream social security on the other hand is a very ambiguous one. As mentioned earlier, some employment measures explicitly aim to transfer applicants from minimum income into mainstream unemployment insurance, thus generating a 'revolving door' effect. At the same time, vulnerable groups are often excluded from unemployment insurance (and its related employment services) through sanctions or suspensions, shifting the burden (back) to the PCSWs. Wets *et al* (1998) investigated the flows between unemployment and the PCSWs for the first time. Of all applicants for minimum income support, roughly one third (32%) appeared to be registered as unemployed, with some of them just applying for advance payments (34%), others for income supplements due to low benefit rates (39%), and a third group being suspended altogether from unemployment benefits (27%). The last category carries a particular burden since people whose unemployment benefit has been suspended often depend entirely on the PCSW for their means of subsistence. A further breakdown of this category is also interesting: it appears that individuals suspended because of long-term unemployment are less likely to apply for support from the PCSW. People suspended because of refusing or leaving work or administrative sanctions are more likely to address the PCSW: roughly one in ten cases. In fact, many of them are victims of the complexity or lack of transparency of the unemployment regulations.

Since 2004, the number of individuals excluded from unemployment benefits has risen considerably, due to tightened eligibility conditions, intensification of controls, and sanctions (see e.g. Martens, 2008). Heylen and Bollens (2006) re-examined the flows between unemployment and social assistance (particularly in the case of sanctions) on the basis of administrative files. First, they found a clear relationship between sanctions and dependency on the PCSW. In particular, one in ten sanctioned people receive compensation from the PCSW directly after their exclusion from unemployment benefits. Secondly, it appears that the duration of the sanction influences the dependency on the PCSW in two ways: the longer the sanction, (a) the higher the proportion of sanctioned that apply for help from the PCSW; and (b) the longer the period of dependency on the PCSW.

The figures of the Federation of Walloon PCSWs, based on a sample of 57 Walloon centres, sound more alarming (Cherenti, 2009). According to this study, the number of social assistance recipients in these PCSWs, affected by sanctions of the federal Employment Agency, amounted to 2 637 on 31 October 2008[91], a 22% increase compared to 2007 and a seven-fold increase compared to 2005. The author estimates that (in the Walloon Region) 38% of all suspended unemployed persons apply for support from the PCSW, while many others 'vanish' from any record. As regards the profile of those applying for social assistance, 60 to 90% appear to have (very) low qualifications, 51% are single parents, and another 30% are single persons.

The main lesson from these studies is that the inflow into social assistance depends to some extent on the (lack of) effectiveness of the primary safety net (mainly the unemployment insurance system). More adequate unemployment benefits and a more humane regulation of sanctions and suspensions may prevent a lot of exclusion. The transfer from unemployment insurance into the social assistance system has more than just financial consequences for the claimants: it may also mean that job seekers lose access to mediation and training services that are linked to the mainstream unemployment insurance.

### 3.3.3    *Access to quality services*

Depending on the local context, PCSWs provide a very wide range of services, covering nearly all areas: social guidance, delivery of hot meals, shelter, home care, proximity

---

91    The figure of 2637 is a 'stock' figure. In terms of 'flow', over the preceding 12 months, 6547 applications had been received by the same PCSWs.

services, parenting courses, educational support, sports, cultural projects etc. This section discusses just a few of the most essential types of support.

The PCSWs can provide (or finance) *medical assistance* so that access to quality health care is guaranteed to anybody who legally resides in Belgium. Medical assistance is included in the RSA – not the RSI. Anybody can apply for it whenever it appears that the medical costs cannot be borne by the individual. Medical assistance covers a wide range of health care costs:

- medical costs;
- pharmaceutical costs;
- hospital costs;
- medical costs and/or pharmaceutical costs for ambulatory care in a nursing facility.

In some cities, clients can apply for a medical card with which they (and their families) can visit agreed care providers. The costs will then be directly charged to the PCSW. Undocumented migrants can also apply for the medical card and medical assistance, although for them only the cost of *urgent* medical care is covered by the PCSW.[92]

**Table 3.5: The number of beneficiaries of (urgent) medical assistance (as a percentage of the number of beneficiaries of the right to social assistance)**

|                          | 1999             | 2004             | 2008             |
|--------------------------|------------------|------------------|------------------|
| Medical assistance       | 3,150 (9.88%)    | 6,610 (14.23%)   | 2,038 (9.53%)    |
| Urgent medical assistance| 220 (0.69%)      | 3,171 (6.83%)    | 2,983 (13.96%)   |

*Source: PFS Social Integration; http://www.mi-is.be*

Table 3.5 displays the number of beneficiaries of (urgent) medical assistance. In the period 1999-2004, the demand for (urgent) medical assistance increased strongly. The importance of medical assistance compared to other forms of social assistance also grew in this period. Whereas one in ten applications for social assistance concerned medical assistance in 1999, the proportion had risen to one in seven by 2004. Applications for social assistance by undocumented migrants have always been mainly confined to applications for urgent medical assistance. Nevertheless, we can observe a rapid increase between 1999 and 2004, followed by a slight decrease in absolute figures after 2004.

---

92    The urgency has to be established by a practitioner.

The PCSWs also intervene in the field of *housing*. First of all, most PCSWs have their own housing stock. In many municipalities, they have their own refuges. The PCSW can let a dwelling for a short period (up to 8 months) to people in emergency situations – e.g. when the previous dwelling has been declared uninhabitable, or in the event of eviction for judicial or family reasons, homelessness caused by a calamity, etc. Secondly, the PCSW has to be notified of every judicial eviction. The centre can then assess which kind of support it can provide to the people concerned. The aim is, in fact, to prevent such evictions. When the eviction order is issued, the conflict between tenant and land-lord has often escalated to the point where it is difficult for the centre to find a solution. Moreover, preventive assistance in this field is time-intensive. The staff is often too small to carry out this task properly (VVSG, 2008). Thirdly, the PCSW can subsidise the rent and/or the rental warranty. The latter instrument is powerful in overcoming barriers to private accommodation. In order to help persons searching for a dwelling, the centre can advance their rental warranty. Finally, homeless people who move into a dwelling can receive a settlement bonus. This bonus amounts to one month's living wage for a family (i.e. € 967). It can only be issued once in a lifetime and for at most two years.

Access to *energy* is another major concern of the PCSWs. For specific support in this area, they can use the Energy Fund (Social Fund for Gas and Electricity) and the Social Heating Fund. The umbrella organisation of Flemish cities and municipalities (VVSG) reports two problems in this context (VVSG, 2008). First of all, VVSG advocates the establishment of a single energy fund (whereas federal subsidies are currently spread over different funds, making efficient delivery more difficult). Secondly, the organisation calls for a refocusing of governmental support to prevention and counselling. For the time being, the PCSWs are called upon when problems have become acute. It is also worth mentioning the existence of debt mediation services. Local PCSWs can create their own debt mediation service, not only in the field of energy, but also in other areas such as housing.

The right to social assistance covers a wide range of other activities and forms of as-sistance. We have only mentioned the more structural forms of assistance. Whereas the proper 'living wage' may be insufficient to lift income above the at-risk-of-poverty threshold, the overall package including additional assistance may be more adequate. Research has indicated that some PCSWs systematically supplement the living wage up to the threshold (Bogaerts and Van Mechelen, 2008); however, the applicant usually has to submit an application. Lack of information still prevents too many applicants from using the available support, while PCSWs keep a large degree of discretion in granting these additional services and in determining eligibility conditions. The absence of stand-ard regulations in the field of social assistance may result in unequal treatment of benefit recipients and in legal insecurity. Some stakeholders therefore advocate the development of supra-municipal assistance standards, and the means to enforce them.

## 3.4 Conclusions and recommendations for strengthening EU action on active inclusion

The 2008 Recommendation on active inclusion has received political endorsement from Member States and has gained a wide range of support from key actors in the Social OMC. However, there remains a significant challenge to translate its objectives into reality on the ground. The minimum income and access to services pillars remain underdeveloped in relation to the inclusive labour market pillar. In many Member States, much remains to be done to ensure that integrated and reinforcing strategies are in place that will lead to greater synergies between the three policy areas. Also effective and regular systems for monitoring and reporting on the implementation of the Recommendation need to be established.

It is clear that the 2008 Recommendation provides a solid basis for developing a consistent and intensive programme of work at EU level on active inclusion. However, whether such a programme develops will depend to a large extent on the development of a renewed and strengthened political commitment to work for the eradication of poverty and social exclusion in the context of the Europe 2020 agenda and a specific commitment to promote active inclusion in the context of a renewed and strengthened EU coordination in the social field with much stronger interactions between the EU's economic, employment, social, and sustainable development agendas. This is especially the case as the Recommendation on active inclusion has been developed on the basis that there is an effective EU coordination in the social field with a strong social inclusion strand in place.

In the light of the above, there are three key tasks which are necessary to ensure the effective development of EU level action on active inclusion post 2010:
- first, it is essential that the eradication of poverty and social exclusion in general and the promotion of active inclusion in particular are given the necessary political endorsement by the European Council when it will adopt the Europe 2020 agenda;
- secondly, effective arrangements must be formally agreed at EU level by the end of 2010 for implementing a renewed and strengthened EU coordination in the social field within which a specific priority ought to be given to focused work on key issues including the implementation and monitoring of the active inclusion Recommendation;
- thirdly, the Commission, Member States and stakeholders should agree on (as part of the new EU coordination in the social field) a detailed multi-annual work programme or road map on active inclusion from 2011. This would bring greater coordination and focus to the work on active inclusion and help to lift it onto a new level of effectiveness in the coming period.

In addition to these three core recommendations, we would make a number of more detailed suggestions for the further development of the active inclusion initiative.

### 3.4.1   Review and Monitoring

- Member States and the Commission should agree a clear framework for monitoring the implementation of the 2008 Recommendation. This should provide the basis for an annual report on progress to the Spring European Council and to the European Parliament as well as to Member States' national (and possible sub-national) Parliaments. This could become a standard part of the annual *Joint Report on Social Protection and Social Inclusion*.

### 3.4.2   Exchange and Learning

- A systematic process of exchange and learning on effective approaches to active inclusion should be developed in the context of the Community Programme for Employment and Social Solidarity (PROGRESS) through Peer Reviews, studies, transnational exchange projects, the work of EU poverty networks and the EU Network of Independent Experts on Social Inclusion.

### 3.4.3   Linkages

- Systematic linkages should be developed with the European Employment Strategy to ensure that in future greater attention is given to an active inclusion approach to integrating those most distant from the labour market.

- The contribution of active inclusion to other key themes in the renewed EU coordination in the social field, particularly child poverty, housing exclusion and homelessness and the integration of migrants and ethnic minorities should be more clearly articulated.

### 3.4.4   Resourcing

- The contribution of EU Structural Funds to the implementation of active inclusion strategies in Member States should be further developed.

### 3.4.5    *Minimum Income*

- In their overview of MISs across EU countries, the EU Network of Independent Experts on Social Inclusion suggests a clear agenda of work on the minimum income pillar of active inclusion. This agenda includes proposals for actions on the issues of adequacy, uprating, coverage, non-take up, disincentives, links with other pillars of active inclusion and monitoring and reporting. All of these will be important to follow up in the context of an overall work programme on active inclusion. However, we would highlight one particular issue which in our view should be a priority for attention. This is the need to address the lack of clarity that currently exists as to what constitutes an "adequate" minimum income to live life with dignity. We would thus recommend that the European Commission and Member States, e.g. in the context of the Social Protection Committee, should initiate a process to agree on common criteria which would assist Member States in ensuring that their MISs meet the requirements of the 1992 EU Council Recommendation on common criteria concerning sufficient resources and social assistance in social protection systems and of the 2008 Commission Recommendation on the active inclusion of people excluded from the labour market. These common criteria could then provide the basis for reporting on and monitoring Member States' conformity with these Recommendations. Once common criteria are agreed the possibility of incorporating them into an EU Framework Directive on the adequacy of minimum income schemes could usefully be explored.

- As an interim step to ensure the adequacy of all MISs, all Member States could consider setting the goal that within a given timeframe (to be defined nationally) the combined effect of their minimum income provisions and other policy measures would be sufficient to lift all persons above the at-risk-of-poverty line of the country where they live (i.e. 60% of the median national household equivalised income). This would be in line with the European Parliament Resolution of 6 May 2009, in which EU deputies stated that "the implementation of Recommendation 92/441/EEC needs to be improved in relation to minimum income and social transfers" and that "social assistance should provide an adequate minimum income for a dignified life, at least at a level which is above the "at risk of poverty" level and sufficient to lift people out of poverty". (European Parliament, 2009) In the light of the above comments (and particularly Section 3.2.1), this may not be achievable in all countries in the short term, but this goal ought to be largely achieved by 2020. Progress towards this would need to be closely monitored and reported on by the Commission.

# References

Barroso, J.M. (2010), *2010 European Year for Combating Poverty and Social Exclusion: Working together towards a society in line with our values*, Speech delivered at the Opening Conference of the 2010 European Year for Combating Poverty and Social Exclusion, Madrid, 21 January 2010. Available from: http://europa.eu/rapid/pressReleasesAction.do?reference=SPEECH/10/12&format=HTML&aged=0&language=ES&guiLanguage=en.

Begg, I., Berghman, J. and Marlier, E. (2006), *Trends, Recent Developments, Active Inclusion and Minimum Resources: Key lessons*, Brussels: European Commission.

Bogaerts, K. (2008), *Bestaan er nog financiële vallen in de werkloosheid en in de bijstand in België*, Berichten / UA, Antwerpen, Centrum voor Sociaal Beleid Herman Deleeck, december.

Bradshaw, J. (2006), "Child benefit packages in fifteen countries", in Lewis, J. (ed.), *Children, Changing Families and Welfare States*, Cheltenham: Edward Elgar.

Bradshaw, J. and Bennett, F. (2009), *Minimum Income Schemes in the United Kingdom: A study of national policies*, Brussels: European Commission.

Bradshaw, J. and Finch, N. (2002), *A Comparison of Child Benefit Packages in 22 Countries*, Department for Work and Pensions Research Report No. 174, Leeds: Corporate Document Services.

Cantillon, B., Marx, I. and De Maesschalck, V. (2003), 'Het trilemma van de sociale zekerheid: verleden, heden en toekomst. De minimumbescherming in de welvaarts-staat', *Belgisch tijdschrift voor sociale zekerheid*, 44, 2, pp.399-434.

Cantillon, B., Van Mechelen, N., Marx, I. and Van Den Bosch, K. (2004), 'De evolutie van de minimumbescherming in 15 Europese welvaartsstaten in de jaren negentig', *Belgisch tijdschrift voor sociale zekerheid*, 45, 3, pp. 509-548.

Cherenti, R., *Les exclusions ONEM: implications pour les CPAS*, Fédération des CPAS – Service Insertion Professionnelle, February 2009, 22p.

Cincinnato, S. and Nicaise, I. (2009), *Minimum Income Schemes: panorama and assessment. A study of National Policies (Belgium)*, http://www.peer-review-social-inclusion.eu/network-of-independent-experts/2009/minimum-income-schemes

COFACE (2009), *Recommendations on active inclusion, a tool for fighting family poverty*, Brussels: COFACE.

Council (2010), *Joint Report on Social Protection and Social Inclusion* (including related supporting document produced by the European Commission), Brussels: EU Council of Ministers and European Commission. Available from: http://ec.europa.eu/social/main.jsp?catId=757&langId=en.

Council (2009), *Joint Report on Social Protection and Social Inclusion 2008*, Brussels: EU Council of Ministers and European Commission. Available from: http://ec.europa.eu/social/main.jsp?catId=757&langId=en.

Council (2008), *Joint Report on Social Protection and Social Inclusion 2008*, Brussels: EU

Council of Ministers and European Commission.

Council (2007), *Joint Report on Social Protection and Social Inclusion 2007*, Luxembourg: Office for Official Publications of the European Communities.

Council (1992), *Council recommendation of 24 June 1992 on common criteria concerning sufficient resources and social assistance in social protection systems*, 92/441/EEC, OJEC, L 245, Brussels: Council.

EU Network of Independent Experts on Social Inclusion: http://www.peer-review-social-inclusion.eu/network-of-independent-experts.

European Anti-Poverty Network (2008), *'Active Inclusion': what is at stake? Policy realities and challenges*, EAPN Briefing, Brussels: EAPN. Available from: http://www.eapn.eu/images/docs/eapnbriefingonactiveinclusion_en.pdf.

European Commission (2008a), *Commission Recommendation of 3 October 2008 on the active inclusion of people excluded from the labour market*, Brussels: European Commission. Available from: http://eur-lex.europa.eu/LexUriServ/LexUriServ.do?uri=OJ:L:2008:307:0011:001 4:EN:PDF.

European Commission (2008b), *Renewed Social Agenda: Opportunities, access and solidarity in 21st century Europe, Comm*unication No. COM(2008) 412 final, Brussels: European Commission. Available from: http://eur-lex.europa.eu/LexUriServ/LexUriServ.do?uri=COM:2008:0412:FIN:E N:PDF.

European Commission (2008c), *Communication on* a *Commission Recommendation on the active inclusion of people excluded from the labour market*, Communication No. COM(2008) 639 final, Brussels: European Commission. Available from: http://eur-lex.europa.eu/LexUriServ/LexUriServ.do?uri=COM:2008:0639:FIN:E N:PDF.

European Commission (2006a), *Modernising social protection for greater social justice and economic cohesion: taking forward the active inclusion of people furthest from the labour market*, Communication No. COM(2007) 620 final, Brussels: European Commission. Available from: http://eur-lex.europa.eu/LexUriServ/LexUriServ.do?uri=COM:2007:0620:FIN:E N:PDF.

European Commission (2006b), *Communication concerning a consultation on action at EU level to promote the active inclusion of the people furthest from the labour market*, Communication No. COM(2006) 44 final, Brussels: European Commission. Available from: http://eur-lex.europa.eu/LexUriServ/LexUriServ.do?uri=COM:2006:0044:FIN:E N:PDF.

European Commission (2005), *Communication on the Social Agenda*, Communication No. COM(2005) 33 final, Brussels: European Commission. Available from: http://eur-lex.europa.eu/LexUriServ/site/en/com/2005/com2005_0033en01.pdf.

European Parliament (2009), *European Parliament resolution of 6 May 2009 on the active inclusion of people excluded from the labour market*, Brussels. Available from: http://www.europarl.europa.eu/sides/getDoc.do?type=TA&language=EN&referen ce=P6-TA-2009-0371

European Social Network (2009), *Pathways to Activity: Active inclusion case-studies from the ESN policy and practice group 'active inclusion and employment'*, Brighton: ESN. Available from:
http://www.esn-eu.org/active-inclusion/index.htm.

European Social Network (2008), *Realising potential: social services and active inclusion*, Brighton: ESN. Available from:
http://www.esn-eu.org/active-inclusion/index.htm.

Frazer, H. (2008a), *Minimum income, minimum wage and active inclusion: some recent developments in Europe*, in: Teil-Haben und Aktiv-Sein: Aktive Eingliederung als Teil des Europäischen Sozialmodells, Vienna: Federal Ministry for Social Affairs and Consumer Protection. Available from:
http://www.bmsk.gv.at/cms/siteEN/attachments/2/8/1/CH0129/ CMS1220604768693/konferenzband_teil_haben_und_aktiv_sein.pdf.

Frazer, H. (2008b), *Yes to an Active Inclusion based on rights! Promoting EAPN Principles on Active Inclusion*, Report of EAPN seminar on Active Inclusion held in Paris on 13 June 2008, Brussels: EAPN. Available from:
http://www.eapn.eu/images/docs/eapnseminarreportonactiveinclusion_en.pdf.

Frazer, H. and Marlier, E. (2009), "Minimum income schemes across EU Member States", Brussels: European Commission. Available from:
http://www.peer-review-social-inclusion.eu/network-of-independent-experts/2009/minimum-income-schemes.

Groenez, S. and Nicaise, I. (2002), *Traps and springboards in European minimum income systems – the Belgian case*, Leuven: HIVA-K.U.Leuven, 138 p.

Heylen, V. and Bollens, J. (2006), *Stromen tussen werkloosheid, werk en OCMW*, Leuven: HIVA-K.U.Leuven.

Immervoll, H. (2009), *Minimum-Income Benefits in OECD Countries: Policy Design, Effectiveness and Challenges*, IZA Discussion Paper No. 4627, Bonn.

Martens, Y. (2008), Le contrôle des chômeurs est bel et bien une machine à exclure, *Le Journal du Collectief Solidarité contre l'Exclusion*, nr.61, p.12-18.

Morissens, A. and Nicaise, I. (2006), *Trends, Recent Developments, Active Inclusion and Minimum Resources: First Semester Report 2006 (Belgium)*, http://www.peer-review-social-inclusion.eu/network-of-independent-experts/2006/first-semester-2006

Nicaise, I., Groenez, S., Adelman, L., Roberts, S and Middleton, S. (2004), *Gaps, traps and springboards in European minimum income systems. A comparative study of 13 EU countries*, Leuven: HIVA-K.U.Leuven, 144 p.

Nicis Institute (2009), *Nine good practices on active inclusion in Europe*, The Hague. Available from:

http://www.eukn.org/binaries/eukn/eukn/practice/2008/09/nine-good-practices-def.pdf.

Peer Review in Social Protection and Social Inclusion (2009), *Developing well-targeted tools for the active inclusion of vulnerable people*, Vienna: ÖSB. Available from: http://www.peer-review-social-inclusion.eu/peer-reviews/2009/developing-well-targeted-tools-for-the-active-inclusion-of-vulnerable-people.

Peer Review in Social Protection and Social Inclusion (2008a), *Initiatives by the social partners for improving the labour market access of disadvantaged groups*, Vienna: ÖSB. Available from: http://www.peer-review-social-inclusion.eu/peer-reviews/2008/initiatives-by-the-social-partners-for-improving-the-labour-market-access-of-disadvantaged-groups.

Peer Review in Social Protection and Social Inclusion (2008b), *The social economy from the perspective of active inclusion*, Vienna: ÖSB. Available from: http://www.peer-review-social-inclusion.eu/peer-reviews/2008/the-social-economy-from-the-perspective-of-active-inclusion.

Peer Review in Social Protection and Social Inclusion (2006), *Integrated Services in Rehabilitation – On Coordination of Organisation and Financing*, Vienna: ÖSB. Available from: http://www.peer-review-social-inclusion.eu/peer-reviews/2006/financial-coordination-within-the-field-of-rehabilitation.

Steenssens, K., Degrave, F., Demeyer, B. and Vanregenmortel, T. (2007), *Leven (z)onder leefloon. Deel 1: onderbescherming onderzocht*, Leuven: HIVA-K.U.Leuven, 194 p.

Tempera and Agence Alter (2006), *Activeringsmaatregelen en de arbeidsmarkt. Hoe vergaat het rechthebbenden op maatschappelijke integratie na een activeringstraject*, http://www.mi-is.be (22/04/2009).

Urbact II (2008), *Active Inclusion: Synthesis of baselines*, Available from: http://urbact.eu/fileadmin/general_library/Microsoft_Word_-_synthesis_on_Active_Inclusion_sept_09.pdf.

Van Mechelen, N. and Bogaerts, K. (2008), *Aanvullende financiële steun in Vlaamse OCMW's*, Berichten / UA, Antwerpen, Centrum voor Sociaal Beleid Herman Deleeck, juni.

Vercauteren, L. and Daems (1995), *Niet-gebruik van sociale zekerheid*, Universiteit Antwerpen, Departement Rechten, Vakgroep sociaal recht, Antwerpen, 142 p.

VVSG (2008), *Reactie van de VVSG op NAPincl 2008-2011*, http://www.vvsg.be.

Wets, J., De Witte, H., Vanheerswynghels, A., Breauchesne, M.-N. and Olivier, M. (1998), *Werkloosheid en sociale bijstand:* communicerende *vaten? Een onderzoek naar de relatie tussen werkloosheid en instroom in de sociale bijstand. Syntheserapport*, Leuven: HIVA-K.U.Leuven.

# 4 Homelessness and Housing Exclusion [93]

This chapter draws on the important material that has been developed on homelessness and housing exclusion (HHE) in the context of the Social OMC. Sections 4.1 (HHE in the EU Social OMC), 4.2 (The extent and causes of HHE across the EU), 4.3 (Necessary elements to prevent and tackle HHE) and 4.4 (Key policy elements) summarise some of the key lessons and conclusions that can be learned on HHE. Section 4.5 then considers HHE in Belgium. Finally, Section 4.6 draws some conclusions and makes recommendations for strengthening EU action on HHE in the future.

## 4.1 HHE in the EU Social OMC

### 4.1.1 No commonly agreed EU definition of HHE

At the moment, there is no commonly agreed definition at EU level of HHE. The European typology of HHE called "ETHOS" was developed by the European Federation of organisations working with the people who are homeless (FEANTSA) and classifies people according to their living situation.[94] There are four conceptual categories: *rooflessness* (without a shelter of any kind, sleeping rough); *houselessness* (with a place to sleep but temporary in institutions or shelter); living in *insecure housing* (threatened with severe exclusion due to insecure tenancies, eviction, domestic violence); and living in *inadequate housing* (in caravans on illegal campsites, in unfit housing, in extreme overcrowding). These in turn are broken down into 13 operational categories[95].

From this approach, Edgar *et al* (2007) have proposed a harmonised definition of homelessness (see Table 4.1).

---

93  We would like to thank Bill Edgar for his major contribution to the drafting of this chapter.

94  http://www.feantsa.org/code/en/hp.asp.

95  These can be found on the FEANTSA web site at:
     http://www.feantsa.org/files/freshstart/Toolkits/Ethos/Leaflet/EN.pdf.

**Table 4.1: Proposal for a harmonised definition of homelessness**

| Operational category | | Living situation | | Definition |
|---|---|---|---|---|
| 1 | People living rough | 1 | Public space / external space | Living in the streets or public spaces without a shelter that can be defined as living quarters |
| 2 | People in emergency accommodation | 2 | Overnight shelters | People with no place of usual residence who move frequently between various types of accommodation |
| 3 | People living in accommodation for the homeless | 3 | Homeless hostels | Where the period of stay is less than one year* |
| | | 4 | Temporary accommodation | |
| | | 5 | Transitional supported accommodation | |
| | | 6 | Women's shelter or refuge accommodation | |
| 4 | People living in institutions | 7 | Health care institutions | Stay longer than needed due to lack of housing |
| | | 8 | Penal institutions | No housing available prior to release |
| 5 | People living in non-conventional dwellings due to lack of housing | 9 | Mobile homes | Where the accommodation is used due to a lack of housing and is not the person's usual place of residence |
| | | 10 | Non-conventional building | |
| | | 11 | Temporary structure | |
| 6 | Homeless people living temporarily in conventional housing with family and friends (due to lack of housing) | 12 | Conventional housing, but not the person's usual place of residence | Where the accommodation is used due to a lack of housing and is not the person's usual place of residence |

\*    The period of one year is chosen to allow consistency with UNECE/EUROSTAT Census recommendations.

*Source: Edgar et al, 2007*

### 4.1.2 Why it is a major issue in the EU Social OMC

The first common objectives for the EU Social Inclusion Process (adopted by the Nice European Council in December 2000) were ambitious and included a specific focus on the need to fight against HHE. As recalled by Spinnewijn (2009): "One of the overarching objectives adopted was to ensure access to resources, rights, goods, and services for all, and within the ambit of this the EU agreed to guarantee access to decent and sanitary housing. A second overarching objective was to reduce the risk of exclusion, as part of which the EU agreed to put in place policies to prevent life crises such as homelessness. While homelessness was not amongst the most important issues, the common objectives provided a sufficiently strong basis for EU intervention." In 2002, the very first *Joint Report on Social Inclusion* highlighted the importance of "Ensuring good accommodation for all" within which "developing integrated responses both to prevent and address homelessness is another essential challenge for some countries" (Council, 2002). So, HHE was identified as a priority from the outset of the process and has in fact always remained a major issue between 2000 and 2010. (See Frazer, 2009).

There are a number of underlying reasons why HHE has been an ongoing priority for the Social OMC during the past decade. These include:

- The growing evidence of the persistence of HHE problems across the EU.
- A growing awareness that the multi-dimensional nature of poverty and social exclusion means that ensuring decent and affordable housing needs to be an integral part of national social inclusion strategies along with access to employment, access to adequate income and access to other essential services.
- As homelessness is one of the most visible and extreme forms of poverty and social exclusion and one which most endangers and damages people, and as the right to decent accommodation is a fundamental human right it must inevitably be a high priority in any EU initiative on poverty and social exclusion.
- Tackling HHE can also boost the economy – for instance:
  - as poverty can result from high housing costs which in turn can affect economic competitiveness (e.g. it can affect wage demands, labour mobility…), addressing such costs can benefit the economy as well as reducing poverty;
  - as a key factor in HHE is the lack of sufficient affordable housing, it is necessary to increase housing production and consumption and this in turn can help to boost GDP.
- As housing is also a social good, the assessment of (and provision for) housing needs is a necessary component of effective governance and it impacts on all aspects of society (health, welfare, social protection, social solidarity etc).

### 4.1.3    Brief summary of key work on HHE in the Social OMC

HHE has featured in the work and activities of the Social OMC in many different ways. For instance:

- *National Action Plans on social inclusion*: HHE issues have been a key element in successive NAPs/inclusion of many Member States since 2001.

- *European Federation of organisations working with the people who are homeless*: FEANTSA has been one of the core groups of EU level networks working on issues of poverty and social exclusion to be funded by the European Commission as part of the Social OMC[96]. Among other activities, FEANTSA has carried out regular analysis of Member States' NAPs/inclusion with a specific focus on HHE.

- *EU study on measuring homelessness*: Edgar, W. Harrison, M., Watson, P. and Busch-Geertsema, V. (2007), *Measurement of Homelessness at European Union Level*, Brussels: European Commission (DG Employment, Social Affairs and Equal Opportunities).

- *EU project on "Mutual Progress on Homelessness Through Advancing and Strengthening Information Systems" (MPHASIS, 2007-2009)*:
  http://www.trp.dundee.ac.uk/research/mphasis/index.html

- *EU work on indicators*: At their December 2001 Laeken European Council, EU leaders called on Member States that in their NAPs/inclusion they report on housing quality, housing costs, and homelessness and other precarious housing. In practice, however, the absence of any commonly agreed indicators in the field of housing has meant that many NAPs/inclusion to date have not satisfactorily (if at all) addressed this essential dimension of social inclusion. A major step forward was made in the second half of 2009 when the EU Social Protection Committee and its Indicators Sub-Group finally managed to develop and adopt commonly agreed indicators and background statistics in the field of housing costs, overcrowded households and housing quality (see Section 4.4.3 below).

- A number of *transnational exchange projects* addressing HHE issues have been supported during the process such as the "COOP" project which examined how different countries and cities deal successfully with the homeless or the

---

96    Other EU funded networks such as the European Anti-Poverty Network (EAPN), the European Foundation for Street Children, the European Social Network (ESN) and Eurocities have also made valuable contributions on HHE. For more information on the EU funded networks, see the European Commission web-site (Directorate-General "Employment, Social Affairs and Equal Opportunities").

"Building Inclusion – Access to Housing and Inclusion in Europe project".[97]

- *EU Peer Reviews on HHE*: 4 peer reviews have been organised at EU level in the field of HHE. For a detailed report on these, see: Vranken, 2004; Meert, 2005; Edgar, 2006; Edgar, forthcoming.
- *Consensus conference*: in 2007, France organised the first national consensus conference on homelessness, paving the way for a national homelessness strategy and developing a model that FEANTSA has subsequently promoted at EU level.[98]
- *Annual EU events on poverty and social exclusion* organised by the European Commission and the EU Presidencies: HHE issues have been regularly highlighted in the EU Round Tables on Poverty and Social Exclusion and the EU Meetings of People Experiencing Poverty.
- *2009 thematic year*: a major focus of the Social OMC activities throughout 2009 has been on HHE, which has led to considerable work by a wide range of actors.
- *2010 European Year*: Addressing the needs of the homeless has been recognised a priority policy area for the EU 2010 Year for Combating Poverty and Social Exclusion.

### 4.1.4    *What the EU dimension adds to country's action*

It is clear from the experience over the past decade that the EU dimension has added significant value to the work on HHE in many Member States. For instance:
- it has raised awareness and understanding of HHE issues in its own right and as a key element in addressing poverty and social exclusion more generally;
- it has advanced debate on definitions of HHE;
- it has enabled considerable exchange of learning and good practice on different aspects of HHE;
- it has led to increased collection of comparable data, thus enabling improved analysis and monitoring;
- it has fostered a number of important comparative studies on HHE issues that Member States can use to develop better policies;

---

97    Information on "COOP" can be found at:
      http://www.eukn.org/eukn/themes/Urban_Policy/Housing/Housing_policy/Homelessness/
      COOP-project_1013.html.
      For information on "Building Inclusion", see http://buildinginclusion.oberaxe.es/en/home/index.
      On the Building Inclusion web-site, see also the page on "Contributions".
98    For more information on the 2007 consensus conference, see: http://sans-abri.typepad.fr/. And
      for information on the December 2010 "European consensus conference on homelessness", see
      FEANTSA web-site: http://www.feantsa.org/code/en/hp.asp.

- it has encouraged Member States to involve a broad range of actors, particularly people having experience of HHE, in developing, implementing and monitoring policies;
- it has raised the awareness in many Member States (particularly through the NAPs/inclusion) of the need for a more strategic approach based on more comprehensive and integrated policies;
- it has helped highlight the need to focus on prevention as well as on alleviation of problems.

## 4.2 The extent and causes of HHE across the EU

An understanding of homelessness and housing exclusion is best articulated by presenting the problem as a condition of vulnerability in the housing market. Across the EU housing markets are dominated (though in varying degrees) by private ownership and market structures of provision and allocation. The *structure-agency model* (see Table 4.2) provides a useful framework for understanding the factors leading to vulnerability in the housing market. (Neale, 1997)

**Table 4.2: Structure-agency model of the causes of housing market vulnerability**

| Cause | Factor of vulnerability | Example |
|---|---|---|
| | Economic processes | Labour market demand / unemployment |
| | Housing market processes | Availability of / access to affordable housing |
| *Structural* | Social protection / welfare | Support for low income and vulnerable groups |
| | Citizenship | Legislative basis of active inclusion for immigrants |
| | Available mainstream services | Capacity of service provision |
| | Allocation mechanisms | Access to mainstream services |
| *Institutional* | Lack of coordination between existing mainstream services | Policy and operational coordination between mainstream services |
| | Institutional procedures | Procedures for discharge from prison and other institutions |
| | Family Status | Support structures |
| *Relationship* | Relationship situation | Married, single |
| | Relationship breakdown | Divorce, violence, widowhood |

| | | |
|---|---|---|
| | Disability / long-term illness | Learning disability, mental illness |
| *Personal* | Educational attainment | Low educational attainment |
| | Addiction | Drug / alcohol addiction |
| | Age / Gender | Life-stage, gender |

*Source: Edgar and Meert, 2005*

Poverty is a major determinant of vulnerability in the housing market especially where the provision of social housing is limited. It is for this reason that the European Union produces poverty risk figures broken down by accommodation tenure status (distinguishing between full ownership, owners still paying mortgage, tenants at market price, and tenants at subsidised price or rent free) and that it has agreed in 2009 an indicator on persons in households with high housing costs (see section 4.4.3). [99] The availability of social rented housing is a distinguishing factor among EU Member States but is not an adequate explanation of differences in homelessness among different welfare regime countries (Stephens and Fitzpatrick, 2007, Edgar *et al*, 2004).

The ability of the local state to meet the needs of vulnerable groups is evident in the capacity and geographical availability of mainstream services and in the allocation mechanisms that control access to these social goods. Equally institutional procedures in relation to rehabilitation and the discharge of people into the community are key components affecting vulnerability and the risk of homelessness. For example, research demonstrates that a high proportion of homeless people had recent experience of prison (Dyb, 2007; Fitzpatrick Associates, 2006).

Undoubtedly, the agency of the individual is a key predictor of the risk of vulnerability in the housing market. Lack of social support and family status is itself a significant factor. In this context the impact of demographic factors (known as the second demographic transition) is leading to the increase in single person households (especially in major conurbations where the housing market is more constrained) and in elderly households.

---

99    The most recent list of indicators that have been commonly agreed by the European Commission and all 27 EU Member States for monitoring the Social OMC was adopted by the EU Social Protection Committee (SPC) in the second half of 2009. This list includes four portfolios of indicators and context information: one for the Social OMC as a whole (overarching portfolio) and one for each of the three social strands (social inclusion, pensions and health portfolios). For each indicator, it provides the agreed definition and socio-demographics breakdowns. See: European Commission, 2009. The national values of these indicators and breakdowns can be found for the various EU countries on the web-site of Eurostat, the statistical office of the European Communities: http://epp.eurostat.ec.europa.eu/portal/page/portal/statistics/themes.

Households such as these, which rely upon a single income, find it harder to cope with the costs of housing or to cope with unexpected life events (e.g. illness, temporary loss of income). Research on the causes of homelessness and on the profile of the homeless population adequately and clearly demonstrates the importance of relationship break-down (and especially domestic violence) and the importance of factors related to personal capacity (e.g. addiction behaviour often linked to mental illness) in predicting the risk of homelessness among the population.

Households relate to the places in which they live by a process of residential mobility and residential choice. The pattern of residential mobility and choice can be analysed using the life course approach (or "theory"). The nature of that residential mobility and choice is narrowly prescribed for some households and can be said to be more prescribed for all households at some stages in their life course. Hence, life-course analysis is helpful in understanding housing market vulnerability. The life course approach is developed and applied across many academic disciplines and is based on a number of fundamental principles. The objective is to look at individual life events and the pattern of life trajectories in the context of social processes that generate these events or trajectories (Golledge and Stimson, 2006). The approach stresses that an individual's developmental path is embedded in and transformed by conditions and events occurring during the historical period and geographical location in which the person lives. Second, it is assumed that periods of life, such as childhood and adolescence, influence positions, roles and rights in society, and that these rights may be based on culturally shared age definitions (Hagestad and Neugarten, 1985).

Elder (1985) observes that time can also be envisioned as a sequence of transitions that are enacted over time. A *transition* is a discrete life change or event (e.g., from a single to a married state), whereas a *trajectory* is a sequence of linked states within a defined range of behaviour or experience (e.g., education and occupational career). The life course perspective emphasises the ways in which transitions, pathways, and trajectories are socially organised. Transitions typically result in a change in status, social identity, and role involvement. Trajectories, however, are long-term patterns of stability and change; they can include multiple transitions.

Explanations of residential mobility and choice have employed the life course concept to structure the decisions of individual households related to their housing needs, aspirations and resources. Classical models of residential mobility (Rossi, 1955) describe a behavioural analysis of residential choice around the main stages in the life course. The conceptual assumption and empirical evidence suggest that the trigger points to residential mobility arise from stresses associated with changes in housing need arising through the life course. It is argued that these transition points in the life course are also points of vulnerability depending upon economic and social circumstances and residential history (Clarke and Davies-Withers, 2007).

The paths of individual households through the housing stock are influenced by broader societal changes such as increasing incidence of divorce, remarriage and de facto household arrangements as well as life transitions and local housing markets. Just as transition points in the life course are employed to explain residential patterns, so the notion of trajectories has been used to specify "housing careers" (Kendig, 1984) as an organising principle to examine the interactions of housing choices and household family composition, linking housing tenure decisions and the life course.

In a similar manner, Chamberlain and MacKenzie (2003) identify distinct pathways into homelessness. The "youth" pathway focuses on teenagers forced to leave their family home prior to securing an independent income or position in the labour market. They identify three pathways into adult homelessness. The first is the "housing crisis career". This draws attention to the fact that for many adults it is poverty – and accumulating debt – that underpins the slide into homelessness. There is no "in and out" stage in the housing crisis career. Once adults lose their accommodation there is a sharp break and their problems usually get worse. The second career path into the adult population focuses on family breakdown, particularly as a result of domestic violence. The third point of entry into the adult population is the transition from youth to adult homelessness. The notion of the homeless career is also used to reflect the progression from homelessness occurring at a crisis or transition point and becoming chronic and long-term homelessness.

The legislative basis and governance of data collection on homelessness is only weakly developed in most countries. As a result responsibility for data collection on homelessness is often not clearly defined or coordinated. In the absence of a systematic and consensual definition of HHE across Europe, it is not possible to quantify accurately the extent and profile of homelessness. Furthermore, the nature of homeless services varies across Europe as does the nomenclature and definition of provision; hence it is difficult to obtain a single comparable figure even for basic services such as emergency overnight shelters and homeless hostels (see Edgar *et al*, 2007). However, some key trends can be discerned in relation to the level of homelessness (Edgar, 2009) and the profile of homelessness (Frazer and Marlier, 2009).

In the EU Member States for which data are available (Edgar, 2009), it can be estimated that, on any given night, there may be a total of 27,500 people sleeping on the streets (data from 14 countries[100]) and a further 51,500 accommodated overnight in emergency

---

100  Data are not available for: Bulgaria, Cyprus, Finland, Germany, Greece, Latvia, Lithuania, Luxembourg, Netherlands, Romania, Slovakia, Slovenia, Malta

shelters (data from 15 countries[101]). Information from 18 countries[102] indicates there are a further 111,000 places available in homeless hostels. Using prevalence rates based on this information, there may be a total of 410,000 homeless people in the European Union on any given night. Based on American research (Burt and Cohen (1989); Culhane *et al* (1994)) this could equate to a prevalence rate of 4.1 million people experiencing homelessness each year. (A first qualification which should be kept in mind concerning this figure is that while it is built up from individual ETHOS categories using the most recent data available in each country it should, like any estimated statistic, be treated with caution and be used as a basis for debate rather than policy-making. A second qualification is that the relevance of using American research which has not been tested in Europe is also open to question. Both qualifications are clearly valid and point to the need for the EU to improve on what is available rather than work blindly.)

Culhane *et al* (1994) show that, although on any day 0.1% of the population of New York City is homeless, 1% of the population (i.e. 10 times more) experiences homelessness over the course of a year, with larger fractions over longer periods. Moreover, turnover among the homeless suggests that point-in-time samples are disproportionately composed of individuals suffering long spells of homelessness. Hence, this composition bias overstates the prevalence of personal problems vis-à-vis structural housing market factors. Improved data availability in the USA has led to a more detailed understanding of the differences between chronic, episodic (or repeat) and transitional homelessness. This in turn has led to a shift in policy approach towards a "rapid re-housing program" (Culhane, 2008).

The evidence also suggests that the profile of homeless people varies across Europe in relation to key demographic and nationality characteristics but that the profile in many countries is changing. While the predominant characteristic of homeless people is middle-aged single men, there is a growing proportion of women, of younger people and of families with children. Furthermore while most homeless people have low educational attainment and are unemployed, there is a growing proportion of people with higher levels of education and in work (albeit mostly part-time and low paid employment). Although most homeless people are national citizens, in many EU countries (especially among the EU-15) there is a growing proportion of immigrants among the street homeless and among homeless service users (in some countries this is the majority).

---

101  Data are not available for: Bulgaria, Cyprus, Denmark, Germany, Greece, Lithuania, Luxembourg, Romania, Slovakia, Slovenia, Sweden, Malta.

102  Data are not available from: Bulgaria, Cyprus, Germany, Greece, Latvia, Luxembourg, Romania, Slovakia, Malta.

## 4.3 Necessary elements to prevent and tackle HHE

### 4.3.1 Governance framework

The locus of responsibility for homeless policies, programmes and strategies differs between Member States. Furthermore, the relationship between homeless policies and housing policies on the one hand and social welfare or support policies on the other hand also varies across Europe. Hence national, regional and local administrations all have a role to play in the development and implementation of homeless policies and strategies. However, evidence suggests that regional and local action depends upon the national government to establish the strategic framework with appropriate funding and guidance. This requires that HHE be a priority issue for government and that this be driven by political will.

While policies, in most countries, are determined at national level, the responsibility for their implementation lies at the local level. Given the range of factors underlying vulnerability in the housing market, policies to address the issue of HHE will involve a range of departmental interests within government. A key feature of the development of HHE policies in countries which have developed national strategies has been the coordination of the main departments (e.g. Ministries of housing, environment, local government, social welfare, health and justice) together with a clear central responsibility for action. This responsibility varies across Europe – e.g., in Finland and Ireland it lies with the Ministries of the Environment, in Sweden and Denmark with the Ministries of Social Welfare, in the UK and Norway with the Departments of Local Government.

Since responsibility for implementation of HHE policies lies at the local level, central-local relationship and decentralisation represents a significant issue requiring vertical coordination between the levels of government. The most significant aspect of this requires clear funding procedures. However, all too often decentralisation has occurred without clarity of matched funding or increased resources to implement the strategic aims of HHE policies.

In addition to ensuring the appropriate level of funding for policies, coordination between levels of government also requires the involvement of local authorities in the development and monitoring of strategic aims as well as guidance and action to improve the capacity of local actors to deliver policies. Good practice can be found in a number of countries on these issues. Ireland and Portugal have developed local network approaches – local homelessness forums in Ireland and local social inclusion partnerships in Portugal. Norway has provided specific funding managed by the Housing Bank and the Social Welfare Executive Agency for building local capacity and local peer reviews. England has developed the concept of champion authorities supported by good practice guidance documents.[103] In the Netherlands, the Ministry of Health, Welfare and Sport has cooperated with the four main cities (*G4 strategy*) to prepare a homeless strategy. In Finland the Ministry of Environment funds the Y-Foundation to act as a facilitator with local authorities in the provision of supported accommodation.

### 4.3.2    Problem definition

A consensual understanding of the nature of HHE is a necessary component for the coordination of strategy development and policy evaluation. The ETHOS typology of HHE (see above) has provided a basis for discussion across Europe. While only a small number of countries adopt broad definitions related to ETHOS, many have adopted a narrower definition, using the ETHOS categories, which gives precedence to homelessness rather than housing exclusion. It was for this reason that the study on Measuring Homelessness in Europe (Edgar *et al*, 2007) suggested a harmonised definition of homelessness.

There may be different reasons why countries prefer a narrower definition focusing on homelessness rather than housing exclusion. This may be partly due to a lack of political priority given to the topic. It may also be due to the perception that homelessness is a social welfare issue rather than a housing issue and a conceptual understanding of the nature of the problem which focuses on personal pathology rather then structural and institutional factors. If the social inclusion objective of ensuring access to decent and affordable housing is to be realised then a definition of HHE which recognises insecure and inadequate housing as a component of exclusion and deprivation is essential to allow for the development of evidence-based policies in each Member State. A more systematic and consistent use of the ETHOS definition across the EU would improve understanding and allow more in-depth international comparisons.

### 4.3.3    Problem analysis

It is an essential prerequisite of the development of appropriate strategies that HHE policies are evidence based. Furthermore, the review and evaluation of policy implementation also requires robust data analysis linked to the main strategic objectives. The Measuring Homelessness study (Edgar *et al*, 2007) proposed the adoption of a Homeless Monitoring Information Strategy and identified a methodology to achieve this. The

---

103   For more information on these (sub-)national practices, see: Edgar (2009).

MPHASIS project (2007 to 2009)[104], which involved 20 countries (19 EU countries plus Norway), tested the study's key recommendations which were, in the main, found to have relevance to build capacity for data collection and analysis (Edgar and Marlier, 2009). The recommended approach was, indeed, built on an understanding of good practice already in operation in a number of countries.

Edgar *et al* (2007) argue for the need for input indicators, "system" indicators and output indicators (see Figure 4.1). They use this understanding to specify the need to utilise different sources of information at each stage. Information for input indicators is mainly dependent on the improved use of administrative data sources. For example, the more systematic compilation of information on prisoner discharge and housing and the court records relating to eviction procedures. Edgar *et al* (2007) specify a methodology for improving the capacity of information from the homeless system by maintaining data-bases on service providers and by collating the client record information held by service providers for policy making purposes. These approaches were piloted in five countries during the MPHASIS project and issues for the implementation of these methods were identified. In relation to output indicators, information is needed on the provision of supporting people and the clients who receive housing support in that accommodation in order to live independently in the community. There is also a need to develop outcome measures to allow for policy evaluation in situations where homeless people have been re-housed into permanent housing (with or without support). While good practice exists in this area in a small number of countries (e.g. the Netherlands, the UK), this is an aspect of policy analysis which is still embryonic.

**Figure 4.1: Homeless system pathways**

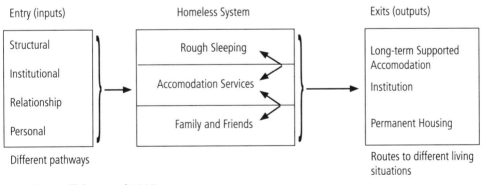

*Source: Edgar et al 2007*

---

104  MPHASIS stands for "Mutual Progress on Homelessness through Advancing and Strengthening Information Systems". For more information: http://www.trp.dundee.ac.uk/research/mphasis/index.html.

### 4.3.4    Strategy

Only a minority (around 10 in total) of the 27 Member States have developed national homeless strategies; though strategies are adopted in some major regions in various countries with a federal structure. In all cases, these strategies have recognised the multidimensional nature of HHE and have involved a range of key central government departments in their development. (See MPHASIS project, *Op. Cit.*; see also: Edgar *et al*, 2007; Frazer and Marlier, 2009.)

It has been argued (Edgar *et al*, 2007) that, in the framework of the EU Social OMC, national and local governments should be developing strategies to:
- prevent homelessness;
- tackle the causes of homelessness;
- reduce the level of homelessness;
- reduce the negative effects on homeless people and their families; and
- ensure that formerly homeless people can sustain permanent independent housing.

Where (national) homeless strategies have been adopted, there is a growing focus on issues of prevention though the approach to prevention varies (see below). Increasingly there is a focus on ending some aspects of homelessness – rough sleeping (in most strategies) or long-term homelessness (Finland, Ireland). A number of strategies include objectives related to the nature and quality of accommodation and/or services for homeless people (e.g. Denmark, Finland, Norway, Ireland, Netherlands).

A thorough review of homeless strategies in Europe (Edgar, 2009) shows that the majority of national strategies have adopted a limited number of key targets linked to survey evidence and that there is an identified source of the evidence which will be used to monitor the implementation of these targets over time. It is apparent also that the adoption of an appropriate or realistic time-scale is a key aspect of monitoring processes. For example, several countries have committed to achieve specific targets within a defined period – end rough sleeping (Ireland by 2012), end long-term homelessness (Finland by 2015), ensure all homeless people are provided with permanent accommodation in a reasonable period (Scotland, 2011). Other countries specify more constrained targets. For example, the "G4 strategy" in the Netherlands (i.e. a strategy covering the 4 largest cities) aims to reduce the level of evictions by 50% in 3 years; the Norwegian strategy has a similar target and also commits to ensure that no one shall have to spend time in temporary housing upon release from prison by the end of the strategy period. (For a detailed discussion of various issues linked to the setting of targets, see Marlier *et al*, pages 201-217.)

### 4.3.5    Delivery and implementation

A key element of policy is that implementation takes place at the appropriate – local – level and that the mechanisms of delivery are effective. This means that the local authorities and actors involved in implementation have the capacity to meet the needs of homeless people and achieve the objectives of policy. Capacity means that local authorities have adequate resources – hence decentralised responsibility requires central government subvention of resources to match demand. Effective delivery also requires a capacity of service providers – i.e., an NGO sector which has organisations whose experience and management structure is capable of providing the services procured with public funds. In most of the new Member States this NGO capacity has taken time to develop and has required state and EU involvement. Involvement of international NGOs can distort local development (see Hradejký, 2008; Salamon and Anheier, 2006). While international NGOs may help to accelerate the development of local NGOs capacity, they can also distort public funding and influence NGOs cooperation. Effective delivery also requires a professionalised and trained staff working within appropriate management structures (Donabedian, 1982).

### 4.3.6    Review and monitoring mechanisms

While evidence is required to develop strategies and determine appropriate targets to achieve policy objectives, data are also needed to review and evaluate policies and to monitor the progress of organisations that use public funds in pursuit of those policy goals. The development of a Homeless Monitoring Information System should establish the mechanism and responsibility for ensuring that the required data are available in the right time-frame and format to allow review of policies. As mentioned above, homeless strategies should specify an appropriate time-frame within which monitoring of targets can be undertaken.

Different mechanisms of review can be identified among countries that have established homeless strategies. First, the provision of information by NGOs is made a condition of funding during the procurement process; for example, information on the *Supporting People* programme is provided on this basis in England[105]. Second, local authorities are required to make returns to central government on key indicators of HHE; so, the Norwegian KOSTRA (*"KOmmune-STat-RApportering"*, i.e. "Municipality-State-Reporting"), system of municipal data has five areas of indicator including HHE. Third, the strategic authority can establish a central committee to undertake continuous monitoring of the strategy. For instance, in Scotland the Homeless Monitoring Group comprises all key stakeholders and reports to the Minister. In France, the *"Observatoire national de la pau-*

---

105  See website: http://www.spclientrecord.org.uk/.

*vrété et de l'exclusion sociale"* (i.e., "National Observatory on poverty and social exclusion") provides a basis for the coordination of statistical research on homeless people. Finally, local homeless forums provide a basis for information collection and policy review. In Ireland and Portugal, local networks of stakeholders provide a platform for information on homelessness including local homeless surveys.

## 4.4 Key policy elements

Governments have a range of policy instruments at their disposal to ensure that citizens have access to decent and affordable housing and that people who are vulnerable in the housing market can be assisted and protected. Bemelmans-Videc *et al* (1998) present a three-fold typology of policy instruments based on the degree of constraint imposed on target groups which can be summarised as:
- Regulatory instruments (sticks): constitute highly choice constraining instruments.
- Economic Instruments (carrots): are moderately choice constraining.
- Information Instruments (sermons): provide information about implications of choices.

It is beyond the scope of this chapter to discuss the range of instruments employed in these areas in relation to housing, social welfare and homelessness policies to prevent and combat housing exclusion. Hence the following sections present a review of selected aspects of policy.

### 4.4.1    *Policies to prevent HHE*

*Housing linked policies*
An adequate supply of affordable housing, access to which is either controlled through social housing mechanisms or by the regulation of the private rented sector, is a necessary (though not always sufficient) condition to prevent HHE. Across the EU, most countries have a relatively small (and often declining) rental sector that is controlled by public policies and agencies. Since access to homeownership is beyond the reach of most people with a low income or unstable employment, the private rented sector is increasingly viewed by Governments across the EU as a crucial element in the mix of housing services that can provide accessible accommodation for households who are experiencing or are at risk of homelessness (O'Sullivan and de Decker, 2007).

As Carr *et al* (2007, page 122) observe, "although it is a commonplace assertion that the private rented sector is deregulated and decontrolled, the types of control and regulation that exist in the sector have been dispersed through, for example, controls on housing benefit, property quality and, less so, security of tenure". Regulation of the private rented sector occurs in the Member States in relation to different aspects of policy. First, many countries require that, in order to rent a dwelling, a landlord must be registered to ensure that the minimum standards of housing and tenancy management are in force. Different aspects of housing management are reflected in such regulatory legislation. Second, vulnerable groups are protected by the regulation of multiple occupation dwellings (i.e. dwellings occupied by three or more unrelated people). Third, the physical standards of rented dwellings are regulated according to minimum housing quality standards.

*Social welfare policies*

The "accommodation with support", i.e. the provision of support to people in their own homes, as well as (purpose built) "supported accommodation" has been a feature of policy in some countries since the de-institutionalisation process of the 1980s (Edgar *et al*, 2000). During that time, an extensive research literature has examined the effectiveness of support in the long-term re-housing of homeless people (see for example, Busch-Geertsema, 2005; Kirkwood and Richley, 2008) as well as the coordination of the provision, funding and management of supported housing (MacPherson *et al*, 2004). Issues have been identified related to the sustainability of funding, the design and management of purpose built accommodation, the nature of ambulant support and the coordination of services between housing providers and social services providers. Two recent examples of the impact of supported accommodation policies on homeless strategies can be cited here: the recent Finnish strategy launched in 2008 which aims to convert all homeless accommodation into small scale supported accommodation (see Tainio and Frederiksson, 2009) and the Irish Homeless Strategy (which has introduced a Supported Living Initiative in 2008 for homeless people). Elsewhere, research has demonstrated the cost-effectiveness of supported accommodation compared to other forms of policy intervention (see Flatau *et al*, 2008; Flatau and Zaretzky, 2008).

*Strategies to prevent homelessness*

Prevention of homelessness can be understood in relation to the main causes or pathways into homelessness. At the structural level, the provision of adequate affordable housing and of social welfare support is a necessary framework of prevention. At the institutional level, removing access barriers to services and non-discriminatory allocation mechanisms are also necessary pre-requisites to ensure that vulnerable groups obtain the services they require in order to prevent their risk of homelessness. At the relationship level, services aimed at the prevention of family breakdown and at mediation and support for dysfunctional families is increasingly adopted as part of prevention strategies. At the personal level, targeted prevention action aims to prevent the risk of repeat homelessness or of long-term homelessness. This overview suggests three distinct approaches to prevention which are summarised in Table 4.3.

**Table 4.3: Prevention of homelessness – Approaches and examples**

| Prevention Approach | Example Focus | Initiative | Good Practice Example |
|---|---|---|---|
| | Youth Homelessness | Education Guidance and Information | Scotland |
| Precautionary Intervention | | Supported tenancies | France |
| | | Children Leaving Institutional Care | None known – some local examples |
| Pre-Crisis Intervention | Prison Discharge | Discharge Protocols | Norway, Netherlands |
| | Eviction | Renters – Funds, Housing | Austria, Germany, Norway |
| Prevention of Recurrent and/ or Long-term Homelessness | Recurrent | Ending repeat homelessness | Denmark |
| | Long-term | Ending chronic homelessness | Finland, Ireland |

*Source: Table prepared by W. Edgar for this volume*

However, some prevention action relates to more than one of these categories. For example, prevention of eviction and family mediation action can occur in all three categories.

### 4.4.2   Policies to combat HHE

Policies to combat homelessness have evolved from more traditional approaches dealing with intervention to address the crisis situation, towards approaches aiming to alleviate the effects of homelessness through rehabilitation and stabilisation allowing the re-integration of the person into permanent housing. These approaches involved the use of emergency hostel accommodation to cope with the crisis situation, transitional or temporary accommodation (normally still in collective living situations) and finally permanent housing. In varying degrees, this involved a "staircase of transition" (Sahlin, 1999). In recent years, evidence has demonstrated that a "housing first" approach is effective even for those people with intensive support needs and that it is also cost efficient (Busch-Geertsema, 2005; Culhane, 2008a). Here, the aim is to reduce the length of time people spend in crisis or temporary accommodation and to re-house the person (quickly) into conventional accommodation as the locus where intervention to deal with their needs can take place. For example, the Homelessness Monitoring Group in Scotland identified a number of key criteria to be monitored as part of the process of assessing progress on programme delivery which included an indicator on the percentage of households placed directly into permanent accommodation. A review of homeless strategies allows identifying policies in a number of countries where the target is to ensure people do not stay in temporary accommodation for more than a defined period. The Irish Strategy, for example, aims that by 2010 no one should be in emergency accommodation longer than six months as part of the strategic objective to eliminate long-term homelessness. Figure 4.2 summarises this shift in policy approach.

This shift in policy focus has been associated, in many countries, with a refurbishment of traditional hostel accommodation into smaller scale living situations with less communal or shared rooms and more privacy. While this re-provisioning of supply has occurred in many countries, perhaps the most ambitious target in EU Member States has been set by Finland where the aim is to eliminate the use of hostel accommodation altogether by 2015. This shift in policy focus has also been associated with the development of supported accommodation or accommodation with support (Edgar *et al*, 2000) though the scale of housing support services has been slow to develop in some countries and the pattern across Europe is variable.

**Figure 4.2: Summary of shift in homeless policy approaches**

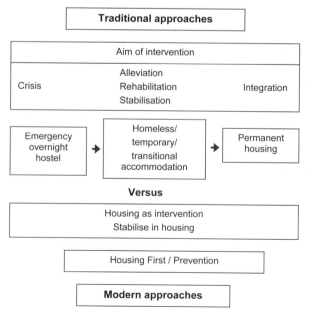

*Source: Figure prepared by W. Edgar for this volume*

### 4.4.3    Policies to ensure quality housing and homeless services

*Homeless services and accommodation*

In examining the range of services provided to homeless people across the EU, a broad typology of services emerges; these are summarised in Table 4.4.

**Table 4.4: Typology of services for homeless people**

| Services for homeless people | Examples |
|---|---|
| Accommodation for homeless people | Emergency shelters, temporary hostels, supported or transitional housing |
| Non-residential services for homeless people | Outreach services, day centres, advice services etc |
| Accommodation for other client groups that may be used by homeless people | Hotels, bed and breakfast, specialist support and residential care services for people with alcohol, drug or mental health services |
| Mainstream services for the general population that may be used by homeless people | Advice services, municipal services, health and social care services |
| Specialist support services for other client groups that may be used by homeless people | Psychiatric counselling services, drug detoxification facilities |

*Source: Edgar et al, 2007*

These services may be provided by a wide range of service providers including the public or state sector (at a national, regional or local level), NGOs and the private sector. Funding for services may be provided by state, private or charitable sources, or a combination of these sources. Accommodation and support services for homeless people are subject to change and evolve over time in response to changing client needs and available resources. The mix of service provision varies in different countries depending upon the nature of welfare provision and the history of development of voluntary sector agencies and thus it is possible to specify different service typologies in the Member States.

It should be an aim of policy, in the framework of the debate on social services of general interest, to ensure that accommodation services meet an adequate standard and that support services comply with minimum standards of care and that mechanisms of inspection and regulation are adequate to ensure compliance (Wolf and Edgar, 2007). In the Netherlands, for example, the umbrella homeless organisation (Federatie Opvang) has developed a kite-mark (ISO) standard for care/support services which member NGOs are encouraged to adopt. While it should be relatively easy to be prescriptive about accommodation standards and to establish mechanisms of inspection and regulation as well as setting normative funding criteria, the diversity of accommodation types makes international comparisons difficult. It should be possible to develop a generic definition of homeless accommodation to allow a mapping of different national nomenclature of accommodation forms (see Table 4.5).

**Table 4.5: Criteria for defining homeless accommodation forms**

| Access criteria | Direct | In person |
|---|---|---|
| | Referral | From agency or statutory body |
| Period of stay | Overnight | Normally not more than 24 hour stay |
| | Short (not defined) | While awaiting assessment/re-housing |
| | Short (defined) | Period linked to training, support or move-on |
| | Longer-term | Linked to resettlement support, rehabilitation |
| Purpose/Intention | Emergency | Crisis |
| | Interim | Assessment for support or re-housing |
| | Transitional | Receiving support or training |
| | Specialist | Resettlement, rehabilitation or refuge |

*Source: Edgar and Meert, 2005*

Key principles can be used to establish standards of accommodation that can be identified by reference to the three domains of physical, legal and social issues. In each of these domains, basic normative standards can be established. For example, the physical space should of course conform to building, fire and health and safety regulations; people should be protected against summary eviction or eviction at night from the accommodation; people should be guaranteed safety from violence or harassment and have access to privacy. Standards of accommodation may then be established depending upon the purpose of the provision – emergency hostels, transitional / longer-stay hostels, supported accommodation. Hence, the size of emergency hostels and the extent of communal dormitories rather than single or small shared rooms can be regulated. Legal rights can also be seen to vary in this respect so that the aim should be that people in supported accommodation have a normal tenancy which is not dependent upon support provision while reasonable notice and protection from summary or night-time eviction may be an appropriate standard in other forms of accommodation. Standards can be established and enforced through appropriate procurement models. The Norwegian homeless strategy, for example, states that homeless people will not be placed in hostels which do not have an approved quality standard agreement (with the municipality).

*Affordable housing*
Policies related to housing exclusion need to address the burden imposed by housing costs and the desirability of capturing situations where an "excess burden" is imposed on

households by these costs (Marlier *et al*, 2007). A clear, consensual and strictly comparable definition of housing costs cannot be achieved across Europe, in particular because of the very different ways housing benefits are allocated to beneficiaries not only across the different EU countries but also sometimes within them. However, in 2009 the European Commission and the 27 EU Member States agreed upon one operational definition which has allowed for the adoption of a "burdened by housing costs" indicator, which measures the percentage of the population living in a household where the total housing costs (net of housing allowances) represent more than 40% of the total disposable household income (net of housing allowances)[106].

Another way of approaching the financial burden of housing costs is to subtract the cash transfers aimed at covering housing costs from the total household income and to calculate a residual household income after housing expenditure net of housing support. Those with a residual income falling below an agreed threshold can be said to experience deprivation or exclusion due to housing costs. This method has been employed in the UK (Scotland) to test the affordability of rent for tenants of social housing (the affordability test stated that rents were not affordable for tenants having a residual income of less than 140% of the income support threshold after paying rent – this was monitored on a continuous basis).

### Quality Housing

The most basic condition of housing quality is that it is fit for human habitation. Different approaches can be used to define "fitness" operationally but essentially the aim is to measure whether the dwelling is structurally stable and wind and watertight, and whether the major elements of the building (e.g. roof, windows, key building fabric elements) satisfactorily meet health requirements or normal expectations of family life. Very few Member States have a statutory definition of "fitness for habitation". The UK statutory definition of fitness for habitation includes the following items:

- be structurally stable;
- be free from serious disrepair;
- be free from dampness prejudicial to the health of the occupants;
- have adequate provision for lighting, heating and ventilation;
- have a suitably located WC for exclusive use of the occupants;
- have a bath or shower and wash hand basin, with hot and cold water;
- have an effective system for the drainage of foul, waste and surface water; and
- have satisfactory facilities for the preparation and cooking of food including a sink with hot and cold water.

---

106   To complement this indicator, the EU has also adopted a background statistic ("context information"): the median share of housing costs in the total disposable household income (for both the total population and the population at risk of poverty). For the detailed definition of these indicator and statistic, see: European Commission, 2009.

If fitness for habitation is an absolute measure of dwelling quality, a normative standard of housing deprivation can be specified in relation to the state of repair of the dwelling. The EU has adopted a background statistic aimed at measuring "housing deprivation" and defined as the percentage of the population deprived of each (or several) of the following housing deprivation items:

- leaking roof, damp walls/floors/foundations, or rot in window frames or floors;
- no bath or shower in the dwelling;
- no indoor flushing toilet for the sole use of the household; and
- dwelling too dark.

In addition to the physical standard of the dwelling, issues of housing quality can also relate to the social dimension related to the occupancy of the dwelling – this is the overcrowding dimension. Three definitions of overcrowding can be identified in use across Europe:

- internal space standards (measured in square metres of habitable rooms – i.e., excluding hall and bathroom);
- cccupancy standards (number of persons per habitable room); and
- involuntary sharing – single family occupancy; household should not be required to share a dwelling with people to whom they are unrelated due to lack of housing.

These definitions relate to different types of measure – physical (space), social (occupancy) or normative (single family). In 2009, the EU adopted an indicator of overcrowding which is defined as the percentage of persons living in a household that does not have at its disposal at least (European Commission, 2009):

- one room for the household;
- one room for each couple;
- one room for each single person aged 18+;
- one room for two single people of the same sex between 12 and 17 years of age;
- one room for each single person of different sex between 12 and 17 years of age;
- one room for two people under 12 years of age.[107]

---

107 The calculation includes single households and considers them as overcrowded if they live in a studio with a bedroom not separated from the living room. A variant, excluding single households, is also included in the EU portfolio of Social OMC indicators.

## 4.5 Homelessness and housing exclusion in Belgium

The study of national policies in relation to HHE, conducted by the EU Network of Independent Experts in 2009 (Frazer and Marlier, 2009), revealed a very fragmented landscape in Belgium. The 'national questionnaire' filled out for this purpose actually consisted of a set of uncoordinated forms reflecting partial approaches at different (national, regional, community) policy levels. This applies to housing in general as well as other relevant policy areas (social protection, migration, social work etc.)[108]. For example, whereas the Belgian NAP/inclusion for the period 2008-2010 includes a quantitative target in relation to the availability of public tenement housing (8% by 2010), the implementation of this target depends entirely on the regions, and no regional breakdown of the target has been agreed upon – nor any coordination mechanism if regional implementation plans diverge or fall short of their commitments.

There is not even a 'national' definition of HHE: the ETHOS definition proposed by FEANTSA has been welcomed by all stakeholders as a useful basis for coordinated data collection. Actually, most (national or regional) definitions refer, at least implicitly, to the two first ETHOS categories, i.e. the roof- and homeless.

The only coordinated policy document in this field is probably the housing chapter of the NAP/inclusion 2008-2010. The objective as formulated by this document is the provision of decent and adequate housing for everyone. Hereby, the national authorities commit themselves to a very ambitious and important task. In order to achieve this goal, the plan takes into account the complex nature of the housing problem. It focuses not only on the provision of housing as such, but also on various related issues such as access to (and use of) energy, integration into the neighbourhood, etc. The housing policy chapter of the NAP/inclusion will be discussed at length in section 4.5.5.

The thematic year on HHE in the context of the European OMC (2009) has further encouraged coordination at the national level. A recent report produced by the Belgian Resource Centre for the fight against Poverty (*'Towards a coherent approach in the fight against homelessness and poverty'* – SLPPES, 2010) upon request from the federal govern-

---

108  Whereas the federal government is responsible for legislation on the operation of the private housing market and social protection, homelessness and housing exclusion are principally a 'regional' competence. 'Regional' should be understood here as a competence of the Regions (Flanders, Wallonia, Brussels) as well as the Communities (French, Flemish, German-speaking). The Regions have authority over matters concerning property, and thus housing and housing exclusion. The Communities are competent in matters that concern people, and thus homelessness. Moreover, the municipalities have certain competences as well – mainly through the actions and policies developed by the PCSWs.

ment provides a comprehensive framework and agenda which will hopefully foster an integrated policy approach. This report was drafted by a 'dialogue group' gathering all relevant stakeholders, including associations of homeless people. The 70 policy recommendations in the report cut across all policy levels and cover a very wide range of policy areas, from the ratification of international treaties to the prevention of family disruption. Interestingly, social services for the roofless occupy the sixth position in the list of thematic sections, while the first section deals with access to fundamental rights. This reflects a structural, preventive and rights-based approach to the issue. The main headings of the policy recommendations include:

- access to fundamental rights,
- knowledge about HHE,
- income, work and social protection,
- health,
- housing,
- procedures of discharge from institutions,
- social services to roof- and homeless people, and
- coordination of policies.

### 4.5.1.   Counting dark numbers

It is no easy task to estimate the *number* of homeless people, as they are generally excluded from all statistics. FEANTSA estimated the number of homeless in Belgium at 17,000 in 2003. An estimate for Flanders in 2007, based on the figures of the Resource Centre for Social Work (SAW), was that 7,980 homeless people were staying in night shelters or hostels and 2,335 were receiving an ambulant form of assistance, representing a total of 10,315 people. 54% of them had an income at or below the social assistance level, and 90% were unemployed (De Decker and Van Menxel, 2005). In the Tellus customer registration system of the Centres for Social Work (CAWs), we find that scarcely one in eight of the homeless people draw an income from work, and that 30% of them have no income when they are taken in. In the past 15 years (Table 4.6), an increase has been recorded in the proportion of women, of the relatively well educated, and homeless people of non-Belgian origin. In 2007, 27% of homeless people were of non-Belgian origin. Contrary to what might be expected, these are not generally people residing illegally on Belgian territory: they are predominantly people staying legally in the country.

**Table 4.6: Socio-economic profile of the homeless population (Flanders, 1982-2007, %)**

| Characteristic | 1982 | 2007 |
|---|---|---|
| Women | 18 | 33 |
| Young homeless < 30 years | 50 | 52 |
| Homeless 30-50 years | 31 | 34 |
| Older homeless > 50 years | 19 | 14 |
| Non-Belgian origin | 9 | 27 |
| Single | 66 | 66 |
| Divorced | 13 | 19 |
| No education or only to primary level | 44 | 30 |
| Educated to lower secondary level only | 30 | 23 |
| Rate of employment | 21 | 12 |
| Main income from work | 24 | 13 |
| Unemployment benefit | 19 | 37 |
| Assistance (OCMW) | 28 | 18 |
| Debt | 25 | - |

*Source: Van Menxel et al (2003); Vranken et al (2008, page 376).*

In the Brussels Region, the Support Centre for Aid for the Homeless *La Strada* (2009) performed a count of the number of homeless (ETHOS categories (a) and (b)) at the end of 2008. 145 counting personnel travelled round the city, counting all homeless people in a variety of public locations (streets, stations, etc.), in squats and in shelters and reception centres, in the space of one hour. In total, 2,766 homeless people were counted. The authors note that this is a minimum estimate, and that this overall figure comprises a very heterogeneous population: young mothers with children, illegal immigrants, drug addicts, loitering young people, and so on. A number of striking observations also emerged from the exercise: the importance of 'negotiated squatting' as a stepping stone to a more stable living situation; the considerable role played by railway and underground stations as a place where homeless people stay; and the substantial proportion of unrecognised centres among the reception facilities.

On the French-speaking side, the association of hostels and shelters published a book in 2008 in which (as well as more qualitative analyses) a number of profile data of the clientele of reception centres in Wallonia and (French-speaking) Brussels are summarised (De Backer, 2008). Over the year 2006 as a whole, 18,000 (in principle distinct) individuals were accommodated in these reception centres: 55% adult men, 24% adult women and 19% children. Note that the number of individuals on an annual basis represents a multiple of the number on a daily basis, since the total reception capacity is only 2,860 places.

Apart from several trends which are consistent with the findings of the Flemish Resource Centre for Social Work, De Backer also mentions the following trends (partly based on interviews with key informants from the sector):

- the increase in the number of children in the reception centres;
- the severe shortage of reception places (with approx. 14,000 requests for accommodation turned down on an annual basis);
- the sluggishness of the housing market is also contributing to the lengthening of the average duration of stay in reception centres;
- the issues are becoming more complex: among other things, there is an increasing incidence of mental health problems, which make reintegration into society more difficult.

The prevalence of inadequate and insecure housing is even more difficult to assess than genuine homelessness. In 2000, the number of undocumented migrants, for example, was estimated at 87,000. The itinerant population (such as mobile home residents and bargees) was estimated at 20,000. The problem with these figures is that the corresponding populations do not necessarily live in inadequate or insecure conditions. The closest we get to a systematic representation of insecure or inadequate housing are the figures provided by the EU-SILC. In 2006, it was estimated that 25% of the population lived in a dwelling with two or more structural problems, 18% in Flanders and 36% in Wallonia[109]. The proportion of the population living in a dwelling with less than one separate room per person was estimated at 4.9% for Belgium as a whole, 4.6% in Flanders and 2.8% in the Walloon Region[110]. 29.6% of the Belgian population lived in a situation characterised by a housing problem, or a dwelling affected by comfort or structural issues, 22.9% of the Flemish population and 37.8% of the Walloon population[111].

### 4.5.2    A basic rights approach

While it is probably a commonplace to state that homelessness is a symptom of multidimensional exclusion rather than a housing problem, it is less obvious to recognise that it obstructs the access to fundamental rights, such as the right to social protection, to pri-

---

109  Structural problems are: leaking roof, no adequate heating, mould and humidity, and decaying casing and doors. The estimates for Brussels are unreliable and therefore not presented. Source: FPS Social Security.

110  Source: FPS Social Security.

111  Source: FPS Social Security.

vacy, to work etc. Sleeping rough can be seen as the final stage in a process of systematic disruption of all social and economic links between an individual and his/her environment. A person who has no legal residence, for example, cannot claim any social benefit or conclude a work contract. Emergency shelter or health care cannot restore the links that are required to re-integrate into society. The participants in the 'dialogue group' that prepared the report *'Towards a coherent approach in the fight against homelessness and poverty'* (SLPPES, 2010) therefore stressed three guiding principles for an effective eradication of the problem: strengthening basic rights, taking into account the experience and aspirations of homeless people, and reaching out to the poorest among the poor.

To begin with, *existing laws should be fully implemented*. For example, municipalities have the legal right to occupy unused private buildings for emergency housing; tenants can be protected against unlawful evictions; homeless people have the right to take a 'reference address' at the municipal social service (PCSW)… but these laws are not applied due to the ignorance or powerlessness of the poor vis-à-vis public services or landlords. In some cases, the administrative procedures are unnecessarily long, or unnecessary additional conditions are being imposed on applicants.

Referring to the French example, grassroots organisations demand an "invocable right to housing" in emergency situations, and the automatic assignment of rights wherever this is possible. They notice that Belgium still needs to ratify article 31 of the revised European Social Treaty (about the right to housing).

Similarly, in other policy areas, the effective guarantee of basic rights may prevent exclusion leading to homelessness. The tightening of access to *social protection* (including social assistance) and, above all, the proliferation of sanctions and suspensions, irrespective of the household income of beneficiaries,[112] appear to take their toll. Grassroots organisations point to the federal activation plan on unemployment insurance, (introduced in 2004 and advertised in the NAP/inclusion as one of the measures for social inclusion!) as one of the new triggers of homelessness.

On the other hand, some regulations in the social protection system appear to hinder exits from homelessness. For example, when a single homeless person is received in a shelter or a private household, his/her benefit may be reduced from the 'single' to the 'cohabitant' level. This may even apply to a private person who decides to host a homeless friend, if the host draws a benefit. Such legal clauses obviously discourage solidarity and prevent the development of informal solutions (SLPPES, 2010, page 14).

---

112  In the past, long-term unemployed were 'immunised' against suspension if they had dependant family members. This protective measure is no longer applied in the new activation plan.

### 4.5.3    *Preventing homelessness and fostering reintegration*

A sensible social policy should foster the *economic and social ties between vulnerable house-holds and their environment* (or, wherever possible, prevent their disruption). The previous paragraph on sanctions and cohabitant benefits in social protection schemes can be seen as an illustration of this principle. But it also applies in various fields:

- some situations of homelessness are triggered by family disruption or debt crises. *Family support* and *debt mediation* services may thus prevent homelessness;
- *supported accommodation*, combining housing with social guidance should facilitate reintegration;
- Legal restrictions on *eviction* do exist (e.g. during the winter), but they are not always respected due to ignorance or powerlessness among poor people. Compensation of the victims by their landlords should be provided by law;
- Many homeless people have lived in *institutions* (youth care, psychiatric hospital, prison). Not only should they be better prepared for an independent lifestyle, but their social protection should be improved and guidance should be provided after they have left the institution. For example, young people should have access to counselling services beyond the age of 18 in order to avoid being 'dumped' in society at that age. Ex-offenders, in particular, should be entitled to more decent reintegration benefits, and while in prison, contacts with their family and social environment should be fostered with a view to easing their reintegration;
- all preventive and reintegration measures in the field of *housing* will be discussed in section 4.5.5.

### 4.5.4    *Services for the homeless*

The rising imbalance between the capacity of existing services on the one hand, and the growing demand for shelter on the other, means that some homeless people are even excluded from bare survival services. The ongoing crisis in the reception of asylum-seekers and undocumented immigrants contributes to growing tensions in shelters and hostels. The report of the Resource Centre (SLPPES, 2010, pages 67 ff.) advocates prompt access to decent services, arguing that lack of capacity tends to exacerbate problems and to make the rehabilitation of clients more difficult.

Some shelters or hostels impose conditions that actually exclude large numbers of homeless people: unaffordable rent prices, no accommodation for pet animals, strict house rules, exclusion of some categories etc. Homeless people excluded from these services have to address the 'secondary segment' of non-accredited provision, which sometimes offers poor-quality services or exploits clients. Service standards should be imposed by law in order to avoid a segmentation of provision into 'luxury' and 'poor' accommodation.

Rough sleepers in public spaces should have access to drinkable water and sanitation, free of charge.

The municipal social services (Public Centres for Social Welfare) are responsible for social assistance (see section 3.3). The right to social assistance mainly includes the 'integration income' (living wage), employment, and access to (affordable) healthcare. In practice, the applicant often receives a medical card, with which most medical expenses can be directly charged to the PCSW. Other specialised organisations such as CAWs, homes or the Social Links can act as intermediaries between the homeless and health workers and PCSWs – or in some cases offer healthcare themselves.

Social assistance can be very broadly and openly interpreted. The law does not provide an exhaustive list of the different types of assistance provided by the PCSWs. Regarding the homeless, it is worth noting that many PCSWs (and CAWs) have their own debt mediation services and services for legal assistance. Moreover, these services are in principle free of charge. It is also worth mentioning that PCSWs can act as a 'reference address' for homeless people. Every person with no legal residence can take a reference address with the PCSW or a private household. This is important with a view to obtaining a living wage or other social benefits. In theory, the PCSW cannot refuse the assignment of a reference address, but field workers claim that some PCSWs prevent its application by imposing additional conditions (e.g. that the claimant already draws a benefit…). Last but not least, many PCSWs have their own transit accommodation, which is often less extensive than that of the CAWs but more suitable for homeless families. PCSWs can thus offer integrated services at the local level.

### 4.5.5    Housing policy

This section focuses on housing policy in particular, but widens the issue from homelessness to 'access to decent and affordable housing'. As mentioned earlier, the competencies in housing policies are shared between the federal and regional authorities.

#### 4.5.5.1 The context

The Belgian housing market is characterised by (a) a very high (and still increasing) share of private ownership (70%), (b) a small share of social tenement housing (6%). For the younger generation, however, ownership of a dwelling has become a privilege – see Table 4.7. Between 2000 and 2008, the average cost of an ordinary house more than doubled, both at regional and national level. In Brussels, prices have almost tripled. The change in prices is less pronounced for apartments, but they have still more or less doubled.

**Table 4.7: Average cost of a dwelling and relative price change between 2000 and 2008 (EUR and %)**

|  | Ordinary house | | | Apartments | | |
|---|---|---|---|---|---|---|
|  | 2000 | 2008 | Change | 2000 | 2008 | Change |
| Flanders | 84,772 | 181,846 | 115% | 92,979 | 178,176 | 92% |
| Wallonia | 68,559 | 135,454 | 135% | 68,640 | 138,228 | 101% |
| Brussels | 113,394 | 317,835 | 180% | 89,309 | 188,022 | 111% |
| Belgium | 79,661 | 172,611 | 116% | 88,943 | 174,155 | 96% |

*Source: FPS Economy, SMEs, self-employed and Energy – Directorate-general Statistics Belgium.*

As regards rents, data are more scarce and slightly outdated; however, the trend is more moderate (+10% in eight years), with the average stagnating around 495 €/month in 2005.

The share of social housing (6.2%) has not risen significantly since 1995. In recent years, regional governments have committed themselves to more substantial investments; however, a very serious and sustained catch-up movement would be required to meet the demand. The number of households on waiting lists is equivalent to 66.3% of the existing stock in Flanders, 45.6% in Wallonia and 79.2% in Brussels.

*4.5.5.2 The federal level*
The federal government is mainly responsible for legislation governing the private housing market. Given the marginal share of social housing in the overall housing market in Belgium, the private rental market remains crucially important. Many stakeholders would advocate a stronger regulation of the private rental market, for example, through collective bargaining mechanisms. Experiments with 'parity rental committees' negotiating controlled rent prices are met with enthusiasm, but have not been mainstreamed so far.

A recent reform of the Belgian rent act obliges landlords to publicise rent prices and to register rent contracts. It also puts a ceiling on rent guarantees and creates the possibility for banks to advance the guarantee. However, banks generally refuse to apply the law. The Resource Centre for the Fight against Poverty and its partners therefore advocate the creation of a national rent guarantee fund to take over this role.

Another hot issue in the federal legal framework relates to local authorities being able to declare a dwelling uninhabitable, which may lead to eviction of the tenants. Grassroots associations demand that landlords be obliged to provide alternative housing, or that an 'invocable' right to housing be introduced in Belgium, following the experience of France. The 'invocable right' may solve a wider range of situations of homelessness.

The federal government also coordinates (at least, partly) the PCSWs which deliver, as mentioned earlier, a range of integrated services to households faced with HHE. The federal government uses earmarked funds to support specific services, such as the 'fuel fund' (to help needy households pay for gasoil) and the 'energy fund' (for electricity and gas). Both funds are under-utilised due to complex regulations and lack of promotion by the PCSWs.

One option that has never been seriously debated is the introduction of a housing benefit, linked to the living wage. Belgium is one of the few countries in the EU which do not have a specific housing benefit. Two factors may explain this gap: (a) political opposition on the part of the liberal parties; and (b) the question of whether housing benefits should be developed at federal or regional level. The Flemish Community has already introduced a (rather marginal) rent subsidy system. A federal initiative would probably be justified only if the housing benefit were explicitly linked to the guaranteed minimum income.

### 4.5.5.3 The Brussels Region

In the policy declaration 2009-2014 of the government of the Brussels Capital Region (Brussels Hoofdstedelijk Gewest, 2009) the main objective with regard to housing is to guarantee the 'right of residence'. The declaration contains nine goals:
- framing the rent prices through the application of recommended rental prices
- helping tenants in their search for decent housing
- safeguarding and developing social housing
- expanding the public housing patrimony and balancing the dispersal of public and social housing
- developing the offer of affordable middle-class housing
- fighting against unoccupied and unsound dwellings
- mitigating energy expenses for both tenants and owners
- continuing the construction of new housing
- supporting the acquisition of housing and supporting new habitation formulas.

Together, these goals look like a well-balanced programme. The focus, however, is especially on the provision of (decent and affordable) housing. This declaration does not include measures to combat discrimination in the housing market. Moreover, it does not provide any objective or target regarding homelessness – nor are any of the goals accompanied by concrete targets.

Regarding the policy framework in the Brussels Capital Region, three important supplementary instruments can be identified:

- the Housing Code,
- the Housing Plan,[113] and
- the Regional Development Plan.[114]

The Housing Plan and the Regional Development Plan share a common focus on decent and affordable housing. Moreover, they attempt to balance policy in this domain by concentrating both on the social and public sector on the one hand, and the private sector on the other. The Regional Development Plan is especially interesting because besides a housing plan, it covers wide areas such as social cohesion and development, cultural and economic development, and political participation. However, the reader may wonder whether the plan takes into account the potential tensions between economic development and the integration of socially excluded populations – through housing or other policies.

Both plans can be primarily considered as horizontal policies. Their aim is to restructure the housing market in such a way that it will be more adapted to the needs of its current and future inhabitants. Target groups are never really specified – they are broadly defined (e.g. low-income groups, middle-class groups). Specific references to the homeless population are lacking. This does not mean that the authorities disregard homelessness. However, homelessness is not integrated into the comprehensive approach reflected in the Housing Plan and the Regional Development Plan.

*4.5.5.4 Flemish Region*
In line with the objectives set forth by both the federal and the Brussels government, the Flemish government commits itself in its recent policy declaration to provide decent and affordable housing for everyone (Vlaamse Regering, 2009). This goal can be translated into a number of operational objectives, including:

- expansion of the social housing patrimony,
- continued support to property acquisition,
- evaluation of the social rent decree (and its potential adaptation),
- renovation of the current social housing patrimony, and
- better functioning of the social rental offices.

A first reading, this policy declaration gives a rather balanced impression. Contrary to the policy declaration of the Brussels government, the Flemish government commits itself to develop and evaluate its legal instruments in the fight against housing exclusion.

---

113  http://planlogement.irisnet.be/.
114  http://www.gewop.irisnet.be.

A further difference is the focus on the efficiency of the institutions (social rental offices, social housing companies) which administer the social housing market. In common with the Brussels policy declaration, a specific reference to the issue of homelessness is lacking, and targets are missing in most cases. In fact, only a few targets are formulated with regard to the expansion of the social housing patrimony: 43,000 additional social housing units for rent, 21,000 additional social housing units for sale, and 1,000 additional social parcels by 2020.

In the Flemish policy framework on housing, we can identify three main policy instruments:

- the Housing Code,
- the Decree regarding the policy on land and property,
- the creation of a rent-subsidy scheme for the people in greatest need of housing.

The Housing Code is the most comprehensive of these instruments. First of all, it confirms the right to decent and affordable housing as a basic human right. Secondly, this legislation aims to open up access to social housing and to raise the level of protection enjoyed by tenants[115]. However, some field work organisations fear that some provisions of the Code achieve the opposite effects[116]. In fact, the new quality standards may reduce the accessibility of subsidised housing for socially weaker tenants; they may also reduce the level of protection which incumbent social tenants and candidate-tenants enjoyed until now.

The recently adopted Decree regarding the policy on land and property allows for the expansion of the social housing patrimony (for rent, for sale, and parcels), as well as additional housing for lower-income groups. Interestingly, the government also decided to start up a database for monitoring the affordability of the Flemish housing market (in all different segments).

Finally, the creation of a rent-subsidy scheme for the 'people in greatest need of housing' aims to guarantee decent and affordable housing in the private rental market for low-income households and specific target groups. In practice, applicants for a social dwelling

---

115  These provisions include the following points: 1) linking access to the unrestricted right of stay, 2) an allocation policy adapted to the local context, 3) consideration of the taxable income and the quality of the dwelling in the calculation of the rental price, 4) a new funding system for the social rental offices, and 5) regulation of the supervision.

116  These provisions are: 1) linguistic and settling-in conditions, 2) a trial period, 3) the dissolution (of contract) by right by the landlord, and 4) abolition of the upper limit in the stipulation of the rental price.

who have been waiting for five years or more can also apply for a rent subsidy. Nevertheless, the number of potential beneficiaries remains rather marginal.

The Flemish approach is very 'categorical', i.e. focused on target groups. And yet, in the documents mentioned above, any specific reference to home- and roofless people is lacking. Again, this does not mean that policy instruments regarding homelessness do not exist – primarily the law on general social work – but the link between these instruments and the housing policy instruments remains to be elaborated.

### 4.5.5.5 *Walloon Region and French Community*

As regards the *French-speaking part of Belgium*, two policy declarations have to be considered: one from the government of the Walloon Region, and one from the French Community government. Of these documents, the declaration of the regional government is probably the most important one. In line with the Flemish and Brussels policy papers, this declaration aims to ease access to decent, affordable and sustainable housing for everyone (Gouvernement de la Région wallonne, 2009). This general objective can be translated into more specific goals in five areas:

- decent housing for everyone,
- energy efficient housing,
- solidarity and housing,
- housing and the living environment, and
- the functioning of the housing sector.

The first two areas appear to be the most important ones – considering the number of goals set forth. These goals are similar to ones in the Brussels Capital Region and Flanders. They aim to organise a balanced housing market for both tenants and owners, with affordable social and private housing. These goals are not accompanied by target-setting. In common with the other declarations, it also lacks a policy outline regarding homelessness.

Likewise, the declaration of the government of the French Community (Gouvernement de la Communauté francophone, 2009) does not outline any specific policy regarding the home- and roofless population.

In the Walloon policy framework, the main instruments include:

- the Housing Code,
- the Exceptional Investment Plan, and
- the Permanent Habitation (of camp sites) Plan.

Like the Flemish Housing Code, the Walloon Housing Code proclaims the right to decent and affordable housing as a basic human right. Besides procedural matters, it also regulates the social housing sector and assistance to residents.

The Exceptional Investment Plan is an important instrument in the fight against housing exclusion. The plan aims to increase the quantity of social housing, and to modernise the existing patrimony. But these two objectives do not necessarily go hand in hand. First, the average age of the patrimony in the Walloon Region is 35 years, and part of the patrimony is no longer fit for renovation. Secondly, as modernisation can no longer be achieved within the regular budget, it has to be funded partly through privatisation. Private owners, for their part, have a tendency to take the costs of these renovations into account when determining the property and rental prices. Finally, the sector has traditionally shown greater interest in building middle-class dwellings. A marked decrease in the number of dwellings available for the most vulnerable groups may thus be the result.

The Permanent Habitation Plan aims at containing the current trend towards permanent residence on camping sites and in tourist accommodation. At the same time, the plan aims to adequately equip these sites for more permanent habitation. This kind of policy is sometimes regarded with scepticism as these sites, even with adequate accommodation, do not conform to what is commonly understood by decent and affordable housing. Nevertheless, some residents explicitly prefer this environment to a 'regular' house or apartment. The plan attempts to guarantee them decent housing. Moreover, for certain groups such as the homeless, it may be a springboard towards sustainable integration into society and the housing market – provided they receive suitable guidance and counselling.

Contrary to Flanders, and similarly to Brussels, the policy framework is primarily horizontal. This does not exclude targeted policy measures, but overall, the Walloon Region and French Community governments aim at restructuring the housing market as a whole.

### 4.5.6  Concluding remarks

Homelessness and housing exclusion are probably among the most complex policy areas, as they are related to many other dimensions (citizenship, social protection, energy provision, debt management, social guidance etc.) and cut across many policy levels (from federal to local). The social OMC at EU level, and the thematic year on homelessness in particular, have undoubtedly raised awareness in Belgium about the need for an integrated policy framework. The NAP/inclusion 2008-2010 has integrated policy objectives and instruments in a well-meaning way, while the recent report of the Resource Centre for the fight against Poverty provides a broad consensus on a normative framework, endorsed by a wide range of stakeholders, with a strong emphasis on the fight against homelessness.

It is worth repeating briefly a few key principles from the report of the Resource Centre:

- homelessness is not just a housing problem. It is in the first place a matter of basic social rights to privacy protection, social protection, citizenship, etc.;
- effective policies need to take into account the independent voice of homeless people, and reach out to the most excluded groups;
- preventive policies need to foster economic and social links between vulnerable individuals and their environment; remedial policies should focus on the restoration of these links.

It seems that the policy agenda has now been set, and that the time is ripe for comprehensive, strategic and coordinated action. What is most needed, is a political consensus about the key instruments to conduct a 'social housing policy': the marginal share of social housing accommodation as well as rent mediation services, and the absence of (federal) housing benefits seem to reflect a lack of political commitment by some majority parties.

## 4.6 Conclusions and recommendations for strengthening EU action on HHE

The Social OMC has played a valuable role in bringing increased attention to HHE issues and has served to highlight their importance in the wider struggle against poverty and social exclusion in the EU. It has also deepened the analysis and understanding of the nature of HHE and the range of policies necessary to both prevent and address them. The process has created considerable opportunities for Member States to learn from each other's experience and it has supported the networking of people active on these issues. Important progress is being made in many Member States and this has been encouraged in several countries by the process of developing NAPs/inclusion. However, many countries still lack a sufficiently comprehensive approach and much remains to be done to develop effective responses to HHE. Also, although progress is being made on issues of definition, measurement and evaluation, there is still much to be done in these areas if the potential benefits of transnational comparisons and learning are to be maximised.

In the light of this, it is vital that the work started between 2000 and 2010 on this issue under the auspices of the Social OMC be consolidated and further developed in the context of the Europe 2020 agenda. It is important that this is done in the context of a renewed and strengthened EU coordination in the social field. Indeed: "If there is one thing above all else we have learned from the EU process since 2000 it is that poverty and social exclusion are multidimensional phenomena which need to be addressed in an integrated and coordinated manner. Issues such as homelessness, inadequate income, child poverty, poor access to services, exclusion from the labour market and discrimination against minorities all overlap. While at certain moments, focused action may be needed to assist particular groups, such action needs to be set in the broader context of effective overall social inclusion policies." (Frazer, 2009) Thus, HHE should continue, along with child poverty and social exclusion and active inclusion, to be one of the key themes of a renewed EU coordination in the social field. However, the work needs to move on to a new level of effectiveness that generates real outcomes. It needs to be planned in a more systematic and integrated manner. Monitoring and reporting on progress should also be greatly enhanced. Furthermore, in line with the 2008 Commission Communication on reinforcing the Social OMC it could be useful to work towards a Commission Recommendation on this issue.[117]

In the light of the above, we would make the following recommendations for strengthening EU action on HHE in the future.[118] They cover six key areas: strengthening political commitment; developing a multi-annual work programme; developing national strategies; improving definition, measurement and monitoring; improving the quality of services; and enhancing exchange and learning.

### 4.6.1    Strengthen political commitment

Without strong political commitment to address HHE issues, future progress is likely to be quite limited. In our view, three things are essential to guarantee that there is a strong political and institutional basis for addressing HHE issues at EU level in the future:

- The Member States and the Commission must ensure that the new Europe 2020 Agenda contains a strong political commitment to prevent and eradicate poverty and social exclusion and, within that context, a specific commitment to prioritise HHE issues.
- This political commitment needs then to be operationalised through the establishment of a renewed and strengthened EU coordination in the social field with a distinct social inclusion strand, including enhanced NAPs/inclusion, and with clear provisions for developing work on key thematic issues including HHE.

---

117  The Commission Communication on reinforcing the Social OMC suggests that "The subjects that are part of the OMC could be further consolidated by formalising convergence of views whenever it arises. The Commission will contribute to this by making, where appropriate, use of Recommendations based on Article 211 of the Treaty, setting out common principles, providing a basis for monitoring and peer review." (European Commission, 2008)

118  The conclusions of the MPHASIS project (see *Outcome Statement from the Final MPHASIS Conference*: Edgar and Marlier, 2009) and the work of the EU Network of Independent Experts on Social Inclusion (Frazer and Marlier, 2009) have been very useful sources of ideas when drafting these recommendations.

- An annual report on progress on HHE issues should be made to the Spring European Council and to the European Parliament as part of the annual *Joint Report on Social Protection and Social Inclusion*. This annual report should also be addressed to national and possible sub-national Parliaments of Member States.

### 4.6.2 Multi-annual work programme

A more systematic and structured approach to addressing HHE at EU level could significantly contribute to more tangible results. We would therefore recommend the following:

- In the context of the SPC, Member States and the Commission should agree to develop a multi-annual work programme on HHE, which ought to reflect the recommendations outlined below. The first work programme, which could usefully be launched in 2011 (as an integral part of the post-Lisbon EU coordination in the social field), could include working towards a Commission Recommendation on HHE by 2012 or 2013.

### 4.6.3 Development of national strategies

Having an effective, well planned and multidimensional approach to HHE is key to making progress at national and sub-national levels. We would therefore recommend the following:

- Member States should be encouraged to develop comprehensive and integrated national strategies to prevent and address HHE and to report on these in the context of the NAPs/inclusion strand of the National Strategy Reports on Social Protection and Social Inclusion (NSRSPSIs). In developing such strategies, Member States should ensure that: the necessary arrangements are in place for the effective coordination and integration of policies relating to HHE; that effective links are established between the different levels of governance (national, regional and local) on HHE issues; that appropriate structures exist to ensure the ongoing involvement of all relevant stakeholders in the design, implementation and monitoring of policies; and that at local level partnerships involving all relevant actors are established so as to ensure the coordinated and integrated delivery of policies and programmes on the ground in a flexible manner which is tailored to the needs of individuals.
- Member States who have not yet done so should be encouraged to set quantified targets for the reduction of HHE appropriate to their situation.
- Member States should be encouraged to ensure that there are effective synergies

between their Active Inclusion policies and their efforts to prevent and tackle HHE. Thus, their national strategies on HHE should be multidimensional and adopt a balanced "active inclusion approach" aimed at not only improving access to quality housing and other quality services, but also to ensuring an adequate income and to increasing access to employment.

- The Commission and Member States should be encouraged to make as much use as possible of EU Structural Funds in support of their HHE strategies.[119]

### 4.6.4   *Definition, measurement and monitoring*

Inconsistencies in definition and the lack of adequate data and effective tools for measuring and monitoring Member States' performance severely limit the added value that the EU level can bring to efforts to tackle HHE. We would therefore recommend the following:

- To enhance the EU involvement in HHE issues and to foster greater transnational exchange and learning the Social Protection Committee (SPC) and its Indicators Sub-Group (ISG) should promote agreement amongst Member States to apply a consistent official definition of homelessness.
- The European Commission and Member States should, in the context of the SPC, agree a common framework and common guidelines for measuring, monitoring and reporting on HHE.
- Given that the legislative basis and governance of data collection on homelessness is only weakly developed in most countries, Member States should be encouraged to put in place a system for regularly collecting data on HHE and, as necessary, collating data from the regional and local levels. Because a single data source will not be enough for a proper count and monitoring of HHE, each country will need to identify a good national "package" of available data sources (e.g. surveys, registers, clients' record data) and develop its statistical capacity as required.
- In the next Census, which will be carried out in 2011, for the first time it will be compulsory for all EU countries to collect information on homelessness. Therefore, the Commission and Member States, in the context of the SPC, might consider taking an initiative in consultation with all key stakeholders (i.e. Ministries and other public bodies in charge of HHE, statistical institutes, service providers, academics and people having experience of HHE) to develop

---

119   See section 1.3.8 in relation to recent amendments to the regulations of the European Regional Development Fund to increase the eligibility of housing interventions in favour of marginalised communities in the newer Member States. This could play an important role in increasing resources for initiatives in these countries.

broad guidelines with a view to ensuring that data on at least ETHOS categories 1 and 2 be collected in an effective and (reasonably) consistent way.[120]

- The ISG should continue to enrich the new indicators on housing deprivation (especially in the field of poor quality housing) and should work towards common EU indicator(s) on homelessness.

### 4.6.5 Improving the quality of services

The quality of services that are in place to assist those at risk of HHE is critical to their effectiveness. We would therefore recommend the following:

- Member States should be encouraged to adopt good practice (e.g. the Netherlands) in relation to the development of standards of accommodation and service provision for homeless people and to support this with mechanisms of inspection, regulation and funding.
- Member States should publish their official definitions of overcrowding and dwellings unfit for habitation. The NAPs/inclusion strand of the NSRSPSIs should report on these definitions and on official information related to dwelling quality and to overcrowding.

### 4.6.6 Exchange and learning

The Social OMC to date has demonstrated the great benefit to Member States on learning from each others' experience. We would therefore recommend the following:

- The promotion of transnational exchange and learning through methods such as peer reviews, studies, networks, improved data collection and conferences should continue to be a key priority under the Community Programme for Employment and Social Solidarity (PROGRESS). However, such learning should be further enhanced by a greater clustering of stakeholders and different activities concerned with HHE in line with what was achieved in the context of

---

120 Independent of this possible initiative, most important is that the National Statistical Institutes publish their methodology or plans to count primary homelessness (i.e., ETHOS 1). EU comparative data on some aspects of HHE could also usefully be collected through: a) questions on "hidden homelessness" that could be included in a module in the *Community Statistics on Income and Living Conditions* (EU-SILC) instrument – i.e. questions aimed at identifying people living with family and friends due to a lack of housing (e.g. parents and married children sharing a dwelling), people living temporarily with family and friends due to homelessness (e.g. young people 'sofa surfing', homeless who move from hostel to friends to hostel...), etc.; and b) a comparative research project using consistent methodology in the capital/ main cities of each Member State to document the extent of and reasons for ETHOS 1 homelessness.

the MPHASIS project (Edgar and Marlier 2009) and has been recommended by FEANTSA (Spinnewijn 2009).

# References

Bemelmans-Videc, M.L., Rist, R.C., and Vedung, E. (ed.) (1998), *Carrots, Sticks, and Sermons: Policy Instruments and their Evaluation*, New Brunswick, New Jersey and London: Transaction Publishers.

Burt, M. and Cohen, B. (1989), *America's Homeless: Numbers, Characteristics, and the Programs that Serve Them*. Washington D.C.: Urban Institute.

Busch-Geertsema, V. (2005), Does re-housing lead to reintegration? Follow-up studies of re-housed homeless people, *Innovation – The European Journal of Social Science Research* 18 (2), pp. 205 – 226.

Carpentier, S. and Van den Bosch, K. (2006) *Situering van de leefomstandigheden van cliënten van welzijnsorganisaties t.o.v. de volwassenen die in bestaansonzekerheid leven volgens SILC*. Nota.

Carr, H., Cowan, D. and Hunter, C. (2007), Policing the Housing Crisis, *Critical Social Policy* 27(1) pp. 100-127.

Chamberlain, C. and MacKenzie, D. (2003), *Homeless Careers: Pathways In and Out of Homelessness*, Australian Housing and Urban Research Institute, Adelaide: RMIT University.

Clark, W.A.V., and Davies Withers, S. (2007), Family migration and mobility sequences in the United States: Spatial mobility in the context of the life course, *Demographic Research* 17(20), pp. 591–622.

Council (2002), *Joint Report on Social Inclusion*, Brussels: EU Council of Ministers and European Commission.

Culhane, D.P., Dejowski, E., Inanez, J., Needham, E., and Macchia, I. (1994), Public shelter admission rates in Philadelphia and New York City: the implications of turnover for shelter population counts, *Housing Policy Debate* 5(2), pp. 107-140.

Culhane, D.P. (2008), *Re-arranging the deck-chairs or re-allocating the lifeboats?: homelessness assistance and its alternatives*, Research Conference European Observatory on Homelessness, The Hague, September 2008.

Culhane, D.P. (2008a), The Costs of Homelessness: A Perspective from the United States, *The European Journal of Homelessness* (2), pp. 97-114.

De Backer, B. with Lodewick, *Les cent portes de l'accueil. Héberger des adultes et des familles sans abri*, Ed. Couleur Livres, 150 p.

Donabedian, A. (1982), The Quality of Care. How can it be assessed?, *Journal of the American Medical Association*, vol. 260 (12), pp. 1743-1748.

Dyb, E. (2007), *Preventing and Tackling Homelessness in a Context of Homeownership: The Norwegian Case*, ENHR conference Rotterdam, June 2007.

Edgar, W (2009), *A Statistical Review of Homelessness in Europe*, Brussels: FEANTSA.

Edgar, W. and Marlier, E. (2009), *Outcome Statement from the Final MPHASIS Conference*, Paris, September 2009, available from:
www.trp.dundee.ac.uk/research/mphasis/.

Edgar, W. (2006), *Norwegian Homelessness Strategy: Pathways to a permanent home*, Social Inclusion Peer Review, Vienna: ÖSB.

Edgar, W. (forthcoming), *Counting the homeless – improving the basis for planning assistance*, Social Inclusion Peer Review, Vienna: ÖSB.

Edgar, W. and Meert, H. (2005), *Fourth Review of Statistics on Homelessness in Europe*, Brussels: FEANTSA.

Edgar, W. Doherty, J. and Meert, H. (2004), *Third Review of Statistics on Homelessness in Europe*, Brussels: FEANTSA.

Edgar, W. Doherty, J. and Mina-Coull, A. (2000), *Support and Housing in Europe: tackling social exclusion in the European Union*, Bristol: Policy Press.

Edgar, W. Harrison, M., Watson, P. and Busch-Geertsema, V. (2007), *Measurement of Homelessness at European Union Level*, Brussels: European Commission (DG Employment, Social Affairs and Equal Opportunities).

Elder, G.H. (ed.) (1985), *Life Course Dynamics: Trajectories and Transitions*, Ithaca, New York: Cornell University Press.

EU Network of Independent Experts on Social Inclusion:
http://www.peer-review-social-inclusion.eu/network-of-independent-experts.

European Commission (2008), *A renewed commitment to social Europe: Reinforcing the Open Method of Coordination for Social Protection and Social Inclusion*, Communication No. COM(2008) 418 final, Brussels: European Commission.

European Commission (2009), *Portfolio of indicators for the monitoring of the European strategy for social protection and social inclusion. 2009 update*, available from:
http://ec.europa.eu/social/main.jsp?catId=756&langId=en.

Fitzpatrick Associates (2006), *Review of Implementation of Homeless Strategies*, Dublin: Department of the Environment, Heritage and Local Government.

Flatau, P., Zaretzky, K., Brady, M., Haigh, Y. and Martin, R. (2008), *The Cost-Effectiveness of Homelessness Programs: A First Assessment, Volume 1– Main Report*, AHURI Final Report No.119, AHURI, Melbourne.

Flatau, P.R. and Zaretzky, K. (2008), The Economic Evaluation of Homelessness Programs, *The European Journal of Homelessness* (2), pp. 305-320.

Frazer, H. (2009), Response to 'How to Use the Open Method of Coordination to Deliver Policy Progress at European Level: The Example of Homelessness', *The European Journal of Homelessness (3), pp. 317-327.*

Frazer, H. and Marlier, E. (2009), "Homelessness and housing exclusion across EU Member States", Analysis and recommendations of the EU Network of independent experts on social inclusion, available from:
http://www.peer-review-social-inclusion.eu/network-of-independent-ex-

perts/2009.

Golledge, R.G. and Stimpson, R.J. (2006), *Spatial Behavior: A Geographic Perspective,* New York and London: The Guildford Press.

Hagestad, G.O. and Neugarten, B.L (1985), "Age and the Life Course" in: Robert H. Binstock and Ethel Shanas (eds.) *Handbook of Aging and the Social Sciences.* New York: Van Nostrand Reinhold, pp. 46-61.

Hradejký, I. (2008) Building Capacity of Homelessness Services in the Czech Republic, *The European Journal of Homelessness* (2), pp. 177-190.

Kendig, H. (1984), "Housing careers, life cycle, and residential mobility: implications for the housing market", *Urban Studies,* vol. 21, pp. 271-283.

Kirkwood, S. and Richley, T. (2008), *Supported Accommodation Services for Offenders: A Research Literature Review,* Edinburgh, Scotland: Criminal Justice Social Work Development Centre.

La Strada (Centre d'appui au secteur bruxellois d'aide aux sans-abri, 2009), http://www.thuislozenzorg.org/Files/media/imports/res-denombrement-19-novembre-2008.pdf)

La Strada (Steunpunt voor Thuislozenzorg Brussel, 2009), *Een eerste poging om het aantal dak- en thuislozen in het Brussels Hoofdstedelijk Gewest te tellen,* Brussels, 10p. (http://www.thuislozenzorg.org/Files/media/imports/res-telling-van-19-november-2008.pdf)

Macpherson, R., Shepherd, G., and Edwards, T. (2004), Supported accommodation for people with severe mental illness: a review, *Advances in Psychiatric Treatment* 10, pp. 180-188.

Marlier, E., Atkinson, A.B., Cantillon, B., Nolan, B. (2007), *The EU and Social Inclusion: Facing the challenges,* Bristol: The Policy Press.

Meert, H. (2005) *Danish Homelessness Strategy – Our Collective Responsibility,* Social Inclusion Peer Review, Vienna: ÖSB.

Neale, J. (1997), Homelessness and Theory Reconsidered, *Housing Studies,* vol12 (1), pp. 47-61.

O'Sullivan, E. and De Decker, P. (2007), Regulating the Private Rental Housing Market in Europe, *The European Journal of Homelessness* (1), pp. 95-118.

Rossi, P.H. (1955), *Why Families Move; a study in the social psychology of urban residential mobility,* Glencoe Illinois Free Press.

Rowntree, B.S. (1901), *Poverty: A Study of Town Life,* London: Macmillan and Co.

Sahlin, I. (1999), *The Staircase of Transition,* National Report of the European Observatory on Homelessness, Brussels: FEANTSA.

Salamon, L.M. and Anheier, H.K. (eds.) (2006), *Social Origins of Civil Society: Explaining the Non-profit Sector Cross-Nationally,* John Hopkins University, Baltimore.

Service de Lutte contre la Pauvreté, la Précarité et l'Exclusion Sociale (2010), *Rapport 2008-2009, partie 2: Pour une approche cohérente de la lutte contre le 'sans-abrisme' et la pauvreté,* Bruxelles : SLPPES, 84 p.

Spinnewijn, F. (2009), How to Use the Open Method of Coordination to Deliver Policy Progress at European Level: The Example of Homelessness, *The European Journal of Homelessness* (3), pp. 301-316.

Stephens, M. and Fitzpatrick, S. (2007), Welfare Regimes, Housing systems and Homelessness: How are they linked?, *The European Journal of Homelessness* (1), pp. 201-212.

Tainio, H. and Fredriksson, P. (2009), The Finnish Homelessness Strategy: From a "Staircase" Model to a "Housing First" Approach to Tackling Long-Term Homelessness, *The European Journal of Homelessness* (3), pp. 181-199.

Van Menxel, G. *et al* (2003) *Verbinding Verbroken*. Steunpunt Algemeen Welzijnswerk, Berchem.

Van Menxel, G. *et al* (2007) *De meervoudige kwetsbaarheid van cliënten in het algemeen welzijnswerk*. Steunpunt Algemeen Welzijnswerk, Berchem.

Van Regenmortel, T, Demeyer, B., Vandenbempt, K. and Van Damme, B. (2006) Zonder (t)huis. *Sociale Biografieën van thuislozen getoetst aan de institutionele en maatschappelijke realiteit*. Leuven: Lannoo Campus.

Vranken, J. (2004), *The English Rough Sleeping Initiative*, Social Inclusion Peer Review, Vienna: ÖSB.

Vranken, J., Campaert, G., De Boyser, K., Dewilde, C. and Dierckx, D. (ed., 2008) *Jaarboek Armoede en Sociale uitsluiting 2008*, Leuven: Acco.

Vranken, J., De Boyser, K and Dierckx, D. (ed., 2006) *Jaarboek Armoede en Sociale uitsluiting 2006*, Leuven: Acco.

Wolf, J. and Edgar, W. (2007), Measuring Quality of Services and Provision in Homelessness, *The European Journal of Homelessness* (1), pp. 15-40. www.trp.dundee.ac.uk/research/mphasis/.

# 5 Making social inclusion a cornerstone of EU and Member States policies

The diagnosis established in the preface of this book, that a decade of coordinated social inclusion policies has failed to reduce poverty and social exclusion in any substantial way, necessitates a thorough reflection on the current European social model. How is it possible that the EU has largely failed in its 2000 declared objective of making a *decisive step towards the eradication of poverty*? The answers are many and varied.

On the one hand, external factors can be cited which EU leaders were either unable to foresee in 2000 or whose course they were not able to alter sufficiently.

- First, there were two severe economic crises: in 2001, the explosion of international terrorism and the Gulf War were accompanied by the bursting of the dot-com bubble; and in 2008 came the worst financial crash since the 1930s. Crises such as these naturally take their toll, and the first victims are the most vulnerable groups in society.
- Secondly, EU enlargement to include countries from Central and Eastern Europe (CEE) meant that, at a stroke, the EU population gained large numbers of poor and socially excluded people.[121] The eight CEE countries that acceded to the EU in 2004 had an *average* per capita income which was only half that of the "old" EU-15 Member States; in the two newest Member States (Romania and Bulgaria), which joined in 2007, the average was even lower, at just one third.
- In addition to these macroeconomic factors, there are also a number of important socio-demographic trends which tend to drive up poverty and social exclusion. Population ageing is one, but above all rising immigration and family fragmentation (see e.g. OECD, 2008). The risk of poverty is much higher among migrants, people living alone and lone-parent families. Where the size of these groups increases, therefore, that is sufficient to push up poverty and social exclusion in a country.

---

121 Note that the observations in the foregoing section (specifically that income poverty has not fallen) would also hold true without EU enlargement. In other words, the stabilisation or increase in poverty risk rates is not the result of a statistical artefact caused by the accession of the 12 newer EU Member States. (See Preface for some poverty risk and material deprivation figures; for full detailed evidence, see web-site of Eurostat, the Statistical Office of the European Communities: http://epp.eurostat.ec.europa.eu/portal/page/portal/living_conditions_and_social_protection/introduction.)

Leaving aside these exogenous factors, the EU policy itself has in our view also failed to reduce poverty, inequality and social exclusion, due to a lack of coherence between general and social policies. This manifests itself in an ever-changing variety of policy domains. In essence, European policy is driven by a free-market logic, which in addition to key benefits in terms of prosperity and freedom also causes substantial "collateral damage" to vulnerable groups as it often does not take sufficiently into account the social impact of the policies that are being promoted.

Another risk which is inherent in European policy making concerns the lack of active participation of socially excluded groups in policy debates. Despite efforts on the part of the European Commission and, as we indicated in Chapter 1, despite some progress on this issue a lot remains to be done to get the voices of the poor heard in Brussels (and indeed at any policy level – EU, national, regional and local). This chapter concentrates on those two key issues, "Putting social inclusion at the heart of policies" (Section 5.1) and "Building participation of all stakeholders, including the most excluded" (Section 5.2), and puts forward some general governance principles aimed at making the EU more inclusive "by nature".

## 5.1 Putting social inclusion at the heart of policies

Coordinating and strengthening social policies at EU and country levels is undoubtedly a major challenge; preventing the reproduction of poverty and social exclusion in mainstream (economic) policies is even more crucial. Poverty and social exclusion would certainly be lower today if social inclusion were put at the heart of the mainstream policies, as required under the 2009 Lisbon Treaty's "horizontal social clause" (see Section 1.3.4). By way of illustration, we look briefly at three key policy strands from the past decade: EU enlargement, the liberalisation of basic services and the Lisbon Strategy.

### 5.1.1   EU enlargement

Nobody will question the historical importance of the re-unification of Europe after the fall of communism, for the sake of peace as well as prosperity. Nevertheless, it is worth examining *how* the EU enlargement took place. At the very least, the enlargement policy demonstrates a heavy predominance of economic over social priorities. Kvist (2004) refers in this connection to "negative integration" (removal of obstacles and loss of privileges) in contrast to "positive integration" (in the sense of a common social policy). This has undoubtedly also exacerbated the problem of poverty and inequality.

Of course, the upsurge of poverty and social exclusion in the newer Member States started well before their accession to the EU; the implosion of the old industrial base and agriculture in the former planned CEE economies had begun following the 1989 revolution (Kogan *et al*, 2008). The structural changes that took place in CEE were enormous, and entire sectors and labour markets were further undermined. In the Baltic States and Bulgaria, for example, average real income levels fell by between 35 and 50% within the space of a few years. Moreover, the artificially compressed pay differentials from the Communist period burst apart, as it were, leading to very sharp falls in real income for the lowest-skilled. At the same time, the socialist welfare states collapsed: full employment made way for high, lasting and structural unemployment; the newly introduced unemployment insurance and social assistance systems were very Spartan and inefficient; subsidised basic services such as housing, childcare, education, and so on, were systematically privatised, further undermining the purchasing power of families with modest incomes. Here and there this gave rise to a real exodus, especially among the elite, which has by no means ended.

Accession to the EU did little to mitigate this economic and social crisis in CEE. While it did bring new growth opportunities thanks to foreign investments, new markets in the West and the growing shift towards a service economy (tertiarisation), accession also made severe (excessive) demands on the candidate countries. They were subject to stringent financial and budgetary discipline (the so-called convergence criteria) as a condition for accession to the EU, and that "discipline" had the effect of undermining the social policy of the countries concerned. The European Structural Funds, despite their focus on CEE, were nowhere near big enough to compensate for the shortfalls in the social budgets of the newer Member States. In any event, the "old" Member States which were providing the finance were themselves faced with budgetary constraints.

There was moreover no political support for a common social policy. Older Member States such as Sweden and Finland were reluctant to agree to norms which fell well short of their own national minimum incomes; but, remarkably, it was the new, liberal elites in the "new" Member States (led by Poland and the Baltic States) who swore by the free market as the solution to their structural crisis of adaptation. They slashed their pension systems and healthcare spending, and some countries introduced a flat tax to enable them to compete better with their Western neighbours.[122] Although the EU compelled its new members to adopt the "acquis communautaire" – the entire body of social EU rules in relation to non-discrimination, health and safety at work, etc. – informed observers argue that this *acquis* is not a heavy burden, and monitoring its application tended to be rather lax.

It therefore comes as no surprise that, according to the sparse data available, poverty in

---

122  A flat tax is a uniform low tax rate, for both personal taxation and VAT, which mainly benefits those on higher incomes.

the new Member States continued to increase after accession to the EU; of the seven Member States in which Lelkes *et al* (2009: 30) observed an increase in poverty, five are new Member States. There is a strong possibility that the problem will be further exacerbated by the financial crisis (especially in Latvia): more drastic sacrifices are being imposed at all levels, at the behest of the International Monetary Fund (IMF). The European Commission, meanwhile, looks on fairly powerlessly.

The social decline in CEE boosted migration to the West. The European Commission has repeatedly played down the fears in the old Member States of a flood of immigration from the new Member States (see e.g. European Commission – High Level Group, 2004): after a peak of 300,000 migrants per year in the first years after accession, it was argued that the influx would fall to around 50,000 per annum. However, a number of old Member States (including Belgium) decided to play safe and imposed temporary restrictions on immigration, or tightened up the eligibility criteria for their social security and social assistance systems (Kvist, 2004). They were not necessarily wrong to do so, because the actual migration flows mask sometimes worrying figures about the scale of migratory *aspirations* in CEE, especially among the well-educated and the young. In fact, perhaps precisely because of this, the potential damage caused by this migratory pressure is possibly greater for the home countries than for the EU-15: the countries of origin need these emigrants the most, because CEE is also confronted with an ageing population and a scarcity of skilled workers.

In short, it is apparent from this brief outline of the trends in CEE that the acute and greatly underestimated problem of poverty and social exclusion in the 10 new Member States[123] has been exacerbated rather than mitigated by "negative integration". But there is more. In combination with other factors, this form of integration is slowly but surely eroding the famed European Social Model in the old EU (characterised by high wages, high productivity and high levels of social protection). In the past, social dumping by the new Member States was the nightmare of the old EU members; that nightmare is slowly becoming reality. The further liberalisation of the markets, especially in the services sector, may have a favourable effect on employment in CEE, but in the longer term it too contributes to the erosion of wages and working conditions in all segments of the labour market (from seasonal employment in the agricultural sector, through domestic services and road transport to scientific research). The first of these segments are particularly relevant here, as these are the segments where there is the greatest risk of finding the "working poor". This brings us to a second structural factor.

---

123  The use of relative yardsticks such as the 60%-of-the-median threshold strongly underestimates real poverty in the 10 new Member States. So, even though deprivation indicators have significantly improved in these countries, they still remain on average 2.5 times as high as in the older Member States. (see Preface)

## 5.1.2   Liberalisation of basic services

In addition to the integration of several "low-wage countries", the EU has given further impetus to the liberalisation of markets in the last decade. The "Services Directive"[124], which creates a general framework for the liberalisation of the service sectors, was implemented in revised form after heavy opposition (mainly from Western trade unions) in 2006. Henceforth, everyone within the EU has the right to provide services anywhere in the EU territory, and to set up a service company wherever they choose within the Union. It goes without saying that this relaxation presents a major challenge to the 27 national (and many more regional) governments in monitoring the accessibility, conformity with local legislation and quality of those services. For service-users who are in a weak position, this entails considerable risks, for example with regard to the quality of home care or the continuity of electricity supply. On top of this, a number of sectors which have traditionally fallen within the public services are being systematically privatised: telecommunications, electricity, gas, water, railways, etc. In principle, services such as these will henceforth be exposed without restrictions to competition within the internal EU market. The notion of "restrictions" may also include accreditation conditions, grant schemes, obligations or prohibitions which are socially inspired, if this means that providers are *de facto* kept at a distance. Public authorities have even found themselves pushed on to the defensive in this regard, for example because they are obliged under certain circumstances to justify government aid to the European Commission, or where new players (foreign or otherwise) challenge the imposed rules as being trade restrictions, at the European Court of Justice, arguing that they distort competition. Once again, the logic applied is pure free market economics: privatisation and competition are expected to lead to greater efficiency, a better qualitative match between demand and supply, lower prices and thus greater prosperity. Any market correction by the government is subject to scrutiny, as if it were to be re-invented.

Past experiences with transferring public services to the private sector (e.g. rail transport, education or employment services) are mixed, however. On the one hand, there is some evidence supporting the arguments in favour of efficiency and the responsiveness of markets; on the other, the quality of the service will not necessarily improve, and almost always becomes more unequal. Consumer satisfaction surveys conducted by Eurobarometer in relation to "network services" (telephony, water, electricity, gas, postal services) show that, while the average user is in favour of liberalisation, more than three-quarters of them notice little or no improvement in terms of prices, choice, quality and consumer protection (Clifton and Diaz-Fuentes, 2008). Moreover, there are signs of growing dissatisfaction as regards affordability and legal certainty; in 2006, for example, one in three consumers felt that electricity and gas were "exaggeratedly expensive or unaffordable".

---

124   Directive 2006/123/EC of 12 December 2006 on services in the internal market.

In part, the negative side-effects of liberalisation can be ascribed to a range of factors:

- the fact that in some cases public monopolies were in practice replaced by private monopolies (e.g. in the electricity market) or "monopolistic competition", so that prices did not fall;
- the lack of transparency of the markets after privatisation; the wide differentiation of products and prices means customers are no longer able to find their way through the administrative maze, are virtually unable to access alternatives and are no longer able to enforce their rights; and above all,
- the primacy of the drive for profits over providing (basic) services in the ethics of private service companies; this makes it difficult in practice to force companies to conduct a social policy with respect to weak service-users.

In Belgium, too, the privatisation of utilities (especially electricity and gas) has to date not proved to be an unmitigated success: with the exception of the telecommunications sector, the hoped-for price falls have not materialised; even worse for the poor is the fact that the delivery of basic services such as gas and electricity is less secure than in the past, and that private suppliers often display a marked lack of scruples in their supply conditions. Weak service-users are "parked" or even excluded from service; they are not offered preferential tariffs, and so on. The poor are often the first victims here. As an example, the Flemish government was forced to put months of pressure on Belgacom, the former state telephone company, just to maintain the special tariffs for poorer subscribers.[125]

Yet the intention had been that liberalisation would be socially corrected; there was to be a free minimum supply, "social tariffs" for specific categories of households, and monitored procedures for dealing with payment defaults (to prevent households being cut off). In practice, the private companies have proved to be very creative in circumventing the rules – or the government lacked the power to enforce the rights of the weakest service-users. Despite the statutory provisions, energy companies in Belgium continued to cut off customers who did not pay their bills, simply by replacing the criterion of "inability to pay" in their argumentation with the term "manifest unwillingness to pay". They even began exchanging "black lists" of customers who were bad payers, which meant that some households were no longer able to find any suppliers who were willing to supply gas or electricity. Other companies began demanding prohibitive security deposits before (re) connecting these customers; and so on (Nicaise *et al*, 2004).

Less well-known than the problems in the utilities sector is the unrest in the *social services*: the wind of privatisation is also blowing through the world of care for the elderly, childcare, healthcare and related sectors, putting pressure on public services and grant

---

125 *De Standaard* newspaper, 31 January 2005. Initially, those concerned had to fill in a relatively complicated application form for the continuation of their 'social subscription'.

schemes. These sectors, too, are seeing the effects of internationalisation and competition, and in a variety of ways:

- The free movement of workers means that the proportion of employees of foreign origin is increasing. These employees are flexible and help resolve bottlenecks in the care professions, but are also often less well trained.
- The free movement of persons occasionally also leads to the risk of "social tourism", "care migration" and, according to some sources, even to "social raids" (i.e. migration with the aim of enjoying the social benefits in other European countries – Kvist, 2004).
- Then, there is the entrance of multinationals into local and neighbourhood services. These major players use the European Court of Justice to enforce their right to access these "growth markets", using the Services Directive as a lever. The traditional non-profit providers, often themselves no small players, fear that they will be forced out by the competition because the big companies are less scrupulous about quality standards.

These three trends have a potentially mutually reinforcing effect on (subsidised) social services, leading to a downward levelling off of subsidies and of quality. The EU itself contributes to this pressure with its Services Directive and its stance as a watchdog guarding against competition-distorting state aid. Once again, it is the less well off client who is at risk of losing out in this interplay. For example, the discretionary authority of national or regional governments to subsidise services as compensation for the fulfilling of a public task is constrained: large subsidies must be submitted in advance to the European Commission, which scrutinises them to ensure that they do not distort competition. From the standpoint of social inclusion, the EU has to date done no more than provide for a few "exceptions" to the competition rules, mainly concerning the subsidising of small-scale services.

It took the EU no less than ten years to establish a Protocol, which among other things defines the concept of "services of general interest": energy supply, telecommunication services, transport, the audiovisual sector and postal services, education, water supply, waste management, health services and social services (European Commission, 2007). For these services, Europe allows government intervention in the various markets (for example in order to combat social exclusion) and *Member States or regions are permitted* to impose obligations on the producers which meet the public utility nature of their service, for example in relation to universal service, quality, accessibility and affordability. This does not however alter the fact that, as regards the "economic" (i.e. tradable) services, the EU rules on the internal market and competition continue to apply.[126] It is in any event

---

126  Only services such as the police, justice, etc., escape entirely from the EU rules on the internal market.

striking that the free market (and therefore the profit motive) remains the norm, while the arrangements concerning services of general interest count as "exceptions". This cannot be described as a genuinely positive contribution to the development of these services. There is no European law which guarantees a basic service or automatic allocation of a social tariff to disadvantaged clients. What Europe does do is tolerate the fact that a lower authority takes such measures: the national and regional inclusion policy *is permitted* to act in a compensatory way. Paradoxically, its social impact is then evaluated by the EU in the context of the Social OMC.

Here, again, Member States have clearly opted for "negative integration". From the perspective of the fight against poverty and social exclusion and of the recognition of fundamental rights, a more proactive policy of social minimum standards could have been expected. Prior to liberalisation, the Union could perfectly well have set out a framework guaranteeing the right to basic services for EU citizens. Clifton and Diáz-Fuentes (2008) in fact recall that this possibility was already raised in the middle of the 1990s. Eventually, the EU pushed through the free market thinking, and left the social corrections to the Member States and regions. The calls from the social sector for the setting of "minimum social standards" across the EU have only recently resulted in the adoption of an article in the new EU Treaty (article 14) that provides the basis for a (potential) EU-wide legal framework concerning social services of general interest.

Building on the European Commission's White Paper on Services of General Interest (European Commission, 2004) and a study produced by the European Anti-Poverty Network (EAPN, 2007), a broad coalition of national and European civil society organisations and European parliamentarians, united under the label "Spring Alliance"[127], have included in their Manifesto a concrete agenda for the further implementation of minimum social standards at EU level. Section 8 of the Manifesto lists the following demands:

- "Ensure that the EU internal market and competition legislation does not negatively impact on the provision of or access to quality public services, and that it takes into account the specificities of public services. Specifically:
    o   Revise as necessary EU internal market and competition legislations to ensure universal access to public services. This could be done by adopting a Framework Directive on Services of General Interest
    o   Enforce the implementation of the requirement for universal and affordable access to services in existing EU sectoral directives, e.g. by adding a provision on the access to a minimum supply of energy and water for households

---

127   The Spring Alliance is managed by four leading European civil society organisations: the European Environmental Bureau, the European Trade Union Confederation (ETUC), the Social Platform and Concord.

- o   Amend EU Public Procurement rules to require mandatory quality criteria for the public tendering of social services
- o   Evaluate and revise as necessary regulation on State Aid that adversely affects the development and provision of social services provided by non-governmental, non-profit actors
- o   Implement the European Parliament request for an independent assessment of the impact of liberalisation and privatisation on essential services, involving all stakeholders but particularly users
- Earmark European Social Fund and European Regional Development Funds for investment in education, social housing, social and health services, particularly for the most disadvantaged
- Develop an EU action plan outlining how EU macroeconomic policies can increase support to individuals with caring responsibilities (e.g. to children or older parents) and recognise the economic value of care services provided by family members.
- Renew the commitments to achieve the Barcelona targets on childcare provision that aim to lift the barriers and disincentives for the participation of women in the labour market
- Implement the EU Energy Package requirements to develop National Action Plans and reduce energy poverty, and coordinate them with the National Action Plans for social inclusion and social protection
- Provide an appropriate EU financial and legislative framework to support social economy activities in the provision of public services, particularly social services
- Adopt a directive on financial inclusion to establish universal access to a bank account and to fair and sustainable credit and loan facilities for all." (Spring Alliance, 2009) [128]

We would suggest in this context a particular priority for guaranteed basic services that can be characterised as *investments in the (material, human, social and cultural) resources* of socially excluded groups. Education and child care deserve a special mention here, as instruments in the fight against child poverty and social exclusion.

---

128   Similar demands are increasingly being developed at national level by civil society and trade union movements for change. For example, in Ireland a recent civil society initiative has launched a manifesto (Is Feidir Linn, 2009) which has as one of its goals "a model of development which prioritises, invests in and develops high quality, efficient and effective public services" and amongst the related policy objectives argues for "legally enforced minimum standards".

### 5.1.3   The Lisbon Strategy

*"Making the EU the most dynamic and competitive knowledge-based economy in the world capable of sustainable economic growth with more and better jobs and greater social cohesion":* that is the familiar core objective of the strategy that was adopted for the decade 2000-2010 by EU Heads of State and Government at their Lisbon Spring Summit in 2000. The reference to competition and social cohesion in one and the same sentence requires some degree of mental gymnastics. Yet to our knowledge, the link between the two has never been fully explained. As we have highlighted in Chapter 1 the reports of the EU Network of Independent Experts on Social Inclusion (Frazer and Marlier, 2009) evaluating Member States' National Reform Programmes have shown clearly that there has been very little "feeding in" or "feeding out" between economic and employment policies and social policies to ensure that they are mutually reinforcing. Other evaluation reports suggest that the Lisbon paradigm should be interpreted primarily as a linear line of reasoning: the knowledge-based economy makes the EU more competitive and therefore generates more economic growth, and that growth in turn translates into higher employment and thus less poverty and social exclusion.

In our view, some of the links in this line of reasoning are less clear-cut than others. For example, there is a reasonable degree of certainty about the positive impact of investments in knowledge on economic growth; both the generation of knowledge (through research and development) and its dissemination (chiefly through education, but also by the media and via the Internet) bring about economic growth. But to what extent does this growth translate into employment, and above all, what is the quality of that employment and how is it distributed? The dominant pattern appears to be one of *"skill-biased technological growth"*, which means that technological innovations boost the demand for better-skilled jobs, while low-skilled jobs either disappear or sink even lower on the status and pay ladder. This raises inequality on the labour market, an inequality that increases the risk of poverty for low-skilled workers.

Empirical research into trends in inequality produces a pervasive picture of growing inequality in *individual labour* incomes in the EU, which has in fact risen significantly more than inequality in *total household incomes*, due partly to widening wage gaps and partly to an increase in atypical employment, especially among the low-skilled (part-time work, temporary work, etc.).[129] This confirms that labour markets in the EU (as in the rest of the OECD) have indeed undergone a radical shift towards being more knowledge-intensive, *at the expense of greater inequality and social exclusion* (Gottschalk and Smeeding, 1997; Katz and Autor, 1999; Gottschalk and Danziger, 2005).

---

129  The growing inequality in individual labour incomes is partially compensated for at household level by increased labour participation by several family members and, in some Member States, through reducing taxation on low wages and enhancing social transfers and in-work benefits.

This critical observation does not mean that the knowledge-based society is per se harmful for social cohesion. It just necessitates a better policy mix, with a stronger emphasis on investments in education and training, especially at the bottom of the education ladder. The dissemination of knowledge through education and training is equally favourable for economic growth, but not at the expense of greater inequality. Education and training transform low-skilled labour into high-skilled labour, reducing the labour supply at the bottom of the ladder whilst increasing the supply in the higher-skilled segments. This means that the composition of labour supply is better able to track the trends in demand. As a consequence, the employment rate and pay levels of vulnerable groups should both increase, reducing the risk of poverty. Eurostat (2010) has shown that the poverty risk of highly educated adults is less than one-third of that of low-educated adults.

Returning to the Lisbon strategy, however, it appears that thus far the strategic link between social inclusion and the knowledge-based economy has not been adequately thought through, despite solemn declarations. Yet it should be obvious: international organisations such as the World Bank, United Nations Development Programme (UNDP) and others see education and lifelong learning as *the* lever to escape poverty. Investment in preschool education programmes for disadvantaged children, for example, are rightly regarded by economists as the most effective way of breaking the poverty circle, and at the same time one of the most profitable investments that can be made. This viewpoint is insufficiently reflected at EU level, at least not in the policy texts on social inclusion, though it was highlighted in several Joint Reports on Social Protection and Social Inclusion. However, it is encouraging that in its May 2009 adoption of a strategic framework for European cooperation in education and training the European Council has adopted as one of its strategic objectives the promotion of equity, social cohesion and active citizenship and that within this it has recognised that "Educational disadvantage should be addressed by providing high quality early childhood education and targeted support, and by promoting inclusive education". (European Council, 2009) The 2008-2010 Integrated Guidelines for growth and employment did include a number of targets which are also highly relevant for combating poverty and social exclusion, and which are informed by the EU set of social inclusion indicators (see Section 1.2.1): improving literacy, reducing the number of students leaving school with no qualifications, and increasing the participation in adult education. However, not a single one of these targets was achieved by 2010.

Within the Education and Culture policy domains, the European Commission has formulated an "Education and Training 2010" action plan, in which the equal opportunities policy is one of the crucial elements. However, there is little coordination with the Social Affairs policy domain (which includes Social Inclusion). The Directorate-General for Education and Culture has taken the initiative of setting up a network in relation to education and social inclusion, and recent communications contain strongly argued recommendations for the Member States, for example urging them to invest

more in preschool education programmes for disadvantaged children and young immigrants (European Commission, 2008), and even calling for structural reforms intended
to lead to a further democratisation of education (European Commission, 2006). In
the light of the subsidiarity principle, unfortunately, these recommendations carry no
weight of obligation for the Member States. The Open Method of Coordination is
also applied in education policy, but is even weaker than in the social inclusion field –
and the connection between the two is also weak. The fact that social inclusion – and
the entire Social Affairs policy domain – has been placed under the responsibility of
the European Commission's Directorate-General for Employment also means that
the inclusion policy is focused more on (re)integration in the labour market than on
education. Whatever DG. has the lead role, there should be effective mainstreaming
and coordination.

It would appear that investments in knowledge have become the *leitmotif* of the welfare
state, but seen through the eyes of the upper and middle classes. When it comes to the
poorest members of society, by contrast, these ambitions are all too often abandoned and
recourse is sought to older paradigms such as the activating welfare state. In a welfare
state which is based on activation, it is not education and training that are central, but
work. In other words, even the discourse about the welfare state is in danger of contributing to a divided society, in which the rich are encouraged to invest in themselves, while
the poor are encouraged… to work.

The Europe 2020 agenda designed by the European Commission seems to acknowledge
at last the necessary links between jobs, growth, education and social inclusion where it
states that "better educational levels help employability and progress in increasing the
employment rate helps to reduce poverty" (European Commission, 2010, page 13) and
proposes to develop innovative education programmes for deprived communities, reiter-
ating the objective to reduce early school leaving to 10% – by 2020 instead of 2010. One
can only hope that the message will now be translated into powerful action.

## 5.2 Building participation of all stakeholders, including the most excluded

### 5.2.1    The challenge

The quality of social inclusion policies depends also on the degree of involvement of all
stakeholders, and in particular those experiencing poverty and social exclusion. As we
have argued in the earlier chapters, stakeholder involvement is not "just" a principle of
democratic decision-making: it also guarantees a more evidence-based design of policies
and improves their effectiveness through stronger consensus and ownership at all policy
levels. In this context, stakeholder participation has at least five dimensions:

- vertical integration of policies across *levels* of government, ranging from EU to local;
- horizontal coordination across different policy *areas* (labour market, health, housing, education, etc.);
- involvement of different *types* of stakeholder, including policy makers, professional bodies, the social partners, civil society organisations, experts, people experiencing poverty and social exclusion;
- the *time* dimension: ensuring involvement from the design of policies to their monitoring and evaluation; and, most importantly,
- the *strength or "depth"* of involvement.

The challenge is enormous. To begin with, social exclusion is by definition a situation of non-participation by the victims of exclusion. The term actually refers to social conflicts between powerful and powerless parties, with the latter being unable to claim their legitimate rights. For example, companies such as electricity providers may have little interest in joining a debate on market regulation based on users' rights. Managing such conflicts requires specific methodologies and appropriate skills on the part of mediators.

The EU dimension adds to the complexity of the exercise, because of the mental distance between EU institutions and the average – let alone, the most deprived – citizen. As we indicated in Chapter 1, many evaluations so far have expressed a strong scepticism about the value added of the Social OMC, arguing that Member States confined their involvement to the mere reporting of existing national policies.

Socially excluded people themselves also tend to show little interest in participating in the process (at any policy level), due to the priority of daily survival, their poor knowledge of policy-making, their feeling of inferiority, and their low level of literacy. Moreover, the lack of immediate, tangible outcomes of policy negotiation often discourages poor people. In sum, building participation is an important but extremely demanding task.

### 5.2.2   A brief overview of responses

EU institutions have invested a lot of energy in developing or supporting stakeholder involvement, particularly the involvement of socially excluded people. The December 2000 Nice European Council emphasised "participation and self-expression of people suffering exclusion" as a key element of the OMC, and the Commission has reiterated this point in its guidelines for the drafting of the 2008-2010 National Strategy Reports on social protection and social Inclusion and indeed its guidelines for each round of the NAPs/inclusion since 2001. The previous Belgian Presidency of the EU in 2001 initiated a process of yearly European meetings of people experiencing poverty, a tradition that has been endorsed by subsequent Presidencies, and supported by the European Commission and EAPN. EAPN has also fostered, through its national member organisations, the participation of poor people in the evaluation of National Action Plans on social inclusion as well as in the annual EU Round Tables on social inclusion.

More recently, the European Commission has ordered a study of stakeholder involvement in social inclusion policies in each of the 27 Member States. Apart from country chapters, the final report contains a series of examples of good practice and draws some lessons for mutual learning (Inbas and Engender, 2010). The following checklist summarises the main preliminary findings (formulated as suggestions or just observations):

- Member States should issue transparent quality guidelines for stakeholder involvement (who should participate, how should involvement be organised, etc.):
- stakeholders should have enough time, not just to comment on documents but also to consult their constituencies;
- national reports should be prepared by multi-stakeholder bodies;
- the gender dimension should be monitored in the reports as well as in the participation process;
- vertical as well as horizontal coordination structures should be established;
- in some countries, regional and local action plans for social inclusion mirror the national plans at the lower levels;
- a variety of approaches are used to mobilise different stakeholders: internet portals, hearings, round tables, conferences, recognition of / support to representative umbrella organisations, establishment of national consultation bodies, legal consultation or approval procedures, etc.;
- a balanced consultation with parliaments, social partners, NGOs, and people experiencing poverty is desirable;
- the duration and phasing of participation tends to differ between stakeholders, with associations being more involved in the preparation of policies while experts are more often engaged in the monitoring process;
- the participation of NGOs with limited resources or people experiencing poverty should be facilitated by compensating their costs;
- participants should get feedback on the outcome of the policy process in which they participated. This impact can be measured using different yardsticks (e.g. better understanding of some issues, agreement reached on some points, inclusion of proposals in the national strategy report, enactment of decisions, budget allocation etc.);
- stakeholders' comments should be published as this guarantees that their voices are heard, even when their claims / recommendations are not retained;
- participation of responsible Ministers in meetings is important as it shows their commitment and valuation of the participation process.

The European Anti-Poverty Network has devoted a specific publication to stakeholder participation (EAPN, 2009), with a particular emphasis on the implications for people experiencing poverty. "According to anti-poverty organisations, time and mutual understanding are two key factors in ensuring the meaningful participation of people experiencing poverty. It takes time for people experiencing poverty to feel prepared to share their lives and to engage in dialogue, and it takes understanding on both sides for participation to have an impact. For people experiencing poverty, participation starts with building their self-esteem and confidence, gaining courage to express their opinions as equals and to participate in making decisions and implementing them. A favourable environment for that should allow individuals and their organisations to contribute actively and not be taken as mere subjects for discussion. Participation by a person experiencing poverty and social exclusion, who is ready to share his or her daily reality, can break the barriers of stigma, question the use and impact of the policies or services concerned and empower people to challenge the inconsistencies of social systems. Often people in organisations, social services or public authorities start with stigmatising preconceptions about the people experiencing poverty with whom they work. Therefore, both parties need to reach a point of mutual trust and understanding for participation to make an impact." (EAPN, 2009, page 4)

Building on the experience of the Irish Combat Poverty Agency, EAPN distinguishes four stages in participation:
- *Information* and the sharing of knowledge is the "life blood" of involvement, as without the full and complete availability of information on the policy initiative, which is made available in good time, it is not possible for either consultation or participation to be meaningful.
- *Consultation* enables those individuals or groups who are interested and involved to express views on a proposal and to influence the final decision, but not to be involved in the making of that decision, which remains the prerogative of the policy-makers who may, or may not, take into consideration the views put forward through a consultation process. Consultation cannot be effective unless those who are consulted have all the relevant information on the proposed policy.
- *Participation* recognises equally the contribution made by all the stakeholders in the decision-making process and it provides individuals and groups with the ability to influence the process and to have their views incorporated in the final outcomes.
- *Co-decision-making* goes one step further by ensuring that a consensus is reached during the decision-making process, that policies are arrived at jointly and that they reflect the concerns and priorities of all those who will be affected by the decision, resulting in all the stakeholders having a joint ownership of the final outcome.

People experiencing poverty have been involved in the design of social inclusion policies to varying degrees. Self-help organisations and advocacy groups have been created, often starting without any recognition or public subsidy, thanks to the strong commitment of volunteers. In some countries, specific fora have been set up to institutionalise a dialogue with other stakeholders and policy-makers: the Combat Poverty Agency in Ireland (now integrated with the Office for Social Inclusion into the Department of Social and Family Affairs), the Local Poverty Conferences in The Netherlands and Poverty Hearings in Norway, the Belgian Resource Centre for the Fight against Poverty etc. In the context of the Social OMC, these fora have experimented ways to accommodate the bureaucratic process of preparing and monitoring the National Strategies for Social Protection and Social Inclusion.

In what follows, we summarise the Belgian experience, by way of example. Belgium is fortunate in being able to enlist the help of many organisations in which poor people have a say. They decided to join forces for the preparation of the General Poverty Report in 1994 (ATD-Quart Monde *et al*, 1995). An important – and in those days unique – element of the document is the participation of the poor themselves. The Report gave a never-seen view of poverty and what it means to the people concerned. It was an important eye-opener for many policy-makers and informed a multitude of projects and initiatives. It can be argued that the General Poverty Report gave the starting signal for a coordinated Belgian anti-poverty policy, six years before the EU initiated the OMC in the field of social inclusion. One of the key recommendations of the Report concerned the creation of a Resource Centre that would continuously monitor social inclusion policies and ensure a permanent dialogue between associations of people living in poverty and other stakeholders. Apart from the grassroots organisations, the steering group of the Centre includes representatives of all levels of government, the social partners, the federation of municipal welfare centres and the mutual health insurance agencies.

Dozens of grassroots associations are currently in existence in Belgium, including small and larger ones (e.g., a Belgian section of ATD-Fourth World). Most of them have now federated at the national and regional level.[130] Some of these associations have agreed on a common methodology, based on principles of community development, and they are now increasingly recognised as valid representatives of people suffering poverty. They are actively participating in the preparation of the two-yearly reports of the Resource Centre. For this purpose, thematic "dialogue groups" have been set up, which initially include only people living in poverty and gradually extend to other stakeholders (professionals, government officials, other associations). The criteria for a genuine "dialogue" have been extensively described in the first report of the Resource Centre (Service de Lutte contre la Pauvreté, la Précarité et l'Exclusion sociale, 2001).

---

130  Brussels Anti-Poverty Forum, Flemish Anti-Poverty Network, Walloon Anti-Poverty Network, Common Front of the Homeless, Belgian Anti-Poverty Network.

The experience with such dialogue groups has revealed a series of key conditions for guaranteeing a genuine participation:

- pre-existence of *representative grassroots associations* that have built up a collective political awareness among the target group. The mere availability of such associations involves a long-term financial and human investment, which is not to be taken for granted as yet;
- an *agenda* (choice of issues for discussion) meeting the priorities and experience of those experiencing social exclusion;
- sufficient *time and resources* for the development of a process of dialogue, including, if necessary, the remuneration of participants;
- a *rigorous methodology*, starting with an exchange of life experience, moving along with training, extending gradually to exchange with other stakeholders and resulting in a negotiation of policy proposals;
- a guarantee of balance between partners with different backgrounds, which necessitates *positive discrimination* in terms of time, support and resources in favour of the target group;
- a process of *"intercultural mediation"* (even when most partners have the same ethnic background) to ensure mutual understanding between people with completely different life experiences;
- a guarantee of participation *until the final stage* (i.e., not limited to testimonies of life experience, but until the re-drafting of final conclusions and even the follow-up of the policy implementation); and, last but not least
- a *climate of confidence* between the partners involved, which means that the authorities asking for advice prove their commitment and sense of democracy in a sustainable way.

To sum up, genuine participation by people experiencing poverty and social exclusion is possible, but it necessitates a serious and sustained human investment. Governments at all levels need to avoid several pitfalls, beginning with the temptation to manipulate poor people's testimonies while ignoring the root causes of their exclusion and excluding them again from the decision-making process. There is now, in part as a result of the Social OMC, a significant body of good practice in this area and this provides the basis for building a much more widespread participation in the future.

## 5.3 Conclusions and recommendations

The overall result of a decade of joint EU social inclusion policies is not really satisfactory. Whereas genuine progress has been made in terms of mutual learning and coordination, the risk of poverty has not decreased. This can be attributed, at least in part, to the disconnection between social and other EU policies. It highlights the need to reform the EU model of development and to better integrate all aspects of policy so that they contribute to greater social inclusion and a stronger Social Europe. A better governance of social inclusion policy would require:

- mainstreaming of the social inclusion objective, as foreseen in the Europe 2020 agenda, through systematic use of poverty and social impact analysis as an essential component of the overall impact assessment of any new policy initiative (see also Sections 1.3.4 and 1.3.5);
- the inclusion of effective legal guarantees, at EU level, of social minimum standards in all policy areas – especially in those where markets are being liberalised; and
- active promotion and monitoring of the quality of participation of all stakeholders, including people suffering poverty and social exclusion, by the European Commission (see also Section 1.3.7).

## References

ATD-Quart Monde, Fondation Roi Baudouin, Union des Villes et des Communes Belges (1995), *Rapport Général sur la Pauvreté*, Bruxelles: FRB.

Clifton, J., Diáz-Fuentes, D. (2008), *Evaluating EU policies on public services: a citizens' perspective*, Munchen: MPRA Paper N° 9420, July 2008.

European Anti-Poverty Network (2007), *Making a decisive impact on the eradication of poverty. Towards an EU initiative on social standards*, Dublin: EAPN Ireland, 47p.

European Anti-Poverty Network (2009), *Small steps, big changes. Building participation of people experiencing poverty*, Brussels: EAPN, 79p.

European Commission (2004), *White Paper on Services of General Interest*, Communication COM(2004) 374 final, Brussels: European Commission.

European Commission (2004), *Report of the High Level Group on the future of social policy in an enlarged European Union*, Brussels: European Commission, 96p.

European Commission (2006), *Efficiency and equity in European education and training systems*, Communication COM (2006) 481, Brussels: European Commission.

European Commission (2007), *Services of general interest, including social services of general interest: a new European commitment*, Communication COM(2007) 725 final, Brussels: European Commission.

European Commission (2008), *Progress towards the Lisbon objectives in education and training. Indicators and benchmarks – 2008*, Commission Staff working document, Brussels: European Commission.

European Commission (2010), *Europe 2020. A strategy for smart, sustainable and inclusive growth*, Communication COM(2010) 2020, Brussels: European Commission.

European Council (2009), *Council conclusions of 12 May 2009 on a strategic framework for European cooperation in education and training ('ET 2020')*, Brussels. Available from:

http://eur-lex.europa.eu/LexUriServ/LexUriServ.do?uri=OJ:C:2009:119:0002:001 0:EN:PDF

Eurostat (2009), *79 million EU citizens were at-risk-of-poverty in 2007, of whom 32 million were also materially deprived*, Statistics in Focus, 46/2009.

Eurostat (2010), *Combating poverty and social exclusion. A statistical portrait of the European Union 2010*, Luxembourg: Publications Office of the European Union, 111p.

Frazer, H. and Marlier, E. (2009), *Assessment of the extent of synergies between growth and jobs policies and social inclusion policies across the EU as evidenced by the 2008-2010 National Reform Programmes: Key lessons*, Brussels: European Commission.

Gottschalk, P. and Danziger, S. (2005), "Inequality of Wage Rates and Family Income in the United States, 1975-2002", *Review of Income and Wealth*, Vol. 51, No. 2.

Gottschalk, P. and Smeeding, T.M. (1997), "Cross National Comparisons of Earnings and Income Inequality", *Journal of Economic Literature*, Vol. 35, No. 2.

INBAS GmbH, ENGENDER asbl (2010), *Study on Stakeholders' Involvement in the Implementation of the Open Method of Coordination (OMC) in Social Protection and Social Inclusion*. Available from:
http://www.stakeholders-socialinclusion.eu/site/en/head.

Is Feidir Linn (2009), *A vision for an inclusive, equal, sustainable Ireland*, Is Feidir Linn, Dublin. Available from:
http://www.isfeidirlinn.org/page/what-is-is-feidir-linn?xg_source=activity

Katz, L. and Autor, D. (1999), "Changes in the Wage Structure and Earnings Inequality", in O. Ashenfelter and D. Card (eds.), *Handbook of Labor Economics*, Vol. 3A, Amsterdam: North Holland.

Kogan, I., Gebel, M., Noelke, C. (eds., 2008), *Europe enlarged. A handbook of education, labour and welfare regimes in Central and Eastern Europe*, Bristol: The Policy Press, 389p.

Kvist, J. (2004), Does EU enlargement start a race to the bottom? Strategic interaction among EU Member States in social policy, *Journal of European Social Policy*, Vol. 14(3): pp.301–318.

Kvist, J. (2004), Does EU enlargement start a race to the bottom? Strategic interaction among EU Member States in social policy, *Journal of European Social Policy*, Vol. 14(3): pp.301–318.

Lelkes, O., Medgyesi, M., Tóth, I.G. (2009), Income Distribution and the Risk of Poverty, in: Ward T., Lelkes O., Sutherland H., Tóth I. (2009), *European inequalities. Social inclusion and income distribution in the EU*, Budapest: Tárki, pp.45-64.

Nicaise, I., Kerkhofs, R., Vandenbempt, K., Rea, A. (2004), *Policy at work. Local implementation of the Belgian National Action Plan for Social Inclusion. Report of the Belgian non-governmental experts to the European Commission*, Leuven: HIVA, 33p.

Nicaise, I. (2009 – assisted by K. Holman), *Social Impact Assessment, Peer Review in Social Protection and Social Inclusion – Synthesis Report*, Brussels: Eur. Commission, DG Employment and Social Affairs, 47p.

OECD (2008), *Growing unequal. Income distribution and poverty in OECD countries*, Paris: OECD, 308p.

Service de Lutte contre la Pauvreté, la Précarité et l'Exclusion sociale (2001), *En dialogue, six ans après le Rapport Général sur la Pauvreté: premier rapport bisannuel*, Bruxelles: SLPPES.

Spring Alliance (2009), *Manifesto for a European Union that put people and planet first*, http://www.springalliance.eu/images/sa_manen.pdf

# 6 Overall conclusions

2010 is in many ways a turning point in the fight against poverty and social exclusion. The European Year aims to raise awareness about the persistence of the problem, to give voice to the concerns of those experiencing poverty and social exclusion and to renew political commitment of the EU and its Member States. The observation that poverty has not decreased in the past decade, despite real efforts to coordinate social inclusion policies at the EU level, necessitates a thorough reflection about the design of the European economic and social model. We need to ensure that in future the European economic and social model is better at reducing (excessive) inequalities and at both preventing and alleviating poverty and social exclusion. This means ensuring a combination of comprehensive and universal policies aimed at promoting the inclusion of all and complementary targeted policies to assist those facing particular difficulties or barriers. At the heart of this model must be comprehensive social protection systems which are needed both to ensure that all citizens have access to high quality services and to an adequate income and to support sustainable and inclusive economic growth.

The ongoing financial, economic and social crisis adds to the urgency of action, as the poorest citizens are the main victims of this crisis: tougher treatment of over-indebted households, unemployment and cutbacks in social budgets combine to make their lives even more difficult. This year is also a milestone for the EU as a whole, with the EU Lisbon Treaty that entered into force in December 2009, the appointment of the new European Commission, the evaluation of the Lisbon Strategy and the design of the "Europe 2020" strategy for the coming decade. The latter process is a window of opportunity to give social inclusion a more central place in the overall strategy of the Union and to ensure that the EU as a whole as well as all its individual Member State develop smart and sustainable social inclusion policies alongside inclusive economic policies.

The Belgian Government has decided to give maximum weight to the fight against poverty and social exclusion during its EU Presidency in the second half of 2010. It has prioritised putting in place more effective EU coordination and cooperation in the social field, and in particular in three thematic priorities: active inclusion, child poverty and social exclusion, and homelessness and housing exclusion. It will also focus on a horizontal priority, namely the active involvement of all stakeholders, including those experiencing poverty and social exclusion. This book takes stock of the progress made in 10 years of Social Open Method of Coordination (OMC) and formulates a series of recommendations for further action in the next decade, at EU level as well as at country (national, regional and local) level.

Despite the fact that social inclusion is now officially recognised as a key objective of EU policy, the present legal framework for action is rather weak. Nevertheless, the *Social Open Method of Coordination (and, more broadly, EU coordination and cooperation in the social area)* has gained substantial credit and deserves to be further strengthened in the future. For this purpose,

- an explicit policy statement about the interdependence of economic, employment, social and environmental policies is needed in addition to the explicit target of reducing the number of poor people by 20 million in the next decade.

- This overall objective should then be translated into "smart" (i.e. not only knowledge-based but also specific, measurable, agreed upon, realistic and time-based) national and sub-national targets and strategies.

- Progress in achieving the targets should be monitored on a yearly basis and assessed in parliaments at sub-national, national and EU level as well as in the Spring European Council. Adequate monitoring also requires further investment in statistical and analytical capacity building.

- The European Commission and the Social Protection Committee (SPC) should be able to make clear recommendations (endorsed by the EU Council of Ministers) to Member States. Apart from the (essentially soft) OCM, the use of 'harder' instruments such as Commission Recommendations and Framework Directives should be further explored.

The need for *both* the European Commission and EU Member States to *take into account requirements linked to the guarantee of adequate social protection and the fight against social exclusion* is reflected in the so-called "horizontal social clause" (article 9) in the new EU Lisbon Treaty. This requirement is also explicitly stated in a specific guideline on social inclusion in the new Integrated Guidelines for jobs and growth, where employment policies are linked with equal opportunities, social protection, education, health care and the social economy, while the Structural Funds are mentioned as an instrument to support social inclusion. Of course, this should not mean that the objective of social inclusion is subordinate to employment and economic objectives. On the contrary, as we highlighted in the Chapters 1 and 5, social inclusion should become a key priority embedded in each and every strand of EU and country policy. Past experience has shown that the neglect of distributional effects (e.g. in economic and monetary convergence policies or in the Lisbon Strategy) and the absence of minimum social standards (e.g. in liberalising services of general interest) have undermined social protection systems and caused serious damage to the most vulnerable groups in society. Indeed at times they have contributed to causing rather than preventing poverty and social exclusion. Therefore,

- systematic use of *ex ante* and *ex post* social impact assessment (as part of an overall assessment) should be fully embedded in the policy-making process at EU and national level. The ultimate goal should be to systematically work at identifying possible ways (links/ synergies) of adjusting policies to strengthen their contribution to promoting social inclusion. Future policies in the economic and social sphere will then become more coherent and sustainable.

- The development of the European Platform Against Poverty, anticipated in the Europe 2020 strategy, should contribute to this coherence through systematic monitoring and reporting about the implementation of social impact assessments in other strands of EU policy. It should also be enabled to make policy recommendations to the EU as well as to Member States in the context of article 9.

- Building on article 14 of the Lisbon Treaty, a legal framework should be developed for the establishment of minimum social standards for services of general interest such as energy, water, child care, education etc. The recommendations of the Spring Alliance, referred to in Chapter 5, could be used as a starting point for this purpose.

The (renewed) focus on the *fight against child poverty and social exclusion*, both as a priority in its own right and as a way of breaking the cycle of disadvantage in poor and socially excluded families, can be seen as a major success of the Social OMC. Yet the challenge is enormous: with an average rate of one in five for the EU-27 as a whole, the poverty risk is higher among children than among adults in a majority of Member States; this risk is extremely high among Roma (and other ethnic minority) children, children living in large, single-parent or jobless households. The Belgian Presidency aims to spur the debate at EU level, so as to pave the way for a European Commission Recommendation on the fight against poverty. We would therefore recommend the following elements (see Chapter 2):

- A renewed political commitment of the European Council towards the eradication of child poverty and social exclusion, accompanied with a specific EU-wide target for the reduction of child poverty. This would then be echoed by an agreement to include a "compulsory" chapter on child poverty in future NAPs/inclusion, with annual reporting on the progress made. The Member States should also adopt a joint multi-annual programme including thematic (e.g. Roma children, intergenerational poverty, early childhood services…) as well as horizontal (e.g. monitoring, research…) priorities.

- The general recommendations regarding mainstreaming of social inclusion also apply to child poverty and social exclusion, in particular: child poverty proofing as an integral part of social impact assessment, prioritising the fight against child poverty and social exclusion in the use of the Structural Funds, etc.

- Last but not least, the children concerned (and their advocacy groups) should be given a voice in the debate: not only through interviews on their experience of poverty, but also through genuine involvement in a process of continuous evaluation and improvement of policies.

The second thematic priority of the Belgian Presidency relates to *active inclusion*. Careful study and negotiation on the part of the European Commission has resulted in the adoption, in 2008, of a Recommendation which in itself contains a balanced anti-poverty programme: it combines the development of adequate minimum income systems with access to inclusive labour markets and to quality services for all. The implementation of this Recommendation should now be fostered and systematically monitored. To begin with, some Member States still lack a national minimum income system, while others have set benefit levels so low that they hardly provide any relief and are certainly not adequate. Little information is available on the other strands of the Recommendation. In order to put on track coordinated action in this field, we would recommend the following (see Chapter 3):

- By the end of 2010, a concrete work programme for the implementation of the 2008 European Commission Recommendation should be agreed upon. Here too, a specific chapter on active inclusion should become a standard element of the annual monitoring and reporting in the context of the Social OMC, and mutual learning should be fostered in the context of the PROGRESS programme.
- A systematic link should be established between the active inclusion strand of the social OMC and EU employment policies. The Structural Funds should boost investments in the measures taken in this context.
- The EU Network of Independent Experts on Social Inclusion has suggested a specific agenda of work on the minimum income pillar of active inclusion: the European Commission and Member States should agree on criteria relating to adequacy, uprating, coverage, conditionality, work incentives, etc. and explore the possibility of including them into an EU Framework Directive on the adequacy of minimum income systems. In line with the European Parliament Resolution of 9 May 2009, Member States should ensure that within a given timeframe (to be defined nationally) the combined effect of their minimum income provisions and other policy measures would be sufficient to lift all persons above the at-risk-of-poverty line of the country where they live (i.e. 60% of the median national household equivalised income). This goal should be largely achieved by 2020.

The third thematic priority of the Belgian Presidency for 2010 relates to *homelessness and housing exclusion (HHE)*. Homelessness is one of the most visible and extreme forms of poverty, which severely affects the implementation of the most basic human rights (right to a dignified life, an identity, privacy, health, family life, etc.). One of the overarching objectives of the OMC for social inclusion is to ensure "access to resources, rights, goods, and services for all", and in particular "access to decent and sanitary housing". Growing inequality and mobility within the enlarged EU have also exacerbated the problems of homelessness and absence of basic rights among marginalised people who try to improve their chances for a decent living in other Member States. Yet, a common policy towards homelessness and housing exclusion is still virtually non-existent. Despite relentless advocacy work by FEANTSA (the European Federation of National Organisations working with the Homeless), specific attention within the NAPs/inclusion, the organisation of several transnational projects and peer reviews, and the Thematic Year on HHE (2009), there is as yet no common definition of homelessness, nor are their common indicators to measure the extent of HHE.

Therefore, in addition to the general principles for coordinated action at EU-level (public expression of strong political commitment, integration of HHE as a standard chapter in the NAPs/inclusion and annual reporting, parliamentary debates, agreement on a multi-annual work programme in the context of the SPC), we have formulated in Chapter 4 the following key recommendations:
- Member States should develop comprehensive and integrated national strategies to tackle HHE, ensuring a strong coordination, both vertically (between levels of government) and horizontally (between policy areas, in particular between social welfare, active inclusion and housing). The strategies should include quantitative targets and budgets (using support from the Structural Funds wherever possible). They should adopt a rights-based approach (i.e. guarantee access to basic rights also for rough sleepers), set quality standards for accommodation and emphasise the prevention of homelessness (e.g. by supporting the economic and social links between poor people, strengthening family ties, facilitating mutual solidarity etc.).
- In order to facilitate mutual learning, the "ETHOS" definition proposed by FEANTSA should be considered as a basis for a common conceptual framework. This definition is comprehensive and includes several categories, reflecting an integrated approach that combines preventive and remedial aspects. In the context of the 2011 Census, efforts should be made to enumerate at least ETHOS categories 1 and 2.

Once again, we need to emphasise that this study does not have the ambition to give a detailed account of issues, nor to cover all possible measures in the three selected areas. However, we hope that the recommendations summarised above (and detailed in the respective chapters) will provide a useful basis for the policy debate, drawing lessons from 10 years of OMC in the social inclusion field.

Our final key recommendation concerns the *involvement of all stakeholders* – and those with a personal experience of poverty and social exclusion in particular. Despite the large distance between the EU and its most disadvantaged citizens, it must be acknowledged that both sides (EU institutions as well as grassroots organisations) have invested a lot of energy in bridging the gap. Following a period of scepticism and indeed tension, both parties are learning to communicate with each other on a regular basis, and appropriate methodologies have been developed to support the dialogue. Section 5.2 contains a series of lessons from good practice in this regard. It is obvious that the credibility of EU, national and sub-national policies to prevent and address poverty and social exclusion depends crucially on (a) the coherence between social (protection and inclusion) and other policy strands, and (b) the guarantee of genuine participation of excluded groups throughout the policy cycle.